International Perspectiv ....

Gita Steiner-Khamsi, Editor

The Privatization of Education:
A Political Economy of Global Education Reform
ANTONI VERGER, CLARA FONTDEVILA, AND ADRIÁN ZANCAJO

Institutionalizing Health and Education for All:
Global Goals, Innovations, and Scaling Up
COLETTE CHABBOTT WITH MUSHTAQUE CHOWDHURY

Education and the Reverse Gender Divide in the Gulf States:
Embracing the Global, Ignoring the Local
NATASHA RIDGE

Educating Children in Conflict Zones: Research, Policy, and Practice
for Systemic Change—A Tribute to Jackie Kirk
KAREN MUNDY AND SARAH DRYDEN-PETERSON, EDS.

Challenges to Japanese Education:
Economics, Reform, and Human Rights
JUNE A. GORDON, HIDENORI FUJITA, TAKEHIKO KARIYA,
AND GERALD LETENDRE, EDS.

South–South Cooperation in Education and Development
LINDA CHISHOLM AND GITA STEINER-KHAMSI, EDS.

Comparative and International Education:
Issues for Teachers
KAREN MUNDY, KATHY BICKMORE, RUTH HAYHOE,
MEGGAN MADDEN, AND KATHERINE MADJIDI, EDS.

The Privatization of Education

A Political Economy of Global Education Reform

Antoni Verger
Clara Fontdevila
Adrián Zancajo

TEACHERS COLLEGE PRESS

TEACHERS COLLEGE | COLUMBIA UNIVERSITY
NEW YORK AND LONDON

Education International
Internationale de l'Education
Internacional de la Educación

Published by Teachers College Press, 1234 Amsterdam Avenue, New York, NY 10027

Copyright © 2016 by Teachers College, Columbia University

Cover photo courtesy of Fred Kuipers under a creative commons attribution license.

All rights reserved. No part of this publication may be reproduced or transmitted in any form or by any means, electronic or mechanical, including photocopy, or any information storage and retrieval system, without permission from the publisher.

Library of Congress Cataloging-in-Publication Data

Names: Verger, Antoni, 1975– author. | Fontdevila, Clara, author. | Zancajo, Adrián, author.
Title: The privatization of education : a political economy of global education reform / Antoni Verger, Clara Fontdevila, and Adrián Zancajo.
Description: New York, NY : Teachers College Press, [2016] | Series: International perspectives on education reform | Includes bibliographical references and index.
Identifiers: LCCN 2016009364
ISBN 9780807757598 (pbk. : alk. paper)
Subjects: LCSH: Privatization in education—Cross-cultural studies. | School choice—Cross-cultural studies. | Education—Finance—Cross-cultural studies. | Education—Economic aspects—Cross-cultural studies. | Education and state—Cross-cultural studies. | Educational change—Cross-cultural studies.
Classification: LCC LB2806.36 .V48 2016 | DDC 379.1—dc23
LC record available at https://lccn.loc.gov/2016009364

ISBN 978-0-8077-5759-8 (paper)
ISBN 978-0-8077-7472-4 (ebook)

Printed on acid-free paper
Manufactured in the United States of America

23 22 21 20 19 18 17 16   8 7 6 5 4 3 2 1

Contents

Acknowledgments   ix

Acronyms and Abbreviations   x

PART I: INTRODUCTION

1. **The Globalization of Education Privatization: An Introduction**   3

   Inquiring into Education Privatization Processes   4

   The Scope and Meaning of *Educational Privatization*   7

   The Systematic Literature Review Approach   10

   Book Structure   12

2. **The Political Economy of Global Education Reform**   15

   Global–Local Divide   16

   Material–Ideational Divide   20

   The Scope and Dynamics of Policy Change   26

   Conclusion   31

PART II: PATHS TOWARD PRIVATIZATION

3. **Education Privatization as a State Reform: The Ideological Road to Privatization in Chile and the United Kingdom**   35

   The Neoliberal Influence in Education   36

   An Education Privatization Laboratory: The Case of Chile   37

   From Thatcherism to New Labour: The Case of the United Kingdom   45

   Conclusion   53

4. **Education Privatization in Social Democratic Welfare States: The Nordic Path Toward Privatization**   **55**

The Spread of Global Neoliberal Ideas   56

Political Institutions and Party Politics in the Nordic Region   57

New Social Democracy and the Modernization of the Welfare State   64

Conclusion   66

5. **Scaling Up Privatization: School Choice Reforms in the United States**   **69**

School Choice Reform Breeding Grounds:
   Discursive, Institutional, and Legal Contingencies   70

Policy Outcomes: The (Uneven) Advancement of Charter
   Schools and Voucher Programs   76

Conclusion   86

6. **Privatization by Default in Low-Income Countries: The Emergence and Expansion of Low-Fee Private Schools**   **89**

A Growing Demand for LFPSs   90

The Global Promotion of LFPSs   95

Conclusion   102

7. **Historical Public–Private Partnerships in Education: The Cases of the Netherlands, Belgium, and Spain**   **104**

The Netherlands: *Pillarization* and Religious Segregation   105

Belgium: Ups and Downs in a Private School Financing Agreement   109

Spain: The Consolidation of the Private Sector
   in the Transition to Democracy   112

Conclusion   116

8. **Along the Path of Emergency: Privatization by Way of Catastrophe**   **119**

Education Privatization in Catastrophe Settings:
   Identifying Constant Features   119

Natural Disasters as an Opportunity to Privatize Education   121

Education Reform in Postconflict Contexts   128

Conclusion   132

PART III: ACTORS FOR AND AGAINST PRIVATIZATION

9. The Emerging Role of Nonstate Actors
   in the Promotion of Educational Privatization   137

   Think Tanks: Producing Pro-Privatization Ideas   138

   The Media: Means or Agents in Education Privatization?   140

   Policy Entrepreneurs   141

   Private Corporations and New Forms of Philanthropy   144

   Advocating Privatization: Frequent Strategies of Influence   151

   Conclusion   156

10. Resisting Privatization: The Strategies and Influence of
    Teachers' Unions in Educational Reform   158

    Teachers' Unions Participation in Policy Processes:
        Different Models of Engagement   158

    Unions' Strategies and Repertoires of Action   162

    Conditions of Influence:
        Opportunities, Risks, and Threats for Unions   167

    Conclusion   175

11 Conclusions: A Cultural Political Economy of
    Education Privatization   177

    The Multiple Trajectories of Education Privatization   177

    The Political, Economic, and Cultural Forces
        Behind Education Privatization   185

    Final Remarks: Political Implications, Future Directions   193

Appendix—Methodology: Key Components   196

Notes   201

References   208

Index   230

About the Authors   244

Acknowledgments

This book has benefited enormously from the generous input and feedback given by great colleagues and experts on education privatization trends in different world regions of the world. Thanks to Frank Adamson, Stephen Ball, Nina Bascia, Xavier Bonal, Vincent Dupriez, Brent Edwards, Alejandra Falabella, Kathleen Falkenberg, Julián Gindin, Carolina Junemann, Sjoerd Karsten, Michael B. Klitgaard, Bob Lingard, Nestor López, Christopher Lubienski, Alejandra Mizala, Jorunn Moller, Antonio Olmedo, Susan Robertson, Prachi Srivastava, Florian Waldow, and Susanne Wiborg for acting as key informants at the beginning of our search, and for their insightful comments on previous versions of the chapters included in the volume.

This book was developed with the support of a research grant from Education International (EI) and in the context of the Marie Curie project "Public–Private Partnerships in Educational Governance" (EDUPARTNER, ref. GA-2012-322350). The completion of this book project owes much to the great feedback and constant support received from the colleagues from the EI Research Institute: Guntars Catlaks, Mireille de Koning, Felisa Tibbitts, and Nikola Wachter. Many thanks also to Deirdre O'Flynn and to EI for their important support during the linguistic review of the book's content.

Last but not least, we are very grateful to series editor Gita Steiner-Khamsi for accepting our work in the Teachers College Press series *International Perspectives on Educational Reform*.

Acronyms and Abbreviations

ACADE: Asociación de Centros Autónomos de Enseñanza Privada
ADB: Asian Development Bank
AFT: American Federation of Teachers
APF: Azim Premji Foundation
APS: Assisted Places Scheme
ASSIA: Applied Social Sciences Index and Abstracts
BAEO: Black Alliance for Educational Options
BBC: British Broadcasting Corporation
BESE: Board of Elementary and Secondary Education
BIA: Bridge International Academies
CAI: Creative Associates International
CCT: compulsive competitive tendering
CEI: Center for Education Innovations
CEO: chief executive officer
CONFECH: Confederación de Estudiantes de Chile
CPE: cultural political economy
CPS: Center for Policy Studies
CSR: corporate social responsibility
DFID: Department for International Development (U.K.)
EDUCO: Educación con Participación de la Comunidad
EFA: Education For All
EI: Education International
EPPI: Evidence for Policy and Practice
ERA: Education Reform Act
ERIC: Education Resources Information Center
EU: European Union
FAES: Fundación para el Análisis y los Estudios Sociales

FEPADE: Fundación Empresarial para el Desarrollo Educativo

FMLN: Frente Farabundo Martí para la Liberación Nacional

FUNDEL: Fundación Europea Educación y Libertad

FUSADES: Fundación Salvadoreña para el Desarrollo Económico y Social

GBCE: Global Business Coalition for Education

GESF: Global Education and Skills Conference

GSEA: globally structured education agenda

HCREO: Hispanic Council for Reform and Educational Options

HSBC: Hong Kong and Shanghai Banking Corporation

IADB: Inter-American Development Bank

IBSS: International Bibliography of the Social Sciences

ICICI: Industrial Credit and Investment Corporation of India

ICT: information and communications technology

IDP: innovation development progress

IEA: Institute of Economic Affairs

IFC: International Finance Corporation

IO: international organization

KIPP: Knowledge Is Power Program

LEA: local education authority

LFPSs: low-fee private schools

LOCE: Ley Orgánica Constitucional de Enseñanza

LODE: Ley Orgánica del Derecho a la Educación

LOECE: Ley Orgánica del Estatuto de Centros Escolares

LOMCE: Ley Orgánica para la Mejora de la Calidad Educativa

MDG: Millennium Development Goal

MECE: Mejoramiento de la Calidad y la Equidad de la Educación

MOOC: massive online open course

NAHT: National Association of Head Teachers

NCLB: No Child Left Behind

NGO: nongovernmental organization

NPM: new public management

NSTU: Nova Scotia Teachers Union

NUT: National Union of Teachers

OECD: Organisation for Economic Cooperation and Development

OfSTED: Office for Standards in Education

OPSB: Orleans Parish School Board

PALF: Pearson Affordable Learning Fund

PFI: private finance initiative

PISA: Program for International Student Assessment

PPP: public–private partnership

PSEG: Private Sector Education Group

QCA: qualifications and curriculum authority

REDUCA: Red Latinoamericana por la Educación

RSD: recovery school district

SAP: structural adjustment program

SIMCE: Sistema de Medición de la Calidad de la Educación

SLR: systematic literature review

SNED: Sistema Nacional de Evaluación del Desempeño

SPS: school performance score

TAN: transnational advocacy network

TDA: Teacher Development Agency

TFA: Teach for America

TIMSS: Trends in International Mathematics and Science Study

TPE: Todos Pela Educação

TU: teachers' union

UAE: United Arab Emirates

U.K.: United Kingdom

UN: United Nations

UNESCO: United Nations Educational Scientific and Cultural Organization

UNICEF: United Nations International Children's Emergency Fund

U.S.: United States of America

USAID: U.S. Agency for International Development

WB: World Bank

WISE: World Innovation Summit Education

WTO: World Trade Organization

Part I

INTRODUCTION

CHAPTER 1

The Globalization of Education Privatization

An Introduction

The privatization of education is a global phenomenon with multiple manifestations. Northern and Southern countries and states with very different educational traditions and regulatory frameworks have promoted pro-privatization reforms for many reasons—social, political, economic, and educational. Among the most emblematic policies promoting the role of the private sector in education are charter schools, voucher schemes, or the contracting of private schools.

Privatization solutions are recommended and advocated by a broad spectrum of actors, from local interest groups to international organizations and private foundations. In some settings, even "strange bedfellows" (agents with apparently divergent interests, such as ethnic minority groups and conservative think tanks) end up advocating for similar forms of education privatization (Apple & Pedroni, 2005). To all of these different actors, privatization is seen as a formula to expand choice, improve quality, boost efficiency, or increase equity (or all of these things simultaneously) in the educational system.

At the same time, however, privatization policies tend to generate opposition and political dispute. Significant education stakeholders see privatization as a key challenge to the conception of education as a basic human right and a public good. Further, privatization is a policy that runs the risk of undermining educational equity, and whose presupposed benefits—whether in terms of efficiency or quality gains—have not been empirically and rigorously tested globally. Not surprisingly, different types of organizations, including teachers' unions, family associations, and civil society groups, tend to organize themselves against education reforms when they involve education privatization measures. Of all of the opponents to privatization reforms, teachers' unions tend to be the most active because, aside from the potential risks for education quality and equity, privatization can directly undermine the labor conditions and rights of their members, as well as the status of the teaching profession more generally speaking.

INQUIRING INTO EDUCATION PRIVATIZATION PROCESSES

In academia and in policy circles alike, the general consensus on education privatization is that it is a phenomenon that is expanding internationally. A general overview of some of the most relevant existing indicators concerning education provision and spending confirms this trend in most world locations. As Figure 1.1 shows, the percentage of enrollment in private primary school has increased in most countries, whatever their level of economic development—although this trend is not so marked in high-income and lower-middle-income countries.[1]

Figure 1.2 reflects a similar trend regarding private enrollment, but in different world regions. The only region in which private enrollment in primary education has not increased in the last decades is sub-Saharan Africa. To a great extent, this is the consequence of the removal of fees in public schools implemented in some countries of the region since the end of the 1990s, which has favored the expansion of the public sector. In the last years with available data, however, this trend has been reversed and the weight of the private sector in primary education also is increasing in this region.

Finally, Figure 1.3 shows how private expenditure in education has increased in OECD countries since the mid-1990s. This is, at least, the case in 17 of the 21 countries with data available on this matter.[2]

Scholars who are aware of some of these general trends may be tempted to consider that a sort of convergence prevails around education privatization globally. As we explain below, though, education privatization cannot be portrayed as a monolithic process that is susceptible to be captured with a few quantifiable and

Figure 1.1. Percentage of Enrollment in Primary Education in Private Institutions According to Countries' Level of Income, 1990–2012

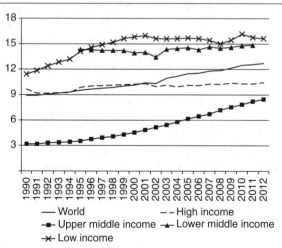

Source: Adapted from data from UNESCO Institute of Statistics, 2015.

Figure 1.2. Percentage of Enrollment in Primary Education in Private Institutions According to World Regions, 1990–2012

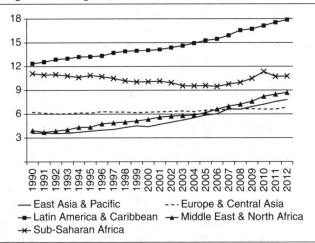

— East Asia & Pacific   --- Europe & Central Asia
-■- Latin America & Caribbean   -▲- Middle East & North Africa
-✱- Sub-Saharan Africa

Source: Adapted from data from UNESCO Institute of Statistics, 2015.

Figure 1.3. Share of Private Expenditure on Education Institutions (All Levels), 1995–2011

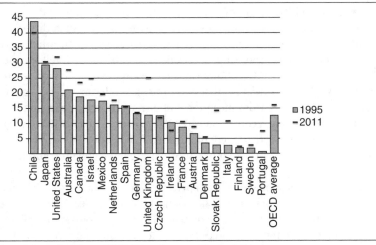

Source: Adapted from data from *OECD Education at a Glance,* 2014.

general indicators. Overall, the specific policies, social mechanisms, and reform trajectories through which education privatization advances internationally constitute a still underexplored research area.

In existing literature, several comprehensive international reviews look at the *effects* of privatization in education systems (see, for instance, Ashley et al., 2014;

UNESCO, 2009; Waslander, Pater, & Vander Weide, 2010). These reviews focus on the impact of privatization on differing dimensions, including student access and learning, teacher quality, and/or educational inequalities. Still, a comprehensive, international, and up-to-date revision of education privatization that, from a political economy perspective, tries to understand why and how education privatization happens has not been produced yet.

This book aims to address these gaps in existing literature by opening the black box of education privatization reform processes at an international scale. No other piece of research looks systematically at the scope of education privatization trends and scrutinizes the reasons, agents, and conditions behind the dissemination and adoption of privatization policies in educational systems from a comparative and global political economy perspective.

As Chapter 2 in this volume outlines, a political economy approach is particularly helpful to understand the multi-scalar dynamics, discourses, and structures through which global education agendas are constituted and education policies are disseminated internationally. Political economy studies are interested intrinsically in understanding how influence and power operate in multiple settings. Paraphrasing Held and Leftwich (1984), political economy studies aim to analyze the forces that influence and reflect the distribution and use of power, and the effects of these dynamics on various aspects and domains, including policy. Political economy, then, is about the transformatory capacity of social agents in constraining (or enabling) political, economic, and institutional contexts.

From a political economy perspective, the main question that inspires the realization of this book is: Why do so many countries, with such different cultural, political, and economic contexts engage in processes of education privatization reform today? By its scope, this question represents a wide intellectual endeavor. To make it more operative, however, the question can be subdivided into more concrete sets of sub-questions that cover the most relevant facets of global education policy processes, from inception and introduction in global education agendas to adoption and recontextualization in particular education settings. These sub-questions can be structured into two main blocks, one focusing on policy diffusion and adoption, and the other one focusing on negotiation and resistance:

- How is the global education privatization agenda constituted, and by whom? How are education privatization policy ideas being diffused at multiple scales? Why are countries adopting privatization policies? What global and domestic forces contribute to them doing so? How do cultural, political, historical, and economic factors mediate in such processes?
- How is education privatization resisted, and by whom? In particular, what is the role of teacher unions and civil society organizations in the negotiation of and/or resistance to privatization trends? Which of the strategies of these organizations are the most effective when in resisting privatization reforms? Which ideational, political, and economic circumstances are more conducive to some strategies being more successful than others?

To address this long battery of questions, as well as to find out how many of the issues included in the questions operate at an international scale, this book adopts a *systematic literature review* approach. This introductory chapter describes the main characteristics and potential of this research methodology, and explains why the authors opted for this approach among other possible options. Before doing so, however, the next section will outline the scope of this book in terms of the type of privatization measures it specifically reviews.

THE SCOPE AND MEANING OF *EDUCATIONAL PRIVATIZATION*

Education privatization can be defined broadly as a process through which private organizations and individuals participate increasingly and actively in a range of education activities and responsibilities that traditionally have been the remit of the state.

The privatization of education does not necessarily mean a drastic transfer of the *ownership* of education services from public to private hands, in contrast to what has been witnessed in other widely privatized sectors such as telecommunications, aviation, and energy, to name a few. At least, this is not the most important way in which education privatization happens in most parts of the world (Lubienski, 2003). Education privatization is a process that tends to happen more at the level of service provision (with a higher presence of private schools) and funding (with families and other private actors paying for a larger portion of total educational expenses) than at the level of ownership in a strict sense.

In their description of education privatization, Fitz and Beers (2002) capture this complexity quite well and show that, although education privatization processes do not necessarily alter ownership relations, they do change in a significant way how education services are coordinated, financed, and controlled. To them, education privatization is described as follows:

> A process that occurs in many modes but in one form or another involves the transfer of public money or assets from the public domain to the private sector. It also includes the provision of services by private corporations, enterprises and institutions that were once provided by the public sector. Privatization also inevitably means a shift in the control of public resources, and changes in the structures through which public money is spent. (Fitz & Beers, 2002, p. 139)

Education privatization can happen *de facto* or for structural reasons that, to a great extent, are external to the education policy domain—namely states' inaction in the face of a growing demand for education and/or the changing educational needs of an emerging middle class. Nonetheless, privatization also occurs because governments promote it proactively by adopting and implementing specific public policies. The education privatization agenda covers policies such as voucher schemes, charter schools, education sector liberalization, tax incentives to private education consumption, contracting out educational services, and so on.

All of these policy measures introduce higher levels of private sector participation, especially in activities of educational services delivery, as well as some level of interaction between the public and the private sectors in education.

Ball and Youdell (2008) famously distinguish between two main types of privatization trends and related policies: (a) privatization *of* public education, or "exogenous" privatization, which involves "the opening up of public education services to private sector participation [usually] on a for-profit basis and using the private sector to design, manage or deliver aspects of public education"; and, (b) privatization *in* public education, or "endogenous" privatization, which involves the "importing of ideas, techniques and practices from the private sector in order to make the public sector more like businesses and more business-like" (Ball & Youdell, 2008, p. 9).

The latter modality is related strongly to the public sector reform program commonly known as *new public management (NPM)*. The adoption of NPM implies the fragmentation of public services into small units, the deconcentration of budget responsibilities in such units, the introduction of a more clear distinction between users and providers, and the promotion of a managerial culture oriented toward the achievement of tangible and measurable results (Clarke, Gewirtz, & McLaughlin, 2000; Kalimullah, Ashraf, & Ashaduzzaman, 2012). In the education sector, NPM often means the promotion of school-based management and a managerialist approach to the governance of schools, outcomes-based incentives for schools and teachers, and, overall, education services further oriented toward families' demands (Gunter & Forrester, 2009). NPM implies that the public sector imports values and techniques from the private sector; however, it is not clear that all types of NPM (such as some forms of teacher evaluation or accountability systems) can be identified mechanically with the privatization agenda in all circumstances (see Bellei & Orellana, 2015; Maroy, 2009).

Despite the clarity of Ball and Youdell's distinction, the two categories of education privatization they define (i.e., privatization *in* and *of* education) tend to be strongly interconnected. Actually, opening public education services to private sector participation may force public schools to compete against private schools for students and, to this end, public schools may end up borrowing values, managerial techniques, and the organizational culture of the private sector. Figure 1.4 shows how some education policies intersect more explicitly with the two categories of endogenous and exogenous privatization, whereas other polices are formally associated with only one of the categories.

Because most education privatization policies lead to the generation of some level of market dynamics in education systems, such as providers' competition and freedom of clients' choice, the concepts of privatization and marketization are linked inextricably (Whitty & Power, 2000). As Marginson (1993) pointed out, although "privatization does not in itself constitute market relations, it creates a potentially favorable environment for market activity" (p. 178).

To make the description of education privatization even more complex, public-private mixes are becoming increasingly central in the organization of educational systems in many parts of the world (Robertson & Verger, 2012). These

Figure 1.4. Types of Education Privatization and Associated Polices

Type of Privatization	Aim	Education Policies	
Exogenous	Promote the emergence and expansion of private providers in the education sector	• Liberalization of the education sector • Tax incentives to private schools and/or private schooling consumption • Public subsidies to private schools	• Vouchers and similar competitive formulas in which financing follows the demand
Endogenous	Introduce norms, rules, and logics of the private sector within education systems	• Performance-related pay for schools and/or teachers • Disaggregation of units in the educational system, school-based management • Standardized evaluation and rankings	• Charter schools • Freedom of school choice policies

Source: Adapted from Ball and Youdell (2008).

public-private mixes, which in recent education policy literature are labeled as *public-private partnerships (PPPs)*, involve a more or less stable contract between the public and the private sector. Through this contract, the public sector buys a service from the private sector for a certain period of time at a certain price and according to results. Both parts, the private and the public, are expected to share risks, knowledge, and other resources in delivering the service (Hodge, Greve, & Boardman, 2010; Patrinos , Barrera-Osorio, & Guáqueta , 2009). Nonetheless, PPPs in education are not necessarily advanced through policies different from those mentioned in Figure 1.4. According to the World Bank, the leading models of PPPs in education are those that include voucher schemes, charter schools, and/or contracting out private education.

This book looks at all of these different types of privatization trends, especially those resulting in the increasingly private provision of education. For methodological reasons, but also for reasons of scope and feasibility, the book deliberately excludes privatization modalities that do not focus explicitly on education service provision, such as: (a) The privatization of so-called peripheral services (cleaning of schools, school meals, etc.) and/or the delivery of education materials (information and communication technology [ICT], books, etc.); (b) partnerships with the private sector for the construction of school facilities and related infrastructures; (c) education-industry links, such as those that are increasingly present in vocational training (e.g., dual education) and universities (e.g., knowledge transfer policies with the corporate sector); (d) education liberalization processes in the context of international free trade agreements.[3] Of course, some of these elements are referred to in other chapters, but they are not the main focus of the privatization processes reviewed.

In terms of education levels, this book deliberately focuses on basic education (primary and secondary education) because the nature of privatization and its main drivers in these levels are very different from privatization dynamics in early childhood education, vocational training, higher education, or adult education. These other education levels also are affected strongly by privatization in many different contexts but, again, they are excluded here for the purpose of feasibility and comparability.

THE SYSTEMATIC LITERATURE REVIEW APPROACH

The investigation presented in this book has followed a *systematic literature review (SLR)* methodology. This methodology is broadly defined as a synthesis of "research literature using systematic and explicit, accountable methods" (Gough, Thomas, & Oliver, 2012, p. 2). The SLR methodology aims at synthesizing the existing scientific evidence in a specific area of knowledge to answer one or more research questions. The investigation used here has followed the standard stages of this methodology, detailed in Figure 1.5. In contrast to other reviews, which are oriented toward testing specific hypotheses, our review has focused on answering more open questions and on the identification of variation dynamics and tendencies.

Figure 1.5. Common Stages in Systematic Literature Reviews

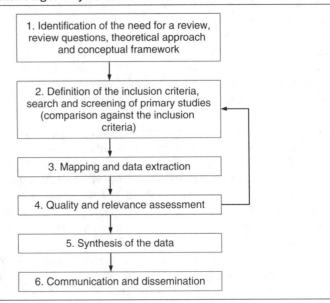

Sources: Adapted from EPPI-Centre (2010); Gough, Thomas, & Oliver, 2012; Gough, Oliver, & Thomas, 2013; Petticrew & Roberts (2006).

As shown in Figure 1.5, the review consisted of six main steps. Because the research questions have been presented already, and the main elements included in the theoretical and conceptual approach (Step 1) are presented in Chapter 2, we describe below how we have developed the following steps (steps from 2 through 5).

Step 2 focuses on the search and screening of primary studies. The keywords used in the first electronic search of primary studies, which can be consulted in the Appendix, were derived directly from the key research questions detailed above. The search protocol restricted the scope of the review to those studies focusing on primary and secondary education, to studies issued between 1999 and 2014, and to those published in English, Spanish, French, or Portuguese. To facilitate the organization of the material identified in the first search, the authors compiled the identified studies according to the country/ies and to the topic/s (e.g., specific privatization policies) being addressed in each of them. This compilation revealed some important lacunas in the literature identified in this first round, which were amended through hand searching and access to key informants.

In total, for the identification of primary studies, four main sources were used: (a) electronic databases (Education Resource Information Center [ERIC], Scopus, Applied Social Sciences Index and Abstracts [ASSIA], and International Bibliography of the Social Sciences [IBSS]); (b) hand searching in a sample of specialized journals and websites; (c) hand searching of gray literature (documents produced by governments, international organizations, and scholars in the form of, for instance, working papers or reports that have not been published by a conventional publisher); and (d) recommendations made by key informants with a country, regional, or thematic expertise. Through these successive screening sequences, a total of 227 studies were selected, reviewed, and systematized in an extraction form.[4]

After all the materials were summarized and compiled into the forms, it was possible to begin identifying, in an inductive manner, the various patterns of educational privatization. Reviewing the literature from a *political economy* perspective enabled us to focus on and discern clusters of contextual dispositions, agents, and mechanisms that frequently were associated with one another, usually in groups of countries or following regional patterns. These clusters represent what we call *paths toward education privatization*. Specifically, the following six paths toward privatization were identified:

1. ***Education privatization as a state reform:*** the ideological road to privatization in Chile and the United Kingdom.
2. ***Education privatization in social democratic welfare states:*** the Nordic path toward privatization.
3. ***Scaling up privatization:*** school choice reforms in the United States.
4. ***Privatization by default in low-income countries:*** the emergence and expansion of low-fee private schools.
5. ***Historical public–private partnerships in education:*** the cases of the Netherlands, Belgium, and Spain.
6. ***Along the path of emergency:*** privatization by way of catastrophe.

Given the scope and heterogeneity of the topic under review, the identification of these six paths—which must be understood as *theoretical models* or as *ideal types* in a more sociological sense—was immensely useful for data synthesis purposes (Step 5), but also from an analytical point of view. We consider that identifying the six paths toward privatization to be one of the most essential contributions of the book in both analytical and content-wise terms. However, as we develop in the conclusions (see Chapter 11 in this volume), we are aware that these six paths do not cover exhaustively all the possible forms/processes of education privatization globally, but, rather, the most significant forms/processes according to existing education research literature.

The data synthesis process followed two main strategies. The first and most important strategy involved the organization of the literature more directly related to each of the six paths toward privatization (Part II of this book). The second strategy focused on those pieces of research that addressed the role of the actors (or groups of actors) actively involved in both promoting and resisting education privatization trends in different country settings, independent of the path toward privatization in which they were inscribed (Part III).

BOOK STRUCTURE

This book is structured in three main sections. In Part I, in addition to this introduction to the theme and the aims of the book (Chapter 1), we present the theoretical and conceptual framework that has guided our research (Chapter 2). The theoretical framework, which is grounded in political economy and global governance literature, identifies and inter-relates a range of variables and dimensions that are key to understanding why countries adopt and implement education privatization reforms. This framework is, we belief, well-suited to analyzing the political advancement of education privatization at a global scale, although it could also be used to analyze the international diffusion of other types of education policies and reforms.

In Part II, a chapter is dedicated to each of the identified six paths toward privatization. In most cases, although a higher number of countries have followed each of these paths, these chapters are grounded on a restricted number of country cases. The focus is on those countries for which more literature of quality and relevance is available, but also on those that fit better within the theoretical model of privatization processes represented by the different paths.

In Chapter 3, the first of the identified paths—"Education privatization as a state reform"—is explored. This chapter shows that, in several countries, education privatization policies have advanced, in a drastic manner, as part of a broader strategy of structural state reform under neoliberal principles. To develop this argument, the chapter focuses on two paradigmatic cases: the United Kingdom and Chile.

Chapter 4, "Education Privatization in Social Democratic Welfare States," focuses on how and why Nordic European countries, which historically have enjoyed active and highly redistributive welfare state models, have engaged with some aspects of the education privatization agenda since the 1990s in a more or less drastic way.

Chapter 5 addresses the path toward privatization that the authors call "scaling up privatization." With a focus on the United States, this chapter explores the expansion of charter schools legislation and voucher programs through an uneven but gradual privatization process. Such a process, as will be seen, has progressively altered a longstanding model of educational governance traditionally characterized by public and uniform provision.

Chapter 6, "Privatization by Default in Low-Income Countries," addresses the growth of the so-called low-fee private school sector. This is an emerging modality of private schooling, driven by profit at the same time that, somehow paradoxically, targets poor households in several low-income countries. This chapter reflects on how the low-fee private school sector is increasingly central in international aid and private sector investment agendas alike.

Chapter 7 looks at "Historical PPPs" as a core privatization modality in countries with a long tradition of religious schooling. The specific focus here is on European countries including the Netherlands, Belgium, and Spain, where the presence and the political influence of faith-based institutions strongly conditioned the design and architecture of the education systems during the educational expansion in the 20th century.

Chapter 8, "Along the Path of Emergency," addresses how episodes of natural disasters or violent conflict set the stage for a sudden and drastic advancement of market-oriented policies in education. It shows how, in several locations that have been affected by this type of disasters, such as New Orleans, Haiti, and El Salvador, the relief and reconstruction interventions have become a window of opportunity for privatization advocates.

Part III discusses the various strategies and agents that have contributed to advancing—but also to mediating and resisting—education privatization trends. Chapter 9 analyzes the political and economic agents behind the promotion of education privatization, as well as the reasons and mechanisms through which they aim to advance their privatization agenda. Chapter 10 explores the role of collective actors, especially teachers' unions, in resisting and opposing such trends. This chapter also scrutinizes the strategies these actors employ and with what outcomes.

The final chapter, Chapter 11, summarizes and discusses this book's main results and presents the major conclusions of the review. Among other things, the chapter includes a synthesis chart (Figure 11.1) that represents, in a more graphic way, the complexity of the global education privatization trends witnessed during the last decades.

Overall, the authors expect this book to work as a global cartography of education privatization politics and policies. Despite its analytical dimension and ambition, the book has been written in a plain language as a way to reach a wide audience. The book has been produced with the explicit purpose of providing students, practitioners, and a broad range of education stakeholders with the necessary clues, ideas, and conceptual tools to better understand how and to what extent education privatization has become a global phenomenon these days, but also to problematize ideas about privatization as a monolithic phenomenon, or as a process that generates policy convergence internationally in a way that is too linear. To this purpose, the book provides conceptual elements and a broad range of quality data to understand how education privatization is translating into differing reform trajectories and policies, why so many governments are embracing measures that promote privatization *in* and *of* education, and the most effective responses to some of these privatization trends at multiple political scales.

CHAPTER 2

The Political Economy of Global Education Reform

This chapter builds a political economy framework to analyze the global spread and adoption of education privatization reforms in different countries and regions. The main aim is to provide the necessary conceptual and analytical tools to respond to this volume's main research question: Why (and how) have so many countries with such different cultural, political, and economic contexts engaged in processes of education privatization reform for decades?

Political economy is a broad and profoundly interdisciplinary area of study that explores the relationship between individuals and institutions, the market, and the state occurring at different interconnections, as well as the specific (policy) outcomes of these relationships.[1] Political economy studies have a keen interest in understanding how and why changes in institutions—including welfare regimes and policy sectors such as education—come about. The interest in power, and powerful forces, is inherent in political economy studies (Sayer, 2001). One of the constant and cross-cutting questions in political economy research is: Who exercises power over whom and with what outcomes?

The objective of this chapter is twofold. First, the chapter identifies the main drivers behind the processes of education policy change in a global era. Second, the chapter explores how various theoretical currents reflect on the trajectory of educational reforms, from inception in policy agendas to enactment and retention at the regulatory level. To achieve these general objectives, the chapter is structured in three main parts. The first part of the chapter elaborates on the main *global* and *local* (or *external* and *internal*) drivers of policy and institutional change. The second part of the chapter distinguishes between the *material* (or *hard*, i.e. political, economic) and the *ideational* (or *soft*, i.e., culture, ideas, semiosis, and so on) drivers of change.

As will be evident in these first two parts, the existing literature quite often focuses narrowly on only one or two of these types of drivers (whether local or global, material or ideational) and neglects the presence and influence of the others. Also, quite frequently, existing research portrays these drivers as dichotomic categories or dualisms. This presents a challenge to undertake a comprehensive analysis of the complex relations and mechanisms behind the processes of policy change. For this reason, when going through both the local-global and the material-ideational debates, and as far as practicable, the authors aim to build bridges between each of these dualisms.

The third, and last, part of the chapter shows how all of these different drivers of change interact in processes of educational reform and, potentially, in adopting pro-private sector reforms. To this purpose it first addresses the different possible types of policy change and, second, divides the concept of policy change into three key evolutionary mechanisms: variation, selection, and retention.

GLOBAL-LOCAL DIVIDE

The global-local (or external-internal, foreign-domestic) divide has become one of the most established cleavages in social sciences in the last few decades.[2] The literature focusing on the role of **local, domestic, or internal drivers** assumes that endogenous factors, such as the role of nationally (or locally) organized lobby groups, national political cultures, party politics, or critical junctures, are keys to explaining processes of institutional change. Some of the more reiterated and well-known theories in this type of literature are: the advocacy coalition frame-work (Sabatier, 1999), the multiple-streams framework (Kingdon, 1995), the punctuated equilibrium model (Baumgartner & Jones, 1993), and the political culture/values approach (Marshall, Mitchell, & Wirt, 1985; Sergiovanni, 1992). Although these theories were produced before globalization became such a central issue in social sciences (approximately, ever since the end of the 1990s), they still are very much in use in contemporary research.

In the study of education privatization reform, these types of theories have been applied mainly in developed countries, and especially in the United States (see Chapter 5 in this volume). This is not a coincidence. Rather, it is because the proponents of these theories work in countries that have more stable liberal democracies and that are not the main target of external pressures from, and conditions set by, international organizations. Many of the studies that apply these theories do not neglect the possibility of national or local policymakers' adopting foreign policy models of reform. Rather, they consider that national decision-makers enjoy great levels of political autonomy in policymaking processes. Thus, in their view, policymakers would engage with foreign policy ideas voluntarily and on their own initiative. If they do receive pressure, it would come predominantly from public opinion and domestic lobby/advocacy groups, not necessarily from external forces.

In contrast, the literature focusing on **external drivers** emphasizes the role of external factors and actors in processes of policy change. This literature tends to look at how certain policies (or policy models) are being globally diffused and adopted by numerous countries, independently of the will and preferences of domestic actors (Drezner, 2001). As a consequence of these external pressures, trends toward *policy convergence* can be identified in different domains.[3] On the basis of an extensive literature review, Knill (2005) outlines what he considers to be the five main causal drivers of policy convergence at the international level, as follows:

1. International convergence can be caused by countries offering similar, but independent, policy responses to the similar problems they face (e.g., climate change, aging population, financial crises).
2. Policy convergence can be the result of imposition (i.e., powerful countries and/or international organizations [IOs] forcing governments to adopt certain policies, via loan conditionalities, debt cancellation, trade deals, and so on).
3. Convergence can be forged by countries that have to comply with international rules and binding agreements (e.g., international trade agreements and United Nations [UN] conventions) subscribed to in multilateral negotiations.
4. Convergence can be the result of *regulatory competition* associated with the increasing economic integration of regional and global markets. In such an internationalized economic environment, countries would adjust policies of a different nature (e.g., taxation, labor, training) as a way to maintain or strengthen their economic competitiveness.
5. Policy convergence can be caused by softer mechanisms such as learning or joint problem solving, which usually happen in the context of IOs and more or less informal transnational policy networks.

IOs such as the Organization for Economic Co-operation and Development (OECD) and the World Bank are becoming key agents and spaces in activating most of the just-sketched policy mechanisms. It is well known that many IOs have formal power to make member states comply with international rules or reform prerogatives via funding or lending programs. However, technical assistance, dissemination of knowledge, and data management are increasingly becoming important sources of authority for IOs. According to Barnett and Finnemore (2004), IOs exercise power by organizing three types of apparently "apolitical" and "technical" actions:

1. Classifying the world by stratifying countries according to, for instance, their level of performance in different domains. International evaluations of students' performance, such as the OECD Program for International Student Assessment (PISA), are well known as instruments that are pressurizing governments to introduce education reforms (Martens, Rusconi, & Leuze, 2007; Meyer & Benavot, 2013).
2. Fixing meanings in the social world by, for instance, defining what educational quality or educational progress means. This is something that IOs can do explicitly, but also indirectly in the form of indicators and benchmarks such as those included in the European Union (EU) 2020 Strategy or in the Sustainable Development Goals.

3. Articulating and disseminating new norms, principles, and beliefs by, for instance, spreading what they consider "good" or "best" practices, or generating spaces for policy harmonization and policy learning among their member countries.

Overall, IOs are active transmitters of various views of educational reform. They have the material and discursive capacity to frame national and subnational education policy priorities and education policy decisions happening at a range of scales (Dale, 1999; Rizvi & Lingard, 2010).

Theorizing Globalization and Education Policy Change

In comparative education, two well-established theories—the Globally Structured Education Agenda (GSEA) and the World Culture Theory (also known as World Society theory)—have elaborated on the external drivers of education policy change, including the role of IOs. The GSEA sees the world's capitalist economy as the driving force of globalization and as the main cause of the profound transformations in today's education arena (Dale, 2000). This approach emphasizes that most current significant educational changes should be understood as being embedded within interdependent local, national, and global political economy complexes. International financial organizations are key agents in this multi-scalar scenario because of their agenda-setting capacities. Among other things, they define the main problems that member states should address if they want to integrate successfully into an increasingly globalized and competitive knowledge economy (Robertson, 2005).

On its part, World Culture Theory argues that global education models spread around the world as part of the diffusion of a culturally embedded model of the modern nation-state. According to this theory, a range of common education policies (but also health, fiscal policies, and so on) have been adopted globally because of both the international dissemination of the values of western modernity and the legitimation pressures on governments—especially in postcolonial settings—to demonstrate to the international community that they are building a "modern state" (Meyer, Boli, Thomas, & Ramirez, 1997).

Nevertheless, the idea of policy convergence often is nuanced and even contested by a range of scholars who, on the basis of locally grounded research, consider that global policy ideas are constantly and actively reinterpreted, modified, instrumentalized, and/or resisted by local agents according to their own symbolic frames, interests, and institutional constraints. This more contextualized perspective to global education policy is advanced, for instance, by:

- *anthropological* studies focusing on the relationship between culture, identity, and dynamics of policy translation and interpretation (Anderson-Levitt, 2003; Phillips & Stambach, 2008),
- *policy sociology* studies, which also focus on dynamics of global policy interpretation and translations, and situate these dynamics within the political and technical disputes that the reception of external models

generate among local constituencies (Ball, 1998; Peck & Theodore, 2010; Rizvi & Lingard, 2009), or
- *historical institutionalist* studies that look at the mediating role of institutional traditions and national regulatory frameworks in the adaptation of global education models. According to this approach, external models will not substitute existing institutions in a drastic way. Due to the path-dependent nature of institutions, gradual changes are more likely to occur (Dobbins, 2011; Maurer, 2012; Takayama, 2012).

In a nutshell, it cannot be expected that—despite its global dimension—education privatization reform ideas (as well as other global education reforms) would be uniformly received and adopted in all places. The mentioned approaches show us that *recontextualization* and *vernacularization* dynamics are central to analyzing the relationship between globalization and national education systems, and to avoid positions of both extreme skepticism and hyper-globalism—as famously characterized by Held, McGrew, Goldblatt, and Perraton (1999) when sketching the globalization debate.

Beyond the Global-Local Dichotomy

The phenomenon of globalization, in its multiple manifestations (such as economic, political, and cultural) has provided opportunities for cross-fertilization between approaches focusing on the *domestic drivers* of change and approaches focusing on the *external drivers*. In a global era, distinguishing analytically between external and internal drivers of change is useful. In ontological terms (i.e., in the "real world"), however, both types of drivers must be seen as mutually influencing or, more precisely, as constituting each other mutually. For instance, the government of country A, making use of its autonomy, may adopt a foreign policy model because it seriously believes that such a change will strengthen the effectiveness of its education system. These beliefs, however, may be the result of an IO (or another international agent) persuading government officials to believe in such a way.

An analogous example is that of government B adopting a new policy in an apparently voluntary way, but at the same time having the desire to comply with globally accepted international norms, or as a result of external pressures from the international economic environment. Of course, some countries are more responsive (or vulnerable) than others to external pressures, although in general, both external and internal factors tend to interact, to one extent or the other, in any process of educational reform.

The external-internal (or the global-local) do not represent a zero-sum relationship. A multi-scalar conception of policy formation and change processes is more accurate. Among other things, a multi-scalar conception of policy processes permits us to unpack the nature of global educational reform by exploring who controls what in which scale, from the local to the global (Dale, 2005). Frequently, the multi-scalar division of education politics makes the global arena more determinant in setting agendas and establishing preferences, with the national arena having the final say in deciding on the specific policies and programs to be adopted, and in retaining them (Dale, 2005). Furthermore, a multi-scalar approach to policy acknowledges that some actors, usually considered as local or domestic agents of change, such as lobby groups, think tanks, or advocacy coalitions, are increasingly transnationalizing their strategies, actions, and networks. As a result of scaling up their activities, these policy actors are challenging global institutions more directly, and are becoming more influential in setting global policy agendas (Ball, 2012; Keck & Sikkink, 1998).

Overall, it is problematic to always see the nation-state as the receiver of external influences, or as an agent whose autonomy is intrinsically restricted in front of global institutions. As shown previously, domestic constituencies and contingencies are expected to play a bigger role at the moment of the recontextualization, resignification, and enactment of the adopted policies. What is more, local actors can also instrumentalise global policies and institutions to advance their preferred policy reforms vis-à-vis other domestic actors (oppositional parties, interest groups, trade unions, etc.). On occasion, national governments resort to global agents and/or to global education models as a coalition builder or as a key *referential* to legitimize certain policy options and changes that, otherwise, would face much more contestation (Steiner-Khamsi, 2010, 2012b). Thus, despite global institutions usually are seen as restricting national autonomy, in some circumstances, they could allow governments to advance their education reform agenda with less opposition (Fulge, Bieber, & Martens, 2016; Grek, 2010).

As a final consideration to overcome the global-local binary, policy diffusion should not be reduced to the simple correspondence between two institutions (i.e., influence between the international organization X and state A, or between state A and state B). It is more accurate to consider that a global education policy field, which interacts with the broader social, political, and economic environment, is being constituted (Vavrus, 2004). Bourdieu's (1999) concept of field forces us to think of global education policy as a social space that each actor struggles to expand and/or transform in a different way and direction. Among other global trends and events, the increasing political dimension acquired by international standardized tests, international comparisons, educational development goals, and cross-border flows in education have generated a growing awareness among a range of education stakeholders of being part of a common *global education policy field*. Despite being open to the participation and involvement of a broad range of actors, however, a field is far from a flat terrain. In all type of policy fields, including the global education policy field, not all of the actors have the same power and capacity to mobilize the different types of capital (such as social, economic, and symbolic) that are necessary to promote their interests and ideas (Lingard, Rawolle, & Taylor, 2005).

MATERIAL-IDEATIONAL DIVIDE

Conventionally, political economy research has tended to focus on the hard or material drivers of policy change (including economic factors, political interests, and institutional constrains). More recently, other authors emphasize the importance of soft or ideational drivers (culture, norms, ideas, learning, semiosis, and so on). As developed below, both research traditions do not necessarily talk to each other.

Hard Drivers: Economy, Politics, and Institutions

The material drivers of change, while highly interlinked, can be differentiated broadly as economic, institutional and political. **Economic factors** can vary significantly in nature, although, among them, a country's *level of economic development* is one of the most commonly used in political economy studies. Economic development is expected, on the one hand, to condition the countries' level of autonomy in defining their own public policy agendas, and, on the other hand, which policy models are affordable or administratively viable. Similarly, policy emulation and diffusion is expected to occur between countries from the same region and linguistic community, and/or between countries that share similar levels of economic and institutional development (Dobbin, Simmons, & Garrett, 2007; Knill, 2005).

A variable of an economic nature that usually is taken into account in policy diffusion studies is the *economic environment* in which governments operate and make decisions (Lenschow, Liefferink, & Veenman, 2005). For instance, a more globalized economic environment is considered to provoke a sort of regulatory *race to the bottom* (cf. Korten, 1995), meaning that countries, as a way to compete for capital and export markets, change their taxation system (and other types of policy systems, including the educational one) to a more business friendly style.[4]

Another economic factor that provokes, conditions, or ultimately legitimizes policy changes is that of an economic crisis or recession. In times of recession, education systems receive more reform pressures and are more conducive to adopting cost-efficiency measures and budget cuts. This premise is especially true when the narratives of the crisis paint education as part of the problem (e.g., the existing education offer is insufficient or inadequate, does not respond to the needs of the economy, and so on) (Ball, 1990). Privatization reforms tend to be consistent with periods of financial crisis and economic austerity because governments usually justify adopting them to overcome public inefficiency or to generate state revenue.

The interplay between economic crises and policy change usually works in a paradoxical way because crises can motivate countries to undertake processes of education reform but simultaneously limit their capacity and resources to do so. Nonetheless, governments, in different circumstances commonly allege economic constraints as a way to avoid adopting policies that they dislike or, conversely, to make decisions that otherwise would be difficult to justify to society (Quiggin, 2006).

Institutions, more than drivers of change, tend to operate as mediators of policy reforms, whether they do so as inhibitors or as facilitators. Understood as stable systems of rules and patterns of behavior that promote social order, institutions influence the direction of future policy changes by generating various forms of path-dependence. As historical institutionalist scholars observe, the weight and legacy of previous policy systems frame the views and perceptions of policymakers concerning the feasibility and/or the desirability of adopting new policy ideas or external policy models (Hall & Taylor, 1996).

In terms of institutional factors, much has been said about the key role of political institutions and systems of political rules in policy processes. Political institutions mediate strongly in both the feasibility and the speed of policy reforms. Reforms that are feasible in unicameral democracies, for instance, may be impractical in other types of democratic regimes with further division of powers. In general, the opportunities for a government to advance ambitious policy reforms are reduced in political systems with more veto points, such as those with a second chamber, constitutional courts, or frequent referenda. A significant presence of interest groups also can make it difficult to adopt new policy changes, because they can exercise an effective veto and because more interests and power groups must be brought together into a winning coalition (Immergut, 2006).

Other scholars, usually coming from a Marxist tradition, focus on the state itself as a key mediating structure in the processes of policy change. To them, the state should not be seen simply as a sum of departments and bureaucrats or as a flat space that intermediates among a range of interests in public policy deliberations (as pluralists assume). Because the capitalist state has intrinsic interests, it must address a set of core problems (i.e., providing the basis of legitimation, supporting the regime of accumulation, and providing a context for its reproduction) (Dale, 2000; Offe, 1987). These problems and inherent contradictions shape policymaking in many sectors including education (Robertson, Bonal, & Dale, 2002). From this perspective, nonstate actors exert influence in policy processes; however, the capitalist state prioritizes the voice and interests of business and elites in decision-making processes over the voice and interests of other organized social groups (Carroll & Carson, 2003).

Welfare-state regimes theory also conceives the state as a type of *institutional structure* that conditions public sector reform processes. The influential classification by Esping-Andersen (1990), distinguishing between liberal, social democratic, and conservative welfare regimes, has been adopted to study how each of these regimes affect reform dynamics and priorities in various policy sectors. For instance, according to this theory, liberal welfare states would be receptive to introducing a more market-based organization in public education; social democratic welfare states would be expected to strengthen citizens' influence through voice and decentralization; and conservative welfare regimes would rather avoid decisions that could alter the prevailing segmentation of the educational system and/or the privileges of private providers (Klitgaard, 2008).

Finally, **political** factors, reasons, and interests can lie behind the adoption of educational reforms. Political parties and governments reform the public sector— and education systems in particular—as a way to gain political legitimacy in the eyes of society and/or the international community (other states, IOs, and so on), but also political power. According to Pollitt and Bouckaert (2004), "announcing reforms, criticizing bureaucracy, praising new management techniques, promising improved services for the future . . . help to attract favorable attention to the politicians who espouse them" (p. 6).

Furthermore, from a political perspective, education reform approaches (especially those involving privatization, decentralization, and others) are direct ways for governments to fragment the trade unions' operational space and reduce the teachers unions' power in the face of the state (Suleiman & Waterbury, 1990).

Soft Drivers: The "Emerging" Role of Ideas

Understanding ideational factors as key variables of policy change has gained centrality ever since the 1990s, with the so-called cultural turn in social sciences.[5] This is a relatively recent shift in education reform studies, though. Traditionally, political economy analysis has not paid sufficient attention to the role of ideas for two main reasons.

First, many researchers base their work on a positivistic epistemology that leads them to study events that can be observed and measured directly. *Ideas*, as a research object, do not seem to fit well within these conditions, because they are rather "vague, amorphous and constantly evolving" (Berman, as cited in Hay, 2002, p. 197). As Kjaer and Pedersen (2001) observed, scholars are not inclined to study ideas because of the difficulty in defining and categorizing them, or even distinguishing them from other social phenomena such as *institutions* themselves.[6]

Second, many social scientists—in particular those coming from a rationalist tradition—do not consider ideas as meaningful variables because, among other things, they assume that rational actors tend to have all relevant information on the consequences of their actions and on the preferences of other actors. For instance, from a rationalist perspective to policy transfer, policymakers, when faced with a new education problem, will scan the international environment in search of policies that have worked well elsewhere, will process the obtained information through a thorough cost-benefit analysis, and will choose the most optimal policy—the one that looks as if it can be best utilized in the country in question (Weyland, 2005). Accordingly, rationalism de-problematizes, to a great extent, the relationship between ideas, interests and decision making.

Against rationalism, many scholars consider that human interests are not necessarily pre-given (they are, to a great extent, socially constructed), and that policymakers, like any other human being, have an incomplete and often precarious understanding of the environment where they intervene. On the basis of these premises, policy adoption cannot be taken for granted as the result of a goal-oriented and rational choice but, rather, the result of the misleading attraction that some innovative or international ideas generate—even when not enough evidence supports them (Steiner-Khamsi, 2010). Actually, once a new policy reaches a certain threshold of adoption in several and sufficiently central countries—which means that this policy reaches the status of a *global policy*—more and more policymakers will be inclined to "take the policy for granted as necessary and will adopt it whether or not they have need of it." Consequently, some policies will "spread to polities for which they were not originally designed" (Dobbin et al., 2007, p. 454).

Because actors' rationality is assumed to be, at most, "bounded," policymakers who intervene in complex policy fields have to resort to inferential shortcuts (Jessop, 2010; Weyland, 2005). To reduce complexity and uncertainty, most policymakers turn to the services and/or are more receptive to the opinion of experts who can tell them about the costs and benefits of potential policy changes. Many consider that the role of experts—external advisers, policy entrepreneurs, consultancies, think tanks, philanthropic foundations, and others—and the mechanism of persuasion should be seen and analyzed as independent causes of policy change (Haas, 2004; Mintrom & Vergari, 1996; Risse, 2000; Schmidt & Radaelli, 2004).

In comparative and international education studies, several scholars are focusing on the dynamics of promotion of and persuasion regarding global policy ideas, and on how a range of policy entrepreneurs and networks of experts (see Box 2.1) predispose policymakers to consider their proposals through various

---

BOX 2.1. POLICY NETWORKS AND THE STATE/NONSTATE INTERACTION

Education policy analysts are increasingly focusing on the strategic role of networks in explanations of institutional and policy change. Networks are key to understanding how advocacy coalitions—and other channels of influence and governance structures—work today. Informality and casualness tend to be intrinsic features in the way policy networks operate. Hence, networks appear to be sustained through social and personal relationships, conversations, face-to-face meetings, social events, discussions, consultations, and so on. At a global level, summits, meetings, and international conferences play a key role in periodically putting in touch companies, investors, policy entrepreneurs, and governments (Olmedo, 2014).

Transnational advocacy networks (TANs) have the capacity to alter national governments' decisions though the international exchange of norms, ideas, and discourses (Keck & Sikkink, 1998). In India, for instance, a national school choice and privatization advocacy coalition termed School Choice Campaign, which operates in the context of a broader TAN, is highly active in disseminating neoliberal policies and in trying to reshape the governance of education in the country (Nambissan & Ball, 2010).

The space occupied by nonstate actors in policymaking also is captured by notions such as the **parapolitical sphere** (the space located at the interstices of business, government, and academia [Horne, in Béland, 2005]), the concept of **heterarchies** (organizational forms located between hierarchical structures and market exchanges and resulting in structures and relationships of governance outside of but in relation to the state [Jessop, 1998; Ball, 2012]), or the notion of the **policy subsystem**, which includes actors from a variety of public and private entities that go beyond the traditional *iron triangle*[7] such as journalists, policy analysts, and researchers who are active in the generation and dissemination of policy ideas on various issues (Sabatier, 1999).

strategies—which include supporting their policy recommendations with sophisticated scientific arguments, or aligning them with international "good practices" and standards (Grek et al., 2009; Olmedo, 2013; Steiner-Khamsi, 2012a). From their point of view, new policy ideas do not necessarily become disseminated because of their inherent quality and rigor but, rather, because of the promotional and framing actions of the experts who back them (Verger, 2012). Policy diffusion and adoption, then, would not necessarily be related to the demonstrated effectiveness of policies but, rather, to the socially constructed *perception* of their effectiveness.

Toward a Dialectical Understanding of the Role of Ideas

Until now, this chapter has developed an understanding of ideas that are much reduced to semiosis (forms of social production of meaning that influence individuals' decisions). Still, ideas and semiosis have an intersubjective dimension that has the potential to constitute broader structures with causal powers over policymakers' individual preferences and decisions in the form of, for instance, institutional norms or policy paradigms. A *policy paradigm* is a well-known example of an ideational-based structure with the capacity to work as a powerful lens for policymakers to interpret their reality and make decisions accordingly. A policy paradigm is broadly defined as a "framework of ideas and standards that specifies not only the goals of policy and the kind of instruments that can be used to attain them, but also the very nature of the problems they are meant to be addressing" (Hall, 1993, p. 279). Policy paradigms are selective in nature because they discriminate for (and against) particular policy ideas and discourses (Béland, 2010; Hay, 2001).

In comparative education, such a "structuralist" understanding of the role of ideas influences a broad range of scholarship, starting with World Culture Theory, which, as discussed previously, attributes world convergence in education to the successful expansion of Western normative frameworks and structures of values. Other scholars adopt a similar conception of the role of ideas when they talk of *education ideology* (Schriewer, 2004), *policy scape* (Carney, 2009), or *political imaginaries* (Robertson, 2005) as ideational frameworks shared by policymakers—usually at a supranational scale—and that shape the way they perceive educational problems and their corresponding solutions. Neoliberalism, new public management and public choice are some of the most often referred to paradigms or corpus of ideas to understand current global transformations in education (Ball, 2009; Gunter, 2009; see also Chapter 3 in this volume).

Public opinion, values, and sentiments also could be seen as necessary components of the ideational environment in which policymakers intervene and that greatly influence their actions and decisions, especially in more advanced democracies (Boyd, 2007). Public sentiments, which are defined as societal "assumptions that constrain the normative range of legitimate solutions available to policymakers" (Campbell, 1998, p. 385), are especially influential in policy decisions on issues that are more topical in the public domain.

So far, this chapter has outlined the multiple roles that ideational factors can play in processes of policy change and policy formation. As with the global-local dichotomy, however, we believe that convincing explanations of policy dissemination, adoption, and change have to combine and integrate both the material and the ideational drivers behind them. Jessop's Cultural Political Economy (CPE) approach, which has been adapted recently by Robertson and Dale (2015) in the education policy field, may be useful for this purpose. To start, Jessop does not see culture and semiosis as providing an alternative explanation to conventional (materially driven) political economy studies. More than as a different domain, the ideational domain has to be analyzed as embedded in both the political and the economic domains. In his own words, CPE "examines the co-implication of semiosis in the interlinked materialities of economics and politics in wider social settings." From this point of view, semiosis would be seen as a key element in the interpretation and construction of economic, political, but also as new, educational realities. Accordingly, policy change would emerge "from the contingent co-evolution of semiotic and extra-semiotic processes that make some meaningful efforts at complexity reduction more resonant than others" (Jessop, 2010, p. 340).

A final conceptual step to overcome the material-ideational dichotomy consists of not conceiving—always and necessarily—ideas as an element of soft power that operate in a diametrically opposed way to hard power. It is certain that the dissemination of ideas operates very differently to hard mechanisms of power such as imposition or coercion (Stone, 2004). Nevertheless, the manipulation of information and evidence, or the monopolization of expertise—in the way that, for instance, some international organizations or think tanks try to do in the education policy field—should be seen as equivalent to more direct forms of coercion (Dobbin et al., 2007).

THE SCOPE AND DYNAMICS OF POLICY CHANGE

Institutional change happens at very different levels of intensity and rhythm. According to Hall (1993), in the policy realm, change can take place from the simple revision of existing policy instruments (which would represent a policy change of low intensity) to the alteration of the legitimate goals that public policy should pursue in a given field (which represents a more radical type of change in nature, with more substantial and probably long-term policy implications). Nevertheless, most changes in policy systems take place at a gradual and evolutionary pace. In part, this is because institutional settings and previously established policy systems condition and mediate in the adoption and enactment of new policy models.

Just because change is usually evolutionary and path-dependent, however, does not necessarily contradict the occurrence of drastic or more radical changes. The *punctuated equilibrium* concept combines both conceptions of change (revolutionary and evolutionary). It refers to a "discontinuous conception of political time in which periods of comparatively modest institutional change are interrupted by more rapid and intense moments of transformation" (Hay, 2002, p. 161).

These types of transformation occur, for instance, when advocacy groups succeed in challenging the *status quo* by redefining issues and replacing old policies with new and more fitting policy solutions. Once the conflict ameliorates and the new constituencies and interests are resituated around the new policy, a (longer or shorter) period of stability follows (Bardach, 2006; Baumgartner & Jones, 1993).[8]

Analyzing the Adoption of Policy Change: Its Structuring Mechanisms

From a political economy perspective that takes ideas and semiosis more seriously, looking at the *adoption* of new education policies is a central element to understand most processes of policy change and institutional transformation. Focusing on policy adoption implies paying attention to the processes, reasons, and circumstances that reflect how and why policymakers aim to apply new education policies (or education models) in their educational realities. Following Bob Jessop's CPE approach, any process of policy adoption and change advances through three key evolutionary mechanisms: *variation* (the contingent emergence of new practices), *selection* (the subsequent privileging of these practices), and *retention* (their ongoing realization) (Jessop, 2010).

The variation, selection, and retention categories can contribute to identifying more systematically the sequence of contingencies, events, and actions involved in adopting new policy models, as well as the specific factors—of both a semiotic and a non-semiotic nature—that conduct or inhibit policy change. A careful analysis of each of these categories separately can contribute to building more complex explanations of why certain education policies—such as pro-private sector policies—are adopted in specific settings. These three categories are explored next, with specific examples.

1) Variation is triggered when dominant policy discourses and practices require revisitation because of a range of circumstances from the perception of an educational crisis (which may be related to internal dissatisfaction with the appropriateness of the education offer and its quality, or induced by the high visibility of countries' unfavorable results in international standardized evaluations) to more systemic phenomena that end up involving the education institution (i.e., global pressures on countries to become "knowledge economies," or the management of an economic crisis). All of these elements and circumstances would put pressure on policymakers to introduce substantive changes into their education systems.

In general, internal or external crises tend to disorient political actors and trigger the mechanism of variation in different policy sectors (Hay, 2002). In moments of crisis, policymakers perceive changing their education systems, or importing new policies from elsewhere, as deemed to be more necessary. The confusion generated by natural disasters or violent conflict can be used similarly as strategic moments to advance policy reforms that otherwise would be difficult to carry out.

Crises, moments of disequilibrium, or rapid changes in the economic, social, or political environment disrupt typical operating procedures and ways of thinking. These situations are conducive to competition and conflict between differing views, and tend to be perceived and used as windows of political opportunity by organizations, policy entrepreneurs, and activists operating at a range of scales to advance their preferred policy solutions.

2) The selection of policy programs implies the identification of certain interpretations of existing problems and the most agreeable and suitable policy solutions. Actually, for a given policy solution to be selected by policymakers from a broader range of options, it has to be empirically credible and consistent with the issues it is expected to address, blend in with accepted ideas on public sector reform and prevailing welfare institutions, and/or fit within the budgetary and economic capacities of the government in question (Verger, 2012). The latter is related to what Hall (1993) calls *administrative viability*, which means that new policy ideas are most likely to be taken up by policymakers if the latter perceive these policies to be technically workable and to fit within their budgetary, administrative, and time-horizon constraints and capacities.

When selecting policy solutions to their problems, more and more governments aim to base their decisions on "evidence." This is why, as Jessop (2015) suggests, researchers now have to pay more attention to the strategic action of policy actors that more actively engage in the construction of meaning, the definition of social problems, and the offer of suitable policy solutions, including intellectual movements, think tanks, IOs, and so on. All of these actors, through their discursive action, contribute to reproduce, shape, and/or challenge hegemonic or sub-hegemonic approaches to public management and/or the governance of education in particular.

Nevertheless, more normatively oriented principled beliefs and ideology still act as important filters in policy processes, including when it comes to screening which evidence from which sources is acceptable to inform policy decisions (Verger, Lubienski, & Steiner-Khamsi, 2016). For instance, in relation to the education privatization debate, many would predict that right-wing governments are more inclined than left-wing governments to outsource educational services (Elinder & Jordahl, 2013). Further, and as mentioned above, beyond what the evidence says, more stable institutions, such as welfare-state regimes and policy paradigms, are expected to influence government positions and choices in the framework of the education privatization debate.

3) Retention of new education policies refers to their institutionalization and inclusion into the regulatory framework, and into the network of educational technologies and practices of a system (Colyvas & Jonsson, 2011). It represents a final and necessary step for the realization of specific policy changes. Of all the mechanisms described here, retention is the most potentially contentious. This moment represents the materialization of the policy change in question and, as such, is more given to the crystallization of conflicts and oppositional movements.

Once a government announces its education reform plans, various political actors and key stakeholders (including political parties in the opposition, teachers' unions, the media, but also groups of civil servants with management responsibilities) tend to position themselves around the new proposals and, according to their level of (dis)agreement, articulate strategies of opposition or support. The consequent negotiation and conflict may result in the transformation or total displacement of the government plans. Accordingly, many policies that are selected by decision makers end up not being finally retained in specific settings. Overall, the retention of new education policies usually means that governments have to face some level of opposition and have to overcome it by deploying a range of technologies of power of both a material and a semiotic base, from persuasion to the repression or co-optation of oppositional forces.

Beyond actors' concrete strategies, the role of political institutions is critical in understanding the final retention of new policies. Prevailing political institutions can work in very different—and even contradictory—ways in retaining education reform ideas. For instance, in some countries, such as Denmark or the Netherlands, the political party realm is so fragmented that governments usually have to be formed by multiple party coalitions, which can be so ideologically diverse that it may be difficult for them to end up agreeing on the adoption of controversial reforms (Kjaer & Pedersen, 2001). At the same time, and as mentioned previously, the role and presence of veto points and veto players in policy processes can be vital to understanding the uneven adoption and retention of education reforms in various settings.

Once the new policies have been retained, there is a *lock-in effect* because these policies usually are associated with the creation of new constituencies and interests (Dale, 2012) and, accordingly, a period of policy stability follows (Bardach, 2006). Actually, the creation of new private constituencies and interests explains why dismounting some policy programs can be so challenging and faces fierce resistance from different fronts.

Because of the political interests and conflicts involved, retention is a more materially inscribed moment in the policy adoption process. It also has a significant semiotic component though. In Jessop's words:

> The greater the range of sites (horizontally and vertically) in which resonant discourses are retained, the greater is the potential for effective institutionalization and integration into patterns of structured coherence and durable compromise. The constraining influences of complex, reciprocal interdependences will also recursively affect the scope for retaining resonant discourses. (2010, p. 341)

Wrapping Up

Many of the factors that intervene in each of the described moments (variation, selection, and retention) have been referred to in the previous sections of this chapter relating to external-internal and material-ideational drivers of change. To avoid repetition, Figure 2.1 organizes and systematizes the cultural, political, and economic drivers that can be more significant in processes of educational reform. Among other things, the table shows that external factors tend to play a significant

Figure 2.1. Unpacking the Drivers of Policy Change: A Cultural Political Economy Framework

Scale	Type of Driver	Variation	Selection	Retention
Global	Hard	• Financial crisis • Race to the bottom mechanism • Catastrophes (externally originated) • Economic migration diasporas	• Loan/Aid conditionality • Welfare-state regimes	• External ideas as a third party to legitimize national positions
	Soft	• Global norms and political imaginaries (EFA, Knowledge Economy) • International comparisons (perception of system failure/mediocrity) • Global education agendas (definition of educational problems and solutions)	• Expert knowledge (evidence, research products, technical assistance); framing strategies of experts and international actors • Prevailing policy paradigm	
Evolutionary Mechanisms				
Domestic	Hard	• Insufficient education offer • Demographic trends • Internal conflict	• Level of economic development • Budget affordability • Administrative viability	• Political institutions (presence of veto points; separation of powers) • Political strategies of resistance/ negotiation/co-optation • Mobilization of resources by key players in the struggle
	Soft	• Key stakeholders perceive profound education problems • Narrative of the crisis points to problems in the education system	• Empirical credibility and resonance of new policy ideas • Public opinion/sentiments/values • Government ideology	• Discursive battles between key stakeholders • Use of evidence to support different positions

role in the moment of variation because, in a global era, agenda-setting processes, as well as other main events conditioning policy change, are increasingly defined at a supra-national scale. It is interesting that the opposite is observed in relation to the moment of policy retention, which is determined more by interactions happening in the domestic arena (although this does not mean that international influences are absent at this stage).

CONCLUSION

This chapter has presented a conceptual and analytical framework that organizes a range of interconnected concepts and variables to guide our research on the processes, reasons, and agents behind education privatization. The categorization used in this framework—the global-local and the material-ideational—is analytically useful, but it should be taken into account that in the real world these categories are not easily discernible. As the authors hope is clear, in the eyes of recent theoretical and conceptual advances in social sciences, a political economy approach to educational reform requires overcoming the understanding of the relationship between the national and the global and the material and the ideational as a zero-sum or as a simple dichotomy. Rather, these categories mutually constitute each other.

Something similar can be stated in relation to the mechanisms of variation, selection, and retention, which are behind the processes of educational reform. In practice, these mechanisms do not necessarily evolve in a linear way, as they generally are loosely coupled and tend to interact dialectically (Jessop, 2010). This is true especially in explaining the selection and retention of contentious and complex policies, such as those behind education privatization, because these are policies that generate heated discussions and, as will be shown in the following chapters, experience much fluctuation in most places.

The cultural political economy framework presented in this chapter highlights the importance of semiosis and related ideational factors at all stages of policy adoption. Specifically, this chapter has argued about the importance of scrutinizing dynamics of persuasion, the generation of meaning and, more broadly speaking, the role of ideas and discourses in the study of any form of policy change. Nevertheless, broader ideational frameworks such as administrative cultures, political ideologies, global norms, and policy paradigms also act as strong ideational structures that tell countries what type of policy goals, instruments, and sources of evidence are acceptable in making policy decisions.

Under all of these different forms, ideas can work as causal factors in policy decisions by shaping the perceptions of decision makers, providing them with rationales for action or filtering interpretations of the external world (Blyth, 2004; Kjaer & Pedersen, 2001). The role of ideas also is significant because ideational or normative changes tend to preclude more observable changes in institutions, such as changes of a regulatory nature or in the way resources are being distributed (Campbell, 2004). In Hay's (2002) words, focusing on ideas, and on the carriers of such ideas, is fundamental because policymakers take decisions according to the views they hold about their social, economic and political environment.

Finally, we must mention that the application of this cultural political economy framework and, in particular, having a comprehensive understanding of policy adoption dynamics requires comprehension of domestic politics, power relations, negotiation, and resistance at multiple scales. This is a huge challenge for a book with a global scope, and one that focuses on a complex and multifaceted education reform phenomenon such as education privatization.

Part II

PATHS TOWARD PRIVATIZATION

Education Privatization as a State Reform

The Ideological Road to Privatization in Chile and the United Kingdom

In several countries, education privatization is the most visible outcome of ambitious educational reforms that have substantially altered the role of the state in the financing, provision, and regulation of education. These privatization processes have brought about a drastic reconfiguration of educational policy in legal, political, and discursive terms (Ball, 2008b). As a consequence of its structural nature, privatization has strongly conditioned the development of future education policies and reforms.

The United Kingdom (UK)[1] and Chile are two of the most emblematic cases in relation to this education privatization path, which we call "privatization as a state reform." Both countries have gone through a privatization process that is grounded on profound structural and legal reforms. These reforms have introduced important changes within education systems that, in the past, had been rather state-centric in their forms of provision and financing. In both cases, the introduction of per capita funding and competition mechanisms between schools became fundamental in understanding the increased participation of the private sector in education. Furthermore, in both the United Kingdom and Chile, privatization became a policy solution accepted and supported by a broad political spectrum. Structural privatization reforms were initiated in both countries by right-wing governments. However, it was the subsequent center-left-wing governments that did not challenge the most crucial privatization policies, but further consolidated them. In the United Kingdom and in Chile, the privatization of education even intensified after the center-left political forces came to power.

The privatization typology discussed in this chapter emerged in a specific historical, political, and economic context strongly marked by the emerging hegemony of neoliberal principles. The fact that the privatization reforms introduced in Chile and the United Kingdom were initiated during the 1980s is not without coincidence. The intellectual and ideological influence of free-market advocate Milton Friedman's ideas in that period is fundamental to understanding the policy changes that occurred in these two countries. At that time, the adoption of education privatization was not simply a policy option; rather, it was a clear political choice driven by strong ideological convictions.

On the basis of the Chilean and the United Kingdom cases, this chapter explores the political and ideological motivations, mechanisms, and instruments used to advance this path toward education privatization. The chapter is structured into four sections. The first section analyzes the influence of the neoliberal doctrine in the structural education reforms that Chile and the United Kingdom went through. Here, the focus is on factors of a different nature (political, economic, and so on) that explain why neoliberalism became so influential in these two countries in particular. A discussion follows of the education privatization reform processes and their more recent consolidation and expansion in Chile (section two) and in the United Kingdom (section three). The last section outlines the most relevant findings and presents the chapter's main conclusions.

THE NEOLIBERAL INFLUENCE IN EDUCATION

The education reforms analyzed in this chapter were initially adopted in the 1980s, under the marked ideological influence of neoliberalism and, specifically, of the Chicago School of Economics, led by Milton Friedman[2] and other influential scholars. Neoliberalism developed in academia during the 1950s, but it started becoming relevant in public policy only in the late 1970s and the beginning of the 1980s (Klees, 2008)[3]. The neoliberal doctrine advocates market economy and market reforms as the best way of promoting wealth and economic efficiency. The application of this principle requires a strong reconfiguration of the relationship between the state, the market, and society. According to the neoliberal approach, the state should intervene as little as possible in the economy and focus on favoring "strong individual private property rights, the rule of law, and the institutions of freely functioning markets and free trade" (Harvey, 2005, p. 64). The policy development of this doctrine is grounded on two core mechanisms: (1) the privatization of traditionally public assets, and (2) the setting of choice and competition as operating principles for public services (Fitz & Hafid, 2007).

In the United Kingdom, education privatization took place in a political context marked by the electoral victory of Margaret Thatcher in 1979, which meant the beginning of the "neoliberal revolution" in this country. The rise to power of Thatcherism[4] represents the victory of the monetarist movement inspired in Friedman's theses and had direct implications for education and the governance of other spheres as well. In the case of Chile, the military dictatorship of Augusto Pinochet, which started in 1973, represented a deep change in the Chilean education system. During the 1980s, Pinochet's military junta also embraced neoliberalism in most policy domains. In education, it implemented diverse reforms, including the establishment of a voucher system, the introduction of competitive mechanisms between schools, and the municipalization of the education system.

From a historical and political point of view, there are evident similarities between the United Kingdom and Chile. According to Fourcade-Gourinchas and

Babb (2002), both cases exemplify the *ideological road* to neoliberalism, in contrast to the *pragmatic transition* that took place in other countries. In the case of Chile and the United Kingdom, the ideological road to neoliberalism is characterized by a pronounced political origin, quick development, and early adoption. At the same time, although the role of globalization and external ideas is important to understanding the initiation of the political debate around neoliberalism, in the two countries, the expansion of neoliberal policies can be largely explained by domestic politics and other intrinsic factors.

Fourcade-Gourinchas and Babb (2002) stress two other common characteristics shared by Chile and the United Kingdom in the development of the neoliberal project, which are important to understand the particular nature of the reforms implemented during the 1980s in different sectors, including education. The first was the radicalism with which the principles of monetarism[5] were embraced and implemented in both countries; the second was the repressive attitude of the governments of both countries toward any form of resistance to the development of the neoliberal project, especially trade unions.

These changes occurred in a particular socioeconomic context that favored the development of neoliberalism and related policies. The low level of economic growth in the United Kingdom and Chile compared to other countries during the 1960s and 1970s undermined the postwar compromise between the state, the unions, and the business sector. Furthermore, the persistent high levels of inflation deepened the economic crisis and increased the level of social unrest. This socioeconomic juncture legitimized the adoption of alternative economic policies in both countries (Fourcade-Gourinchas & Babb, 2002).

In a nutshell, in both the United Kingdom and Chile, the combination of a range of political events and economic circumstances within a particular ideological environment became determinant to understanding the neoliberal restructuring of the state in the early 1980s. Nevertheless, as outlined in the next sections, beyond the common characteristics emphasized so far, there are also some important differences within the processes of selection and retention of education privatization policies that the United Kingdom and Chile have gone through.

AN EDUCATION PRIVATIZATION LABORATORY: THE CASE OF CHILE

The education privatization process in Chile is embedded in a set of broader neoliberal reforms implemented by the military dictatorship between 1973 and 1990 and whose main approach was directly influenced by the monetarist ideas of the Chicago School of Economics (see Box 3.1). During this period, the Chilean government implemented a deep reform of the education system, which facilitated and promoted the privatization of the education system. The main feature of this reform was the implementation of a universal voucher scheme, which transferred state resources to schools according to demand, regardless of whether the schools were public or private. This reform sought to provide families with the complete freedom to choose their schools, as well as to stimulate competition between

---

BOX 3.1. THE CHICAGO BOYS

Chicago Boys is the name given to a group of mainly Chilean economists trained at the University of Chicago who wielded enormous political influence during the military government of Augusto Pinochet.

During the 1950s, the U.S. government implemented a cooperation program between the Catholic University of Chile and the University of Chicago to promote mobility and exchanges between both universities. The main objective of the U.S. government with this program was to create a body of Chilean economists trained in the United States as a response to the increasing influence of Marxist ideas in Latin America. The Chilean students of economics were trained according to the free-market and monetarist ideas of the Chicago School led by the economist Milton Friedman.

The political influence of the Chicago Boys increased in Chile, particularly after the economic crisis of 1975. Pinochet appointed many of the Chileans who had studied in Chicago and placed them in strategic positions as government advisors, or even economic ministers. Under the influence of the Chicago Boys, Chile became a laboratory for monetarist and public choice theory principles, especially in social policies such as education (Hojman, 1993).

---

schools. Competition thus was seen as a core mechanism to improve the quality of and promote efficiency in education.

The first democratic government elected in 1990 after the dictatorship opted not to reverse the market rules and mechanisms implemented during the Pinochet era. These rules and mechanisms were already at the core of the education system and generated a new common sense around how education should be organized, financed, and provided. As a consequence, a high level of privatization was consolidated and even expanded in the 1990s.

The Pinochet dictatorship and the democratic period that followed represent two markedly different phases in Chilean politics. However, there is an intense debate in the academic literature around whether continuity or rupture characterized the education policy of these two periods. For some scholars, the education policies implemented in the last two decades of the 20th century, during both the military dictatorship and the first democratic governments, are part of the same paradigm:

> In 1980, a period of about 20 years of reforms in the school system started [in Chile]. These reforms have become a reference for other Latin American countries due to their innovation and continuity—this is a process that remained practically without setbacks or large disruptions over 13 ministers and 3 governments. (Espínola & de Moura, 1999, p. 1)

According to these scholars, the market approach to education remained unaltered in the two political periods, although in each of them, it was adopted and maintained for different reasons: for ideological reasons during the dictatorship, and for pragmatic reasons during the democratic period.

However, other authors remark that in the democratic period, there were significant elements of departure from the paradigm that prevailed during the dictatorship. For example, Delannoy (2000) characterizes the democratic period as a new political paradigm in education policy, which she labels as "continuity with change." Cox (2003) considers that education was governed under two different paradigms in the two periods analyzed: the paradigm of market and choice during the military dictatorship, and the state or integration approach in the case of the democratic governments of the 1990s. Nonetheless, these authors are also aware of the structural character of the reforms implemented during the 1980s and the impact they had afterward. According to Cox (2003), the privatization process and the market measures implemented during the military dictatorship inevitably marked the educational policies of the following decade. In this sense, the significance of the education reform implemented under the regime of Pinochet lies in its long-standing structural impact on the Chilean education system.

The Dictatorship Period: Imposing Privatization

In 1973, General Augusto Pinochet came to power in Chile through a military coup against the socialist government of Salvador Allende, and he established a dictatorship that lasted until 1990. One of the main features of Pinochet's regime was its open commitment to neoliberalism, which resulted in structural pro-market reforms in multiple policy sectors. In 1981, an ambitious national educational reform based on market ideas such as school choice and competition between schools was approved. This systemwide reform effectively marked the application of neoliberalism in the educational sector and converted the Chilean education system into the largest quasi-market not only in Latin America, but globally.

The military junta was able to advance such an ambitious reform agenda through the repression and political coercion of key education stakeholders (Delannoy, 2000). Gauri (1998) highlights that the repressive political context undermined organized forms of resistance to the controversial market reforms in education:

> The military regime succeeded in implementing the reforms because the authoritarian climate and the regime's repressive strategies disarticulate the resistance that would have been expected in a pluralist setting. (p. 74)

The implementation of neoliberal reforms in Chile should be seen as an incremental process (Fourcade-Gourinchas & Babb, 2002). The neoliberal agenda was not openly adopted by the military junta until 1975, 2 years after the military coup took place. This interlude can be explained by the 2-year internal power struggle between Pinochet and General Gustavo Leigh for the control of the military government. To some extent, this fight for power represented a confrontation between the Keynesian and developmentalist economic policy program advocated by Leigh on the one hand; and the neoliberal agenda embraced by Pinochet, who would end up becoming the president of the country, on the other (Harvey, 2005). The ultimate concentration of power in Pinochet's hands, together with the economic crisis of 1975, is critical to understanding the political influence of the Chicago Boys in Chilean politics (see Box 3.1). In the case of education, the implementation of the new market design starts in 1979, when the minister of education resigned and the responsibility for educational reform was transferred to the Ministry of Finance.

As mentioned previously, the Chilean education market reform was characterized by the creation of a voucher system in which the government provided a fixed amount for each student enrolled in public or subsidized private schools. With the passage of time, this financing model has become almost universal in the country, with about 90% of the Chilean primary and (lower and upper) secondary education being funded—at least partially—through this voucher system (Paredes & Ugarte, 2009). The remaining 10% of students are enrolled in totally private schools not included in the voucher system. Another element that characterizes the Chilean model is the decentralization of the management of public schools to the municipal level (Bellei, 2007). Box 3.2 summarizes the main features of this educational reform.

Cox (2003) identifies four main interrelated motivations or principles that drove the adoption of such an ambitious reform agenda in the education system:

- *Improve efficiency.* Inspired by the neoliberal doctrine, the Chilean military government implemented a market framework in education in keeping with its belief that increased competition and participation of the private sector would lead to efficiency gains.
- *Promote private-sector participation in education.* The adoption of a voucher system and the increase of funds for subsidized private schools were the principal mechanisms to increase private-sector participation in education. These measures were driven by the beliefs that the private sector is inherently more efficient and responsive to social demands than the state sector, and that the competitive atmosphere created between private and public schools would increase the aggregate quality and efficiency of the system.
- *Decentralization of state power.* The transfer of public schools' management to municipalities was based on the belief that the local management of schools would make the education system more responsive to families' demands and concerns. Specifically, it was posited that in decentralized education systems, it is easier for service users to activate the mechanism of *voice,* as enunciated by Hirschman (1970).[6]
- *Reduce the power of teachers' unions.* A political objective of the reform was to reduce the influence of teachers' unions in education policy. With this objective in mind, the military dictatorship implemented

> ### Box 3.2. The pillars of Pinochet's education reform
>
> The reform implemented in primary and secondary education during the military dictatorship introduced drastic changes in four key dimensions:
>
> a. **Financing system:** Establishment of a voucher system to finance primary and secondary education. This mechanism of per capita funding assigns a fixed amount for public and private schools depending on the number of students enrolled and their attendance.
> b. **Management of public education:** The management of public state schools was transferred to the municipalities. This process of decentralization of public school management, known as *municipalization,* increased inequalities between public schools located in the poorest and richest municipalities.
> c. **Evaluation of the education system:** To promote choice and competition, a national assessment of schools and students' performance was introduced. One of the main objectives of this evaluation system, the first of its kind in the region, was to inform parental choice. Nonetheless, its results were not systematically disclosed until the 1990s, in the postdictatorship period.
> d. **Teachers' labor deregulation:** The Teachers' Statute was repealed and teachers lose their condition as civil servants, which meant that teachers' labor conditions were equated to those of other workers in the private sector.

the decentralization of public school management as a way of altering teachers' collective bargaining capacity. Furthermore, as mentioned in Box 3.2, the education reform liberalized teachers' labor conditions and eliminated their status as public-sector workers.

One of the main results of this education reform was a drastic increase in the number of private providers. According to Cox (2003), this can be explained by the financial incentives that accompanied the education reform. In fact, the subsidy per student paid to schools after the reform was 61% higher than the amount previously paid to private subsidized schools (Jofré, 1988, as cited in Cox, 2003). Figure 3.1, which shows the evolution in student enrollment between 1979 and 2009, clearly reflects this privatization trend.

Finally, it is important to note that the last significant legal change passed by the military junta represented the reaffirmation of key market polices in education, which reflects the fact that, for Pinochet, the market model in education was conceived as one of the most important legacies of his regime. The Organic Constitutional Law on Education (known as LOCE, for its acronym in

Figure 3.1. Percentage of Enrollment by Type of Institution in Primary and Secondry education, 1981–2013[7]

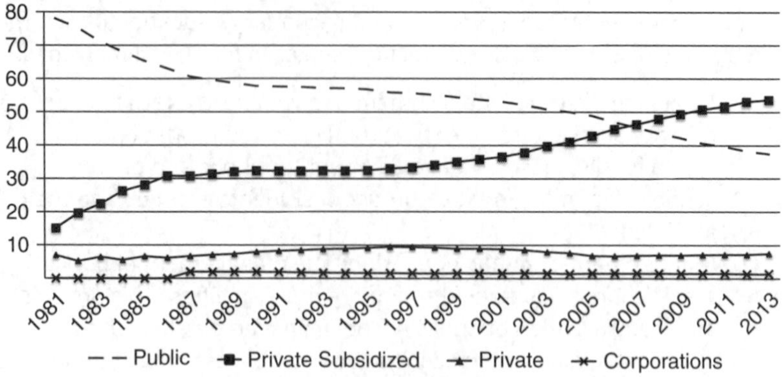

- – Public   -■- Private Subsidized   -▲- Private   -✳- Corporations

Source: Adapted from data from Ministerio de Educación—Gobierno de Chile.

Spanish[8]) was approved on March 10, 1990, the last day of Pinochet's term of office. This law contributed importantly to the longevity of the neoliberal paradigm in the country's education due to the political consensus that was necessary in Chile to change a law with organic status, as was the LOCE. These legal episodes are important for understanding that although the new democratic governments would have wanted to reverse Pinochet's market reform in education, the legal and political restrictions imposed by the dictatorship hindered any in-depth transformation of the education system.

Return to Democracy: The Consolidation of Privatization

The return to democracy raised expectations among a range of education stakeholders—in particular the teachers' union—about the possibility of reversing the reforms implemented during the dictatorship. However, the new center-left coalition (*Concertación de Partidos por la Democracia*), which came to power in the first democratic elections and remained in power during the next two decades (1990–2010), maintained the main features of the school system established in the 1980s. According to Gauri (1998):

> [the center-left coalition] was friendly toward the private sector; and it endorsed decentralization, efficiency in government, and privatization where necessary. Its program for government recognized the principle of *libertad de enseñanza* (with the implicit acknowledgment of the rights of children in private school to equivalent subventions), called administrative decentralization in education "a basic and fundamental principle," supported private sector involvement in education, and advocate the democratization of the municipal and regional frameworks as the best means to improve public education. (p. 87)

Gauri (1998) considers that there are two factors that explain why the democratic government assumed the main market principles of the military dictatorship. First, there was the fact that at least during the first years, the leadership of the coalition was in the hands of the Christian Democratic Party, a political force that supported private-sector involvement in education and other policy sectors. The second factor was the influence that the exile experience had in the way of thinking of many of those that would become government leaders in the 1990s. In the Western European countries where they were exiled, these leaders "grew to believe in the importance of private propriety rights, capitalism, and a sound macroeconomy, as well as in compatibility of these goals with progressivism and a concern for equality" (Gauri, 1998, p. 87).

Obviously, the educational discourse of the new democratic government maintained differences with the policies implemented during the dictatorship. Falabella (2015) qualifies this discourse as the "mantra of equilibrium" between individual freedom and state regulation. The new ministry of education advocated for a new education policy paradigm where state intervention was understood as a way to balance the more negative dynamics of the education market (Falabella, 2015). Despite some factions of the governing coalition expected that the return to a national public education system would be possible, the important ideological differences within the coalition together with other political tensions that emerged within the transition from the dictatorship to democracy "determined that the status quo would be maintained" (Bellei & Vanni, 2015, p. 26).

From the existing literature, it is not clear to what extent or how hard some factions of the center-left government tried to challenge the education market model inherited from the dictatorship. However, several observers agree on the fact that, even if the democratic government had tried to restore the public system, it would have met important barriers to do so. According to Carnoy (2003), who studied the 1990s-era education reforms in Chile, the pressures coming from families and private providers became one of the most important impediments to the reform of the voucher financing system:

> It is politically difficult to disassemble a voucher scheme because, once many students attend private schools, there is a large clientele that keeps the voucher system running. This clientele is not only composed of parents with children in private schools; it also includes the private schools themselves, which have an interest not only in the government subsidies [via the voucher], but also in increasing the value of the vouchers as much as possible. (p. 118)

The *municipalization* of the management of public schools, which was another of the key components of Pinochet's educational reform, was not easy to revert either. In 1991, the government approved the democratic election of local mayors, a figure that was previously dictated directly by Pinochet. Thus, in the 1990s, reversing *municipalization* was challenging because that was associated with higher levels of democracy and accountability, as well as with the possibility of local control over public policies (Mizala, 2007). Overall, the coincidence of the education reform debate with the first municipal democratic elections after the military regime hampered the possibility of legal reforms that could undermine the competence of the municipalities in any way.

The reintroduction of the teachers' labor statute in 1991, which had been abolished during the dictatorship, was an episode that also attenuated the criticism to the continuity of the market model in education during the 1990s. According to Mizala (2007), the reintroduction of the teachers' labor statute was justified by "the need to get teachers to cooperate with the process that began and to mitigate conflict within the sector" (p. 11). For the new democratic government, this was a way of recognizing the principal teachers' union (*Colegio de Profesores*) as a key stakeholder in the education policy arena, but also of reducing the potential for resistance of this union against the continuity of the most important elements of the market approach in education.

Finally, the World Bank's aid conditionality also contributed to this process of policy continuity. Two important education programs, which aimed to promote education equity and reduce the high level of inequalities in the Chilean education system, were launched at the beginning of the new democratic period with the support of the international aid community, namely, the 900 Schools Program[9] and the Improving the Quality and Equity of Education program (MECE, for its acronym in Spanish[10]). The latter started in 1992 with funding from the World Bank. Despite Chile's ownership in the design and management of the MECE program, the approval of the loan came with external conditions. According to Cox and Avalos (1999), two of the conditions that the World Bank tried to impose were (1) a focus on public spending in primary education by the Chilean government (at the expense of public investment in higher education), and (2) the maintenance of policies promoting the involvement of the private sector in education. Although the first condition was not accepted, the second one meant that the Chilean government maintained the main features of the market system established during the military government (namely, the voucher system and *municipalization*).

Continuity and Beyond: The Expansion of the Privatization Agenda in the Nineties

In 1993, one particular episode contributed decisively to accentuate the level of inequalities that the education market system was already generating. The government approved a law on educational cost-sharing (*Ley de Financiamiento Compartido*), which was adopted as a way of addressing the tax burden that Chile was facing. This policy substantially altered the supply-and-demand dynamics in the education system by allowing subsidized private schools to charge a school fee to families.[11] If this fee exceeded a certain amount, the state would proportionally reduce the public funding that schools received via the voucher (although when the fees did not exceed such a threshold, the voucher amount would remain unaltered). For obvious reasons, the cost-sharing policy increased the segmentation of the Chilean education market, as well as the funding differences between private subsidized and public schools. Because of this, some policymakers in the Education Ministry strongly opposed its adoption. However, the measure was imposed by the Parliament, with the consent of the Ministry of Finance. According to Mizala (2007), the implementation of the cost-sharing framework has to be interpreted as part of the negotiations for the approval of a new tax reform. In 1993, the center-left coalition government was trying to renew public income via taxes (which was a mandate from the first democratic election). However, a right-wing party in the opposition, *Renovación Nacional*, made its support to the tax reform conditional on the implementation of the cost-sharing system in subsidized private schools.

Carnoy (2003) summarizes the negative effects of the cost-sharing policy and its apparent contradiction with other education policies and programs launched during the democratic period aiming at promoting education equity and opportunities for the poor as follows:

> While Chile has preserved the main elements of the market system of the eighties, during the nineties' democratic period, the different governments have systematically regulated the market to try to correct their exacerbated effect on educational inequalities. Paradoxically, governmental regulation has promoted greater inequality by allowing private schools to charge fees on the top of the public subsidies received by them in the form of vouchers. (p. 115)

Finally, the agenda of evaluation, standardization, and school rankings, which was approved but not totally developed during the dictatorship, was implemented more faithfully since the mid-1990s. In 1995, the results of the national assessment (SIMCE, for its acronym in Spanish[12]), started to be published and disseminated by the government.[13] In addition, a voluntary program[14] of pay-for-performance for teachers was introduced in 1996. This program was designed to deliver salary incentives to teachers according to some educational quality indicators, with a particular emphasis on the academic performance of their students, measured by the national assessment (Falabella, 2015).

FROM THATCHERISM TO NEW LABOUR:
THE CASE OF THE UNITED KINGDOM

The education reforms implemented in the United Kingdom during the 1980s and 1990s share similarities with those of Chile. One of the most obvious is the policy continuity in the approach to education privatization by both the Conservative and Labour parties. In fact, as outlined next, some scholars consider that the Labour government went even further than the Conservative government when it came to promoting education privatization (Ball, 2008b). According to Lupton (2011), the 1980s and 1990s must be analyzed as a period of policy continuity, constituting what the author identifies as "not one neoliberal period but several" (p. 312). The following sections outline which types of education privatization policies were developed with Thatcherism and New Labour, respectively, as well as how and why they came about.

The Conservative Reform

Margaret Thatcher's election as prime minister in 1979 marked a paradigm shift in economic and social policies in the United Kingdom. The ideological basis of this shift was forged in the 1960s by a range of conservative and neoliberal influential think tanks, such as the Institute of Economic Affairs (IEA), the Center for Policy Studies (CPS), and the Adam Smith Institute (Fourcade-Gourinchas & Babb, 2002).

The privatization reforms implemented by Thatcher's government were not equal in all sectors. In sectors such as gas, water, or telecommunications, the government sold public services to the private sector. According to Fitz and Hafid (2007), this drastic form of privatization became politically strategic for the Conservative government for two main reasons. First, it symbolized the transformation of the governance paradigm, which went from a system guided by the collectivist principles prevailing during the post–World War II period to a governance system guided by the credo of competitive economic individualism. Second, it signaled the abandonment by the Conservative government of some of the key functions that the state had assumed during the previous decades in the United Kingdom.

Nonetheless, privatization in education and other social services was less straightforward. In the case of social sectors, the privatization process started later (in a strict sense, it was not implemented until the late 1980s) and did not mean a drastic transfer of ownership from the public to the private sector. In contrast, the principles of choice, competition, and markets were introduced within the public sector. In education, the most important policy program was the Assisted Places Scheme (APS), a targeted voucher program that offered high-performing students from disadvantaged backgrounds the possibility of enrolling in private fee-charging schools. Criticism within the Conservative Party, low interest from the private fee-paying school sector, and the practical challenges of implementation restricted the scope of this voucher program. Nonetheless, although its impact was limited, according to Fitz and Hafid (2007), the APS exemplified the core principles of the Conservative government in education policy matters: "a critique of the quality of state education, more choice for parents, and the willingness to pay private organizations to provide a public service" (p. 278).

It was not until 1988 that the Conservative government implemented more structural changes in the English education system with the approval of the Education Reform Act (ERA; see Box 3.3). This important reform was justified by two main political arguments. First, the "public education in crisis" argument was proffered, which basically meant that the public system had failed to respond to the needs of the economy and to the demands of the labor market. In line with this argument, the Thatcher government promoted the vocationalization of the curriculum and created the Technical and Vocational Initiative to provide extra funds to secondary schools to develop vocational programs (Fitz & Beers, 2002).

The second argument said that the "monopoly" of public authorities in education represented a barrier to improving the quality and efficiency of education provision, and that market principles and rules needed to be introduced to overcome these problems (Lupton, 2011):

> While other rationales may have been present, the primary ideological motivation for the reform was the Friedman-inspired ideology of the market as a mechanism for increasing public service efficiency. Through having to respond to parental choices, schools would either improve or go out of business. The virtue of choice, in the sense of the right of a parent to choose a school, became more prominent during the John Major governments of the 1990s. (p. 313)

In the case of England and Wales, the ERA represented a paradigmatic change in educational policy that, among other implications, triggered a profound process of education privatization. According to Ball (2008b), the ERA had to be interpreted as a strategic rather than as a substantive reform, in the sense that this educational reform turned privatization and market principles into a real policy option for the education system:

> ERA created the possibilities in legal, political, and discursive senses for a set of profound and inter-linked changes in the paradigm of English education policy. Specifically, ERA and other related legislation made it possible within policy to think about private sector participation in and delivery of state education services. (p. 186)

In the same sense, Lupton (2011) affirms that the ERA placed "markets and competition at the heart of the system" (p. 313), and this normative change had more significant consequences than the particular measures that were implemented within its context. Overall, the ERA converted privatization into a feasible policy option for the English education system and opened a window of opportunity for the entrance of private entities in the provision of education services (Ball, 2008b). Policies and programs such as Compulsive Competitive Tendering (CCT) and grant-maintained schools created a regulatory framework that was highly conducive to private-sector involvement in the provision of education services (see Box 3.3).

Simultaneously, the implementation of the ERA had the capacity to change the perceptions and preferences of key education stakeholders, including teachers and principals, in terms of what are the most desirable forms of school governance. In this respect, although the development of the ERA put a lot of pressure on education professionals by making them dependent on school autonomy and intake according to parental choice, the same professionals naturalized this situation and did not seek to return to the previous structure of the Local Education Authorities (LEAs) (Fitz & Hafid, 2007).

The adoption of the ERA introduced a sort of "fragmented centralization" in the governance of the education system (Ball, 2008b, p. 186). The new regulatory framework of choice, competition, and school autonomy reduced the LEAs'

Box 3.3. Main Features of the Education Reform Act

Fitz and Hafid (2007) summarize the market-oriented features of the ERA, approved in 1988 by Margaret Thatcher's Conservative government, in five main dimensions:

1. **National curriculum**: Business representatives were included in the process of designing the national curriculum to ensure the correspondence between the education system and the labor market needs.
2. **Governance and financing of schools**: Implementation of a per capita funding formula increased school autonomy from LEAs. The reform was designed to promote competition between schools for students and to force the closure of those with less capacity to attract students.
3. **Governing bodies**: The reform promoted the participation of the business sector in different education governing bodies.
4. **Grant-maintained schools**: The educational reform introduced this new typology of schools. Grant-maintained schools are educational institutions outside of the control of LEAs funded directly by the central government. These schools enjoyed a high degree of autonomy, and some of them had selective admissions procedures. To some extent, grant-maintained schools can be considered as the grassroots of current Academies and Free Schools.
5. **CCT**: This principle was introduced to all the contracts established by local authorities for the provision of different services, including services to educational institutions. CCT was a requirement for LEAs to open to competitive tendering the contracts for the provision of certain services in order to use the cheapest option.

---

control over the education system, and schools became stand-alone units with increased levels of state control over some aspects, such as curriculum design and assessment methods. This created a paradoxical situation involving the fragmentation of the education system into small units, which are expected to operate in a more autonomous way, at the same time that the state increases its power and control over schools without the mediation of local authorities. The fragmented centralization approach facilitated the involvement of the private sector in the provision of education services since the isolation of schools in the education market made them vulnerable to closure or takeovers by private institutions.

In a nutshell, the fragmented-centralization framework advanced but ERA, together with other programs such as the CCT or the APS voucher system, contributed significantly to favor education privatization during the Conservative governments of the 1980s and 1990s. As Ball (2008b) highlights, the reforms and the policies implemented by the conservative governments, beyond their practical effects in the education system, produced a *ratchet effect* that explains, at least in part, the development and expansion of education privatization during the New Labour government.

New Labour: The Expansion of Privatization

After 18 years of successive Conservative governments, the Labour Party won the elections in 1997, and Tony Blair became prime minister. This political shift, however, did not mean a substantive change to the existing education policies. In fact, it represented not only the consolidation, but the expansion of the education privatization trend initiated under the Conservative government.

The New Labour discourse contributed to consolidate a pro-private-sector approach to education policy. This discourse was structured around two main pillars: the modernization of society and the need for a national renewal (Poole & Mooney, 2006). The modernization of society and the need to generate high-quality human capital was the New Labour's preferred response to the challenges generated by economic globalization. The national renewal perspective implies a reconceptualization of the role of the state as an "enabler, regulator, and facilitator of change" (Poole & Mooney, 2006, p. 565) that, in the case of education, means that the state should not be seen as a direct provider of services, but as a negotiator and regulator of the contracts with private providers. Overall, the privatization of public services became the central strategy used by the New Labour government to achieve the modernization of the public sector (Ball, 2008b). As a result, contract winning became the new core activity of education businesses (Crouch, 2003).

Nevertheless, according to Fitz and Hafid (2007), the New Labour discourse on education privatization attempted to distance itself from the discourse of the Conservative administration. To these authors:

> These differences have been framed as distinctive approaches to the market, particularly when talking about the motivation for policies encouraging a role for the private sector in providing key public services. In this excerpt and in others, there is the claim in Labour circles that their approach is more geared toward supplying the most efficient services from the public, private, and voluntary sectors. (Fitz & Hafid, 2007, p. 285)

Other than for ideological reasons, the Labour Party would have promoted private-sector participation in education as a way to renew, modernize, and improve the quality of public services. This new political approach of the Labour Party to public services, known as the Third Way, was part of a broader politico-ideological movement that many other European traditional social democratic parties also went through during the 1990s (see Box 3.4).

The New Labour movement was strongly convinced of the necessity to ensure the quality of public services by nonbureaucratic means, as well as the fact

---

Box 3.4. The Third Way

The Third Way is a politico-ideological framework that seeks to reconcile socialism and capitalism and, for this purpose, combines egalitarian and individualist policies. The Labour Party in the United Kingdom, as part of the so-called New Labour movement, played an active role in the development of this framework, which many social democratic parties in the world embraced in the late 1980s and the 1990s.

Giddens (1998) considers that there are two main factors that explain the Labour Party embracing the Third Way and moving away from its classical principles. The first was the hegemony of the neoliberal discourse, based on individual freedom and personal choice, which was forged within the context of Thatcherism. The other was the growing perception that it was necessary to go beyond the traditional Keynesian approach to economic and social development—based on state intervention—and to establish an equilibrium between the public and the private sectors. As Giddens (1998) notes, other European social democratic parties such as those in Norway, Germany, and Italy went through a similar process. The Third Way had important effects on the policies developed between 1997 and 2007 by the Labour Party, particularly in relation to the emphasis this party put on public-private partnerships and market solutions as a way to modernize public services (Poole & Mooney, 2006).

---

that the only way to ensure the renewal of public services, as well as its efficiency and innovation, was through the participation of private providers in education (Fitz & Hafid, 2007). An influential advisor of the Labour government, Michael Barber (discussed further in Box 9.3. in Chapter 9 in this volume),[15] illustrated this idea well when he affirmed that the private sector was "uniquely capable of managing change and innovation" (Hatcher, 2006, p. 599). Even Gordon Brown, who became UK prime minister after Tony Blair, reproduced the generalized belief about the private sector's superiority over the public sector when he affirmed "the public sector is bad at management . . . only the private sector is efficient" (Pollock, 2005, p. 3).

It is important to mention that the Labour government also articulated an equity frame to justify the high level of marketization in education (Lupton, 2011). From an equity point of view, choice and competition would allow disadvantaged families avoiding the bad schools from their neighborhood. Lupton (2011) describes this change in the Labour discourse, which was traditionally against the idea of choice, as a reinvention led by Tony Blair to address middle-class concerns with public services:

> The shift in Labour education policy during the mid-1990s towards a position of considerable overlap ("bastard Thatcherism" according to McKibbin) on principles

of competition, diversity, and some aspects of selection, [is] part of Tony Blair's reinvention of the party to appeal to middle England voter interests. (p. 313)

Despite the New Labour rationale to embrace markets in education is apparently different from that of the Conservatives, it did not translate into a different policy framework in education. When Blair's first cabinet took over, the ERA had already placed choice, diversity, and competition at the core of the education system, the role of LEAs had been reduced, and private providers were actively involved in the provision of education services (Fitz & Hafid, 2007). Similar principles were at the center of the School Standards and Frameworks Act, passed in 1998 by the Labour government. Furthermore, this government expanded the diversity of the school system through the expansion of the Specialist Schools program and the creation of Academies; that is, independent state schools with private sponsors that had to replace "failing" state schools in disadvantaged areas (Lupton, 2011).[16] The Academies program represents the continuity and, to some extent, the expansion of City Technology Colleges (CTCs) and the grant-maintained schools programs implemented by the previous Conservative government (West & Bailey, 2013).

To a great extent, the Labour government promoted the transformation of the governance of the education system through the participation of new agents (principally from the private sector) and the displacement of more conventional educational actors:

[Teachers and LEAs] have been displaced by two new categories of agents: quangos such as the Office for Standards in Education (OfSTED), the Teacher Development Agency (TDA), the Qualifications and Curriculum Authority (QCA), and the Specialist Schools and Academies Trust; and private companies. From this point of view, the principal strategic function of the private sector in the school system is to "discipline and transform the old institutional sites of power." This enables us to explain the centrality in Labour education policy not only of for-profit business involvement but also the role of sponsorship on a non-profit basis by business interests and other agencies. (Hatcher, 2006, p. 600)

Another of the new entities created by the New Labour government was the Private Finance Initiative (PFI). In contrast to other New Labour initiatives, the PFI was not only based on the involvement of private-sector management or the provision of education services, but also in the building or refurbishing of public infrastructures. In this form of partnership, private entities assume the cost of the building and refurbishment of an education facility and local authorities return this cost as a loan. The PFI system was applied not only to the education sector, but also to a number of other areas, such as the health, housing and communications sectors. Many Academies were built under PFI schemes (Gunter, 2010). However, as shown in Box 3.5, this funding modality became a major source of controversy, and different media and academic voices challenged its level of efficiency and accountability.

BOX 3.5. CRITICISMS AND SHORTCOMINGS OF THE PFI

The PFI as an alternative modality to build and manage schools has been the object of increasing criticism for several reasons:

1. PFI schools became more expensive than non-PFI schools. This is due, in part, to the high rates of interest included in these agreements in comparison with other financial options. Furthermore, the costs of caretaking and cleaning were higher in PFI schools than in other types of schools (West & Currie, 2008).

2. PFIs represented substantial benefits for the private sector, but at the expense of the taxpayers. As stated by Fitz and Hafid (2007, p. 289), in the context of PFI schemes, "public revenue is diverted to the private sector as rental income funds."

3. The low quality of the PFI facilities and services. Although according to PFI contracts, private providers would suffer financial deductions if they contravened any aspect of the contract, on many occasions, the facilities constructed did not meet the established quality criteria. This was especially problematic in the education sector since Academies' "buildings and facilities were most frequently cited as the 'worst Academy feature' identified by pupils, parents, and staff" (Education International, 2009, p. 43). As stated in the newspaper *The Guardian,* "A survey by the Commission for Architecture and the Built Environment found that half the schools built between 2000 and 2005 were poor, with only 19% rated as excellent or good. Nine of the ten worst-designed new schools were built using the controversial private finance initiative" (Gillard, 2011; see also Hatcher, 2001).

In conclusion, the privatization policies implemented during the New Labour government represented a deep change in the Labour Party's conception of the role of the state in different aspects of education governance. As Fitz and Hafid (2007) state:

> In their respective ways, each of these policies represents the government justification of the ends—better-quality public services and higher performing schools—justifying the means—the direct involvement of private contractors and sponsors in the arrangements for the design, construction, and operation of public schools. They also represent a reversal of historic Labour Party allegiance to the idea of the state as a producer and the state as the sole provider of public sector services. Both have their antecedents in Conservative Party politics and policies, and we surmise that a change in the party of government is unlikely to change the scope or direction of the privatization of education witnessed under Labour. (p. 292)

CONCLUSION

The education privatization reforms adopted and enacted during the 1980s in Chile and the United Kingdom have many features in common. The ideological foundations of both reforms are found in the principles of neoliberalism in social policies and in Friedman's proposals on education. Competition and choice were presented as the main drivers of higher levels of efficiency and effectiveness in education. Although neoliberal ideas and policies were adopted in several countries during the 1980s and 1990s, the ideological road represented by Chile and the United Kingdom (Fourcade-Gourinchas & Babb, 2002) explain the depth of the transformations that were undertaken, as well as the effects that these transformations still have in both countries.

In both cases, the main objective of the privatization reform was not only to introduce some market features and to involve the private sector in education, but to drastically alter the state's role in education from planner and direct provider to a more hidden role as the regulator and distributor of incentives within the education system. Nevertheless, the political conditions in which these new ideas were adopted were very different in Chile and in the United Kingdom. While in Chile, the military dictatorship, established in 1973, created the conditions for reform via political repression and concentration of power, in the United Kingdom, these reforms had to be advanced in the context of liberal democracy. Despite the authoritarian character of Thatcherism, the education reform that took place in the United Kingdom is a valuable example of how soft power and ideas play an important role in the adoption of drastic reforms. To gain social legitimacy, the government of Margaret Thatcher spread the messages of "public education in crisis" and the "public monopoly" as barriers to achieving a more efficient and better education system that had to be overcome. The privatization policies and market-oriented reforms were presented, very persuasively, as the best solutions to existing problems and as the best way to improve educational services.

The structural changes implemented during the 1980s in Chile and the United Kingdom explain, to a great extent, the consolidation and expansion of privatization policies during the social democratic governments that came later. In fact, one of the most distinctive characteristics of this privatization path is the difficulty of reversing it due to both the structural changes involved in the role of the state in education, and the strong private interests (on behalf of families and private schools) that it originated. In relation to the latter, the promotion of private actors' involvement in the education system usually means the emergence of groups of interest in the maintenance of privatization reforms (Carnoy, 2003).

Nevertheless, the consolidation of privatization policies in Chile and the United Kingdom responded to different circumstances. During the 1990s, the center-left governments in Chile did not aim to dismantle the market education system inherited from the dictatorship period, but rather to find the difficult equilibrium between the market and state interventions which, to a great extent, aimed at addressing the increasing inequalities that market dynamics in education were generating. For political and economic reasons, the reforms of the 1990s did not alter the main pillars of the market system; in fact, some of the measures adopted in that period (such as the cost-sharing policy) even exacerbated the level of education inequalities and segmentation in the Chilean education system.

In the United Kingdom, the Labour government not only consolidated the privatization policies implemented with the preceding Conservative governments but contributed to their expansion. The New Labour movement drastically changed the role of the state in welfare provision that the Labour Party defended in the postwar era and situated the state mainly as a regulator and facilitator in the provision of public services. Again, the discursive dimension of political action became fundamental to explaining the expansion and legitimation of privatization policies during the New Labour government. The messages of modernization of society and the need of national renewal justified the requirement for market and private actors to overcome the presumed limitations that the state faces in providing high-quality public services.

While the privatization reforms explored in this chapter were designed and implemented during the 1980s, they have had long-term repercussions at many levels. Today, 30 years after their adoption, debates about how to transform the education system in both countries are strongly framed by the political and institutional conditions that were embedded with the "privatization as a state reform" path traced in this chapter. Nonetheless, whereas current debates in Chile are about how to reverse market dynamics in education,[17] in the United Kingdom are, in contrast, about deepening the level of *academisation* of the system.[18]

CHAPTER 4

Education Privatization in Social Democratic Welfare States
The Nordic Path Toward Privatization

The privatization reform movement has such a global scope that it has even penetrated countries with a strong welfare-state tradition. In this chapter, we focus on the restructuring of education systems in the so-called Nordic countries, including Denmark, Finland, Sweden, and Norway.[1] In contrast to other cases explored in this volume, some Nordic countries have adopted privatization measures not because private provision is seen as intrinsically desirable or superior to public provision, but rather because it is considered as a way to provide citizens with more educational options in education systems that, traditionally, have been highly comprehensive and cohesive. At the same time, some privatization policies (especially endo-privatization policies) are not seen as necessarily contradicting social democratic welfare state policies in the region, but as a way of modernizing the welfare state itself. In fact, not coincidentally, social democratic parties have played a key role when it comes to favoring privatization reforms in the Nordic region.

Nordic countries are well known for having developed a strong and progressive social policy tradition, and for enjoying a so-called social democratic model of the welfare state. According to this model, high taxes translate into generous benefits and a large public sector intervening in the decommodification of a range of economic and social affairs. Social policies are conceived as "politics against the market" (cf. Esping Andersen, 1985); accordingly, market and private solutions to social problems tend to be rejected. In most Nordic countries, there is a wide social consensus on the desirability of this model that has traditionally been supported by social democratic parties, the biggest trade unions, and the middle class.

In the education sector, this welfare tradition in the Nordic region contributed to the development of a comprehensive and universalistic education system, with a common structure and equal opportunities for all students (Telhaug, Mediås, & Aasen, 2006). This system is grounded in the direct participation of the state in the provision of public education and, accordingly, on very low levels of private education provision. These principles have been at the core of the educational systems of Nordic countries since the 1960s. However, the so-called Nordic education model (Blossing, Imsen, & Moos, 2014) has altered significantly since the 1990s.

Education systems in this region have not remained immune to strong pressures for education diversification and choice, as part of a broader transformation of social democratic welfare politics (see Larsson, Letell, & Thörn, 2012). In Sweden, for example, these pressures fostered the adoption of a very ambitious voucher scheme that has led to the expansion of the private sector in educational provisioning and has even allowed for-profit providers to benefit from public financing.

As is outlined in this chapter, a range of economic and political factors, both globally and nationally inscribed, provide a complex picture of these recent developments in the Nordic region. The chapter is structured as follows: the first part explains how globalization has altered the education policy landscape of the Nordic region in multiple ways. As will be seen, changing dynamics in global politics and economics have contributed to the perception of a welfare state in crisis, which has laid the foundations for future education reform. The second part of the chapter explains how political institutions and party politics have played a key role in the selection, retention, and adaptation of particular aspects of the global education privatization agenda in the various Nordic countries. In this discussion, the specific policies of the education privatization agenda adopted in Sweden, Norway, Denmark, and Finland are detailed. The third part of the chapter reflects on the evolution of social democratic ideas on welfare state reform as a key element when it comes to understanding the adoption—and, in particular, the evolution—of privatization policies in the region's education systems. The main findings of this review are then outlined in the fourth and final part of the chapter.

THE SPREAD OF GLOBAL NEOLIBERAL IDEAS

In the context of Nordic countries, education reform research tends to refer, in very general terms, to the global hegemony of the neoliberal policy discourse as one of the main drivers of the restructuring of education systems in the region (Rinne, Kivirauma, & Simola, 2002). The fall of the Berlin Wall is considered as one of the key episodes underpinning the neoliberal shift in the Scandinavian public policy realm. Until the end of the 1980s, the Nordic model was seen as an intermediary between the socialist and the capitalist worlds. However, with the competition between these two systems being mostly over in 1989, it was more difficult for the social democratic model to keep its distance from the new free market hegemony.

Neoliberalism, as a system of rules and norms, introduced important changes in Nordic societies at many levels, including in people's subjectivities. Among other effects, neoliberalism promotes the individualization of societies; by doing so, it challenges social democratic foundational ideas, such as those of equity and universalism, and legitimates social differentiation in public services (Imsen & Volckmar, 2014). According to Rinne et al. (2002), in countries such as Finland, the individualization of society has even drastically altered the conception of education itself:

> Education was now regarded as existing in order to serve the citizen, whereas, in the past, individuals were educated as citizens in order to serve society. The latest state

education discourse in the new education legislation of 1999 verifies this position of citizens in relation to society in the form of various individual "rights" concerning education. (p. 646)

The global economic recession of the early 1990s, which hit countries like Finland and Sweden strongly, became another significant motivator of change in welfare policies (Lundahl, 2002; Wiborg, 2013). Conservative parties and groups from these countries effectively used this crisis as an opportunity to communicate the message that the Nordic welfare state model was excessively costly and was responsible for the national financial collapses (Wiborg, 2013). The crisis ended up being addressed with austerity policies and important budget cuts in social sectors, including education. These types of policies, to some extent, opened the door for the introduction of privatization and market ideas in public-sector reform.

Other scholars point to the fact that Nordic governments embraced market ideas as a consequence of direct and indirect pressures related to their membership in international organizations like the European Union (EU) and the Organisation for Economic Co-operation and Development (OECD). For instance, countries like Finland adopted managerialist ideas in education so as to be seen as a "good pupil" of the EU (Rinne, 2000; Rinne et al., 2002). In Norway, the low scores in international assessments such as the Program for International Student Assessment (PISA) and the Trends in International Mathematics and Science Study (TIMSS) pressured governments to introduce education reforms and, in particular, to consider the adoption of new public management ideas (Imsen & Volckmar, 2014; Møller & Skedsmo, 2013; Solhaug, 2011).

Nevertheless, the most important way that globalization has affected education policy in Nordic countries is by generating a legitimacy crisis in the welfare state (i.e., the welfare state being seen, in the eyes of public opinion, as too generous, costly, bureaucratic, and so on). This legitimacy crisis has made key stakeholders more receptive to considering welfare reform ideas in different sectors such as education, health, or the pension system. Even the traditional advocates and guardians of the welfare state joined this way of thinking (Klitgaard, 2007). As will be explored in the following sections, welfare state reform has been the object of contentious party politics and has also contributed to generating profound debate and change of direction within social democratic parties themselves.

POLITICAL INSTITUTIONS AND PARTY
POLITICS IN THE NORDIC REGION

Nordic societies are traditionally known for their political stability and policy continuity in many sectors. There are at least two main reasons for these features of the political system. First, important decisions—such as those concerning education reform—are usually made with a high degree of consensus. The most important parties constructively participate in the deliberations that lead to the development of new education laws, and the adhesion that such reforms generate is quite broad across the political spectrum (Rinne et al., 2002). Second, the fact that the political party realm is so fragmented in most Nordic countries means that governments usually need to be formed by multiparty coalitions. This is considered as a factor of continuity because when government alliances are ideologically diverse, as they tend to be, it may be difficult for them to agree on the introduction of drastic changes, such as those represented by education privatization. In other words, multiparty political systems are more conducive to institutional stability than two-party systems (Kjaer & Pedersen, 2001; Wiborg, 2015).

Despite this apparent political placidity in the Scandinavian region, party politics have been especially contentious in the last few decades. In particular, tensions between conservative and social democratic parties are vital for understanding welfare system reform processes, and especially the restructuring of education systems in the whole region. In the 1980s and 1990s, the Scandinavian conservative parties, empowered by the emergence of UK prime minister Margaret Thatcher's and U.S. president Ronald Reagan's New Right movements, as well as the defeat of the Soviet bloc, were able to challenge the idea of a generous and expensive welfare state as a desirable model. Based on neoliberal political orthodoxy, they had a clear diagnosis of what the problem was—namely, "that the public sector caused budget deficits, high taxes, inefficiency, and lack of freedom in choosing services" (Klitgaard, 2007, p. 455). Accordingly, the solution had to consist of embracing the modern privatization agenda, with its emphasis on competitive financing, partnerships with the private sector, and choice.

In the Nordic region, conservative parties have been the main advocates and, when in power, the implementers of the privatization agenda in education (Rinne, 2000; Wiborg, 2013). However, and counterintuitively, social democrats also have become the advocates and, in countries like Norway and Sweden, even the initiators (in a more or less indirect way) of these type of reforms.[2] Meanwhile, in Denmark, social democratic parties directly supported pro–school choice legislation (Lundahl, 2002; Solhaug, 2011). Social democratic parties argue that they engaged with privatization ideas to anticipate the inevitable public education restructuring that would take place when conservative parties were in power. They thought that, by taking the first step, they would be able to introduce the reforms with much more social sensitivity than their political opponents (Klitgaard, 2007), and prevent the right-wing forces from making further demands for privatization (Wiborg, 2015).

Nonetheless, which type of policies have Nordic countries specifically adopted to reform education in such a context of welfare state transformation? In the following sections, we review schematically the adopted education policies in the different countries of the region.

Sweden

The Swedish Social Democratic Party, when in power between 1986 and 1991, transferred the administration of state schools to the municipalities and passed legislation that allowed local governments to outsource different types of services, including education. The decentralization reform aimed at, on the one hand, promoting local and democratic control in education and, on the other, giving more space for professionals to take decisions in schools (Lundahl, Erixson-Arreman, Holm, & Lundström, 2013). Nonetheless, the municipalization process became a necessary step for the privatization reforms that had to come right after (Lundahl, 2002). Specifically, municipalization set the legal basis for the conservative-led government (1991–1994) to approve the implementation of an ambitious voucher system in 1992 that allowed private schools—so-called Free Schools—to receive public financing according to student demand (Wiborg, 2013).

Voucher reform, which aimed at making school choice more effective by promoting the diversification of the types of school offered, accentuated the liberalization of the education sector initiated by the Social Democrats and the competition between the public and the private sector. Private schools were provided with significant resources to operate since the voucher represented 85% of the average costs of a pupil in the public sector. Even for-profit providers could benefit from this public subsidy.

The Social Democratic party was found in the difficult position of having to oppose the reform even though they had already expressed a positive attitude toward school choice policy. As a lesser evil, many social democrats expected that most of the new providers would come from the community, teachers' organizations, or parental associations, and would have a social (nonprofit) ethos.[3] Nevertheless, "the paucity of interested parental and community groups in setting up schools, since they preferred to leave it to the state, made it easy for private business to expand their interests" (Wiborg, 2015, p. 483). Thus, in the context of the voucher scheme, for-profit school companies proliferated and a great majority of Free Schools ended up being run by for-profit providers. More specifically, the number of private schools increased exponentially, from 60 private schools in 1993 to 709 in 2009 (Wiborg, 2015). In the same period, the enrollment of students in private schools went from 1% to 11%, although the percentage is significantly higher in upper secondary education (Böhlmark & Lindahl, 2012). As shown in Figure 4.1, Sweden is the only country in the Nordic region where public school enrollment has decreased substantially in the last decade.

Education has become a very profitable sector in the context of the voucher system in Sweden. In fact, in the first decade of the 2000s, "free-school companies have been more profitable than businesses in other sectors" and several of these companies have expanded abroad and have become "attractive targets for equity companies, whose motivation is to generate profits for shareholders within a few years" (Lundahl et al., 2013, p. 505).

It needs to be emphasized that, in the context of this pro–private sector reform process, the execution of the voucher system was not planned from the beginning, but became the consequence of a chain of smaller changes initiated by the abovementioned decentralization process introduced by the Social Democrats. In this sense, the adoption of the voucher system in Sweden resembles more the type of change characteristic of the punctuated equilibrium model

Figure 4.1. Percentage of 15-Year-Old Students Who Are Enrolled in Public Schools, 2003–2012

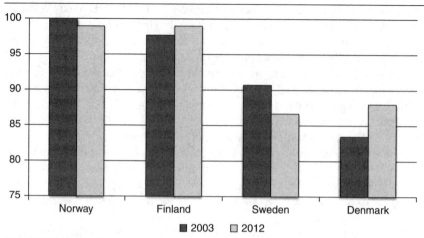

Source: Adapted from data from *OECD–Education at a Glance,* 2014.

(see Chapter 2 in this volume) than a drastic or rupturistic change. According to Blomqvist (2004):

> Promising a "choice revolution" in the welfare services area, the former opposition parties [once in power in 1991] sped up the reforms and encouraged private provision more forcefully than the Social Democrats had, but basically continued along the same reform track. (p. 145)

In the beginning, the Swedish social democratic government was not thinking about privatization as an end in itself, nor did it articulate arguments in favor of school competition or about private schools being inherently better than public schools, as neoliberal advocates often do. At some point, however, education liberalization and vouchers were perceived by an important faction of the Social Democratic Party as an appropriate policy to effectively respond to the new middle-class desire for school diversification and more pedagogical choice. With the introduction of such measures, the Social Democrats thought that they would be addressing an upcoming demand from their potential voters. According to Klitgaard (2008):

> Connected to the strategy of reforming the public sector, the government, in the latter half of the 1980s, initiated a study of power and democracy in Sweden, which conducted a major survey of the Swedish population's attitudes toward public services. This survey revealed a profound feeling of lack of influence in relation to public schools. The attitudes toward schools were that it was difficult to influence the teaching offered to one's children and to choose a school according to one's own preferences. (p. 490)

The fact that the restructuring of the education system was initiated by the Social Democratic Party contributed to the reform being less contested. This is explained by the fact that social democrats are perceived as more "reliable" than conservative forces when it comes to altering welfare policies. As observed by Klitgaard (2007), "social democratic governments engaging in unpopular social policy retrenchment may be more acceptable to the voters because they enjoy more credibility in protecting the system than right-wing market reformers" (p. 174). However, as evident in Box 4.1, institutional factors also explain why Sweden was so effective in advancing such a large-scale education privatization reform, which even allowed for-profit providers to operate in the public sector educational realm.

Nevertheless, it is also fair to mention that in a country like Sweden, the Social Democrats would probably not have initiated these reforms without effective

---

BOX 4.1. EXPLAINING VOUCHER REFORMS:
THE KEY ROLE OF POLITICAL INSTITUTIONS

From a welfare regime perspective, the United States—a country very close to a neoliberal policy paradigm and to free market ideas—would seem more inclined to adopt a national voucher system than a welfare-egalitarian country like Sweden. However, the chain of decisions required in U.S. politics to adopt this type of far-reaching reform is so long and complex that, in the United States, voucher proposals have been interrupted several times at the federal level in the last several decades (see Chapter 5 in this volume). The strong division of powers in the United States (between the President, the Senate and the House of Representatives) does not contribute to efficiency in decision-making processes because it does not guarantee that the party that is governing enjoys a sufficient majority at the legislative level. Thus, there are more chances for the most controversial initiatives to be rejected by legislators.

In contrast, in the Swedish political system, the executive and legislative branches of government are mutually dependent, the state is unitary (in contrast to the situation in federal states), and there is a unicameral political organization. Such a level of concentration of power in the government allowed voucher reform to be advanced in a short time, and with much less opposition than voucher initiatives in the United States (Klitgaard, 2008).

Swedish teachers' unions openly rejected voucher reform. However, in Sweden, due to the institutional rules sketched here, trade unions and other nonstate actors have few possibilities of getting access to decision-making processes if the government cuts them off. When the voucher system was debated, they were left "to organize a demonstration outside the parliament without an opportunity to block the legislative process inside" (Lindbom, as cited in Klitgaard, 2008, p. 491).

pressure from conservative parties and like-minded think tanks. When in the opposition, the Conservative Party put such enormous pressure on the Social Democrats that it forced them to react. According to Volckmar and Wiborg (2014, p. 121), in the mid-1990s, "the right wing's condemnation of the welfare state had become so insistent that the government was goaded into action."

Denmark

In Denmark, the Social Democrats took more time to adopt a pro-market and multitiered approach to welfare state reform than in Sweden. Nevertheless, they also ended up playing a key role in the adoption of some important elements of the education privatization agenda. In this country, right-wing parties have governed for many consecutive years and, specifically, in two main periods: 1982–1993 and 2001–2011. In the 1982–1993 period, the right-wing government did not have the political capacity to advance the proposed drastic political reforms that were supposed to, in their rhetoric, "put an end to the social democratic nanny state" and, in particular, to promote a "neoliberal revolution" in education (Volckmar & Wiborg, 2014, p. 123). The Conservatives were not even able, despite successive attempts, to broaden the coverage of an old program of public subsidy to private schools, which covers around 10% of the school population (Rangvid, 2008).[4]

The main reasons why privatization reforms did not advance at this stage were:

1. The division within the right-wing realm, in particular between the Liberal and Conservative parties, which translated into cohesion problems within the government coalition
2. The determinant role of the teachers' unions, which "were exceptionally powerful" and merged forces with the Social Democrats to prevent these reforms from taking shape (Wiborg, 2013, p. 420)
3. The opposition of the Social Democratic Party

Paradoxically, when back in power in the mid-1990s, some factions of the Danish Social Democrats, very much inspired by the so-called Third Way (see Box 3.5 in Chapter 3 of this volume), wanted to introduce significant welfare reforms, including market mechanisms, into their education system. However, they could not do so because they were locked into their own political discourse—i.e., the discourse that they so effectively articulated when opposing the reforms posed by the outgoing conservative government:

> As they successfully defined market-type reforms as an ideological crusade against the welfare state, it has proved impossible to persuade the rest of the party—and the public—that such reforms are now a tool to achieve cheaper and/or better service' (Green-Pedersen, 2002, p. 283). . . . As a consequence, when the Social Democratic-led coalition governed Denmark between 1993 and 2001, "it stated that the provision of welfare services should remain a public responsibility." (Volckmar & Wiborg, 2014, p. 123)

Nevertheless, in the first decade of the 21st century, when Denmark was governed by a right-wing coalition led by the Liberal Party (2001–2011), the opposition from the Social Democrats to privatization reforms was more diluted. In 2005, the right-wing government passed an act to promote school choice, which allowed parental choice across school districts, and required all schools to create a website to inform families about their educational strategies and the results of national exams. During the negotiations leading to this new regulation, the Social Liberal Party, the Socialists, and the Christian Democrats expressed their reservations and accordingly voted against the reform. However, the Social Democratic Party, despite its initial opposition, supported the government reform. According to Volckmar and Wiborg (2014, p. 124) the Social Democratic Party defended its "act of support in a social democratic manner by purporting that increasing academic standards would help avoiding middle-class flight from state schools and thus promote social cohesion in the Danish society."

Norway

In Norway, it can also be considered that the Social Democrats played a role in initiating pro-market reforms, although they were far more distant and critical than their counterparts in Denmark and Sweden. In the 1990s, the Norwegian welfare system was subject to similar critiques as those of other countries in the region. After taking power in autumn 1990, the Social Democratic Party began to work on reforms in a range of welfare domains, including education. Among other changes, it approved a Municipal Act in September 1992, which promoted decentralization and increased municipal freedom in school administration. This paved the way for the implementation of new public management ideas and related policy measures that would take place later.

When the Norwegian government was in the hands of a center-right coalition (2001–2005), the Minister of Education at the time, Kristin Clemet, a member of the Conservative Party, deepened the decentralization and school autonomy process initiated by the Social Democrats. Such levels of decentralization were complemented by a new management-by-results system, standardized testing, and "back to basics" curricular changes. In 2003, the Free Schools Act was passed, allowing private providers to establish schools with public subsidies covering 85% of the total operational costs (Imsen & Volckmar, 2014; Volckmar & Wiborg, 2014). Nonetheless, as explained next, this law would be abolished by the Social Democrats in 2005.

The Conservatives and the Social Democrats have important disagreements in relation to the more explicit or exogenous privatization and competition agendas in education. Nonetheless, they seem to agree on the desirability of new public management proposals such as school autonomy and the professionalization of school principals. According to the educational discourse of the Social Democrats, school autonomy, outcome-based accountability, and professional school leadership are policies that are "not necessarily in conflict with the legacy of the common school for all as a tenet of equal educational opportunity" (Møller & Skedsmo, 2013, p. 349).

Finland

Finland is an exception to many of the abovementioned trends in the region. In this country, there is not much room for private schools to operate (in primary education, 98.5% of students are enrolled in public schools—OECD, 2012) and, in fact, public enrollment—even though it was already high—increased between 2003 and 2012 (see Table 4.1 earlier in this chapter). The presence of the public sector is so important that schools are not even allowed to use or outsource private pedagogic services. Municipalization and school autonomy policies have advanced in Finland, but in contrast to what has happened in other countries in the region, decentralization has not meant the advancement of privatization. National legislation allows free choice in education. However, "the municipalities were left with the right to restrict parents' choice of school by stating that such a choice must not supersede the right of other children to attend the school designated by the municipal authorities" (Rinne et al., 2002, p. 649).

To some extent, neoliberal changes have not occurred here due to the societal support for public education, which, according to Rinne et al. (2002), is rooted in the national history of the country. Education is widely regarded as a privileged mechanism of nation building and national cohesion to face the recurrent invasions suffered by Finland in contemporary history. Most recently, Finland's success on international standardized tests like PISA, which led to the country being upheld as a model that many OECD countries aim to emulate, has contributed to legitimizing and consolidating such a model of strong public intervention in education (Adamson, Astrand, & Darling-Hammond, 2016).

NEW SOCIAL DEMOCRACY AND THE MODERNIZATION OF THE WELFARE STATE

Understanding the recent evolution of social democratic thinking in welfare politics is key to understanding the engagement with the privatization agenda in Nordic countries. This is especially the case in countries like Sweden and Denmark. In the Swedish context, as we have seen, the Social Democrats seriously believed that, by debureaucratizing welfare policies, they could contribute to improving public education, public health, or the state pension system, as well as the societal perception of how these services work (Wiborg, 2013). Social democratic parties were concerned with the legitimacy crisis of the welfare state and with the increasing social dissatisfaction with the bureaucratization of public services, which has arisen to a great extent because the welfare state is their political flagship and their main avenue to power. To them, marketlike reforms were not a way to undermine the universal welfare state, but rather the opposite: it was a way to dignify and protect the welfare state in the face of its public legitimacy crisis. By reforming the welfare state, the Social Democrats expected to keep on using it as their most valuable political and institutional weapon in electoral disputes (Klitgaard, 2008):

> The reason behind this social democratic break with normalcy is that the Social Democratic leadership acknowledged that the welfare state was being increasingly perceived as a large, state-dominated bureaucracy. It needed recalibration to respond to the needs and demands of the new middle class in an adequate fashion. The welfare state strategy of Scandinavian Social Democracy is built on the assumption that the cohesiveness and political sustainability of the universal welfare state depends heavily on political support from middle class taxpayers (Rothstein, 1998). The continuous satisfaction of a new and less coherent middle class with individualized preferences and demands for welfare benefits was thus a central goal in the reform program developed by the Social Democratic leadership. (p. 491)

When engaging with educational reform, the Social Democrats were careful with language since they did not want to be portrayed as pro-privatizing agents. Thus, in the context of the reform process, they reclaimed the values of freedom, choice, and autonomy, but they never had privatization as a value in itself. For the same reason, they referred to *free* and *independent* schools, instead of *private* schools (Solhaug, 2011).

Of course, this ideological and strategic shift was not peaceful in the context of social democratic parties. For instance, in Sweden, different factions of the Social Democratic party had heated debates and encounters on welfare reform. However, the "true believers," which is how the advocates of the principles of Keynesianism were known (cf. Klitgaard, 2008, p. 489), lost the battle against the pro-market faction, under the lead of the Minister of Finance at that time, Kjell-Olof Feldt, who ended up imposing the official party line (Wiborg, 2013).

Despite the important changes in the social democratic parties corpus of ideas on welfare, it would be incorrect to identify social democratic education agendas with conservative agendas too mechanically. It is true that, in most Nordic countries, the Social Democrats accepted more choice, private sector participation, and new public management. However, they also tried to put limits on market ideas (such as competition, league tables, or tracking), usually from an equity perspective, fearing that such policies would lead to school segregation and education inequalities (Lundahl, 2002). Examples of this distinctive approach between conservatives and social democrats in all the Nordic countries are analyzed as follows:

- In Denmark, while the Social Democrats accepted the application of more school choice freedom and the existence of private schools, they added the condition that these schools should be nonselective (Wiborg, 2013).
- In Sweden, the Conservatives have been arguably more radical than the Social Democrats when it comes to adopting market solutions. When in power between 1991 and 1994, the conservative government allowed

private schools to charge user fees (equivalent to around 15% of private schools' operational costs). Since this was a measure that could clearly favor school segregation, it was abolished by the Social Democrats when they returned to power—although, to this end, they made Free Schools fully funded with public sources instead of only receiving the 85% of the average student cost that they received until then. To social democrats, "the financial situation of parents should not determine the educational opportunities of their children" (Wiborg, 2015, p. 484). In addition, to address socioeconomic segregation in schools, the Social Democrats introduced stricter rules for starting and running Free Schools, including school inspection.

- In Norway, the right-wing government in 2003 passed an Act on Free Schools that was very much inspired by the Swedish voucher model. However, when the Social Democrats took power in 2005, in the context of a broader coalition, they immediately abolished the Free School Act and, in its place, passed an Act on Private Schools, whose focus was on controlling private schools and stipulating how they should operate (Imsen & Volckmar, 2014).

- In Finland, both the Social Democratic and the Conservative parties agreed to promote municipalization and school autonomy. However, for the Social Democrats—as well as for the teachers' unions—autonomy was more about giving power to teachers on pedagogic and curricular matters; for the Conservatives, autonomy was more about managerialism and strong school leadership. In the context of crisis and austerity policies, as ironically stated by Rinne et al. (2002, p. 653), the latter kind of autonomy basically meant "asking those being cut to cut themselves."

CONCLUSION

The way that the global privatization agenda has been recontextualized in the Nordic region is quite uneven. All the countries analyzed have embraced elements of the privatization agenda for similar reasons, and in the context of similar social, cultural, and political transformations. However the policy outcomes resulting from this path toward privatization have been rather dissimilar within the region. Sweden, for instance, has adopted more radical privatization policies, whereas other countries are clearly reluctant to do so and, like Finland, have simply implemented some components of the new public management agenda and promoted school choice in a loose way.

The "Nordic path toward privatization" explored in this chapter challenges a much-extended belief that says that countries with a social democratic welfare state are less prone to pro-market policies in social sectors. Such a belief is often grounded in political theories like the welfare regimes theory, which sees the social democratic welfare model as being grounded in the principles of universalism and egalitarianism and, accordingly, as impenetrable for privatization and market policy ideas. The welfare regimes framework would not have predicted the most recent evolution of the education agenda in the Nordic region, and it seems to be particularly inappropriate for understanding the adoption of more radical pro-market solutions in Sweden, a country that, in fact, has been traditionally considered as the paradigm of social democratic welfare-ism (see Lundahl et al., 2013).

The fact that the privatization agenda has penetrated social democratic welfare states is, apparently, counterintuitive. Nevertheless, three main elements shed some light on this apparent paradox. First, the education reforms analyzed are part of a broader transformation of the welfare state in the Nordic region. The social democratic universalistic welfare model has gradually evolved toward "a multi-tiered welfare state that is more dualistic and individualistic" (Kvist & Greve, 2011, p. 146). In the context of broader welfare reforms, more doses of school choice and school diversification are not to be seen as an anomaly, but as rather the rule.

Second, the effectiveness of political institutions, together with other particularities of Scandinavian politics, contribute to explaining the rapid adoption of several market reforms, which in other countries would have been resisted much more effectively and retained with far more difficulty. This is especially well documented in relation to Sweden (see Klitgaard, 2007, 2008).

Third, social democratic forces themselves have been proactive when it comes to advancing the privatization agenda in the Nordic region. To some extent, the Social Democrats have embraced policies and means that can be considered as neoliberal, but they arguably have not done so (at least explicitly) for neoliberal reasons. In many cases, they have introduced market mechanisms in the public education system because they thought that this was a way of restoring the legitimacy of the welfare state—which not coincidentally is their main asset in political and electoral disputes—and to respond to what they perceive as a growing demand among their middle-class voters: more educational diversification and choice. Thus, in contrast to the conventional neoliberal agenda, privatization was not seen as a tool to undermine welfare politics or to promote market competition among providers as a goal in itself.

However, it needs to be acknowledged that the concrete actions and strategies of social democratic parties does not sufficiently explain these profound educational changes witnessed in the region, and especially in Sweden. At a more macro level, existing research shows that globalization processes in the 1980s and 1990s set the stage for the different changes that would come later. Among other things, globalization has introduced a profound legitimacy crisis, of both a material and ideational base, in the welfare state. Right-wing parties in the region have taken advantage of this situation and mobilized to the extreme the idea of a welfare state in crisis. By doing so, even when they have not been in power for very long on average, right-wing parties have had an enormous agenda-setting capacity that has forced left-wing parties to take action in education and public sector reform.

Furthermore, the demand for more school diversification and choice from middle-class voters (and which put such a reform pressure on social democrats) did not emerge in a vacuum. This demand needs to be contextualized in the individualization process that neoliberalism introduced in Nordic—as well as in other Western—societies in the 1990s. To a great extent, neoliberalism, as a hegemonic project, altered both the ideational conditions and the social context in which policymakers defined their educational priorities and accordingly made policy decisions.

To end, it is relevant to highlight that in Sweden, the Social Democrats are reconsidering their support of school choice and market ideas, as they have been crystallized in the voucher scheme, due to the country's mediocre results in international education assessments on one hand and some recent public scandals associated with Free Schools on the other. The latter is especially the case for JB Education schools, which declared bankruptcy in 2013, and generated an important national debate about the sustainability and future of the model.[5]

CHAPTER 5

Scaling Up Privatization
School Choice Reforms in the United States

In the United States, school choice and market-oriented policies occupy a central place in the national education debate. Nonetheless, and despite their powerful supporters, promarket ideas have advanced unevenly, and not as a consequence of structural changes at the national level (as, for instance, observed in the cases of the United Kingdom and Chile in Chapter 3 in this volume). Although somewhat encouraged by federal legislation, the most visible changes in privatization in the United States have been adopted at the state and local levels.

Overall, the push for education privatization in the United States has been gradual, limited, and uneven in nature. Nevertheless, given the country's long-standing model of a predominantly public and rather uniform system of educational provision, the sum total of education changes that have occurred in the last decades represents a remarkable shift toward privatization. In fact, some of the most emblematic privatization policies implemented in the United States, like charter schools, have become an international model that several countries in both the North and the South have attempted to emulate. It is important to remark that charter schools and related pro–private sector polices, such as voucher schemes, have usually been advanced in the United States in the name of freedom, choice and quality.

In countries such as Canada and Colombia, privatization has advanced through an irregular process, similar to the United States. In these two countries, as in the United States, the adoption of pro–private sector reforms, predominantly at the subnational level, have eventually resulted in the alteration of the governance of the public education system. This chapter exemplifies the "scaling-up path toward privatization" by focusing exclusively on the U.S. case. This is done for two main reasons: (1) the pioneering role played by the United States in theorizing about and experimenting with main privatization measures such as vouchers and charter schools, and (2) the weight and broad coverage of the U.S. case in the existing literature.[1]

The chapter is structured into three main sections. The first section identifies those contextual and historical contingencies that have paved the way to—but also restricted—the adoption of different proprivatization and pro–school choice policies in the country. The second section explores the main policy processes and mechanisms that several U.S. states and municipalities have undergone in advancing school choice policies. Here, as an analytical strategy, particular attention is paid to the reasons why charter school legislation has advanced more than voucher programs across the U.S. territory. The third and final section of the chapter summarizes and discusses the main results.

SCHOOL CHOICE REFORM BREEDING GROUNDS: DISCURSIVE, INSTITUTIONAL, AND LEGAL CONTINGENCIES

The United States comprises 50 states and a federal district, and thousands of local governments, all of which have roles in regulating education. Such a level of education decentralization explains the high fragmentation of the education system and the huge diversity of school reforms that are being adopted throughout the country. Nevertheless, at the national level, a set of shared factors and contingencies strongly frame the privatization debate and condition the adoption of pro-privatè sector state legislation. Specifically, we refer to factors of a discursive, political, and legal nature. In this section, we show how each of these factors incentivizes or restricts the ambition of proprivatization reforms in the United States. We also show that even though the vouchers idea better reflects the "school choice ideal," the charter schools proposal has ended up being more politically and legally viable.

School Choice: The Origins of an Influential and Long-Standing Debate

The advancement of privatization in the United States is closely linked to the growing resonance of the idea of *freedom of school choice* among the general public. In fact, voucher programs (and, especially, charter school legislation) have expanded significantly across the country, largely because both policies fall within the category of school choice policies (Heise, 2012). Nevertheless, the popularity of the school choice concept is relatively recent, since in the 1970s, school choice was still seen as a marginal education policy principle with right-wing connotations (Apple & Pedroni, 2005).

The idea of choice dates to the market-oriented approach to education developed by the economist Milton Friedman more than 50 years ago. In a concept paper (Friedman, 1955), he advocated a voucher system as a means to foster competition among educational providers. The author blamed bureaucracy for the prevailing unequal access to quality education and considered the replacement of the monopolistic public education system by an educational market with choice and consumer satisfaction at its center. However, at that time, Friedman's proposal had only a limited impact and failed to resonate among key policymakers and broad public opinion.

In the early 1980s, Friedman's thinking on education developed in parallel to a political slogan that was acquiring a lot of traction within the administration of President Ronald Reagan—the idea of *freedom*. In the educational field, this new language on freedom of choice penetrated more strongly in conjunction with a social perception of public education being in a deep crisis. According to Terzian and Boyd (2004):

> During the 1980s, public schools in the USA encountered a barrage of criticism from academics, federal officials, and corporate interests. By the early 1990s, many US parents had grown accustomed to hearing that their children were poorly educated (p. 136)

The report *A Nation at Risk,* issued in 1983 and warning about the growing mediocrity of American education in an alarming tone, had a significant influence on the construction of this belief of public education being in crisis (Harris, Herrington, & Albee, 2007; Renzulli & Roscigno, 2005). Pro–school choice ideas were absolutely conducive within the ideological climate of the Reagan administration. "Reaganomics" was known for strong antigovernment rhetoric and for repeated claims about the need to resort to the private sector to provide all manner of public services, and to competition between public and private institutions (Fitz & Beers, 2002; Klitgaard, 2008). In spite of vocal support from political and religious conservatives—including President Reagan himself—the vouchers idea did not translate into concrete policy, failing to appeal to either middle-class or disadvantaged families (Carnoy, 2000; Viteritti, 2005).

Nonetheless, in 1990, the publication of a seminal book, *Politics, Markets, and America's Schools* (Chubb & Moe, 1990), represents a turning point in the progression of the school choice debate. The authors provided Friedman's market model with an empirical base and made an efficiency and equity argument in favor of school choice. They condemned the monopolistic bureaucratic system and the related political dynamics that undermine public sector efficiency, and they considered that these dynamics were particularly harmful to low-income families. Their book generated a great deal of controversy within and outside academia. Although strongly criticized by many scholars, the book had strong supporters in the political domain, including President George H. W. Bush (Ryan & Heise, 2002; Viteritti, 2005).

In the 1990s, the concept of school choice took on a life of its own, evolving in a number of directions. School choice was mainly about freedom and education excellence, but it also became aligned with equity-based arguments. The idea that low-income and minority families should enjoy the opportunity to choose their schools (which was a de facto option for wealthier families) gained in popularity. Lubienski, Weitzel, and Lubienski (2009) recall that:

> Although Friedman and others originally advocated for vouchers largely as a way of liberating supply and demand, a subsequent wave of school reformers echoed Friedman's economic logic for schools in arguing that vouchers would offer new and better educational opportunities to disadvantaged students and create competitive forces that would force schools to improve. (p. 165)

In conclusion, despite being initially considered as a radical market proposal, freedom of school choice became a sort of master frame that gave rise to a confluence of diverse and apparently competing arguments, such as reducing the inappropriate intrusion of the state, promoting so-called traditional family values, increasing competition, and empowering disadvantaged communities.

Political Architecture: The Bipartisan Promotion of Charter Schools

The system of institutional rules for decision making in American politics is key to understanding the particular and uneven path toward privatization in the United States. Such rules have made the translation of drastic proprivatization policy preferences of numerous federal governments into concrete legislation more difficult. In particular, these rules explain the poor advancement of voucher policy frameworks at the federal level. It is quite illustrative of this point that the U.S. Congress rejected three voucher bills submitted by President Reagan during his tenure (in 1983, 1985, and 1986) (Viteritti, 2005).

Klitgaard (2008), focusing on institutionalist theory, points out that presidentialism (involving the independence between the executive and the legislative branches of government), bicameralism, and federalism[2] are features of the U.S. political system that contribute to the fragmentation of political power and to the presence of a larger number of veto opportunities along the decision-making chain. These features result in the federal government's limited capacity for institutional reform, especially in relation to reforms that generate controversy, such as vouchers. Hence, existing rules for political decision making could be considered a mechanism of nonadoption of voucher reforms at the federal level. According to Klitgaard (2008):

> In the USA in the 1980s and early 1990s, Republican presidents experienced that even their modest voucher programs were rejected by Congress. These programs were rejected because the president's party did not control Congress and because an independently elected president could not even rely on legislators from his own party. Later, in the 1990s, a congressional majority in favor of school vouchers was actually formed by a now Republican-controlled Congress. In the meantime, however, a Democratic president had moved into the White House, so that Congressionally passed voucher plans were now vetoed by the president. Divided American government structures have indeed been a major obstacle to the voucher movement and to the advantage of voucher opponents. (p. 492)

Despite the difficulties met by successive federal governments in advancing drastic privatization reforms in the 1980s, more recent federal legislation has included dispositions that encourage and incentivize the adoption of privatization reforms by state governments. Such legislative advancement of school reform began to gain momentum with the election of President Bill Clinton, but particularly in relation to the promotion of charter schools—not the vouchers proposal. In fact, since the Clinton administration (1993–2001), Democrats in Congress have openly rejected and resisted the vouchers concept (DeBray-Pelot, Lubienski, & Scott, 2007; Terzian & Boyd, 2004).

When Clinton took office in 1993, only one charter school existed in the country, and he stated that he would like to see 3,000 charter schools established by the turn of the 21st century (Terzian & Boyd, 2004; see Box 5.1). With Clinton's presidency, both Democrats and Republicans found in the charter school idea a meeting point to promote the principles of choice, competition, and efficiency in education. According to Terzian and Boyd (2004):

> The burgeoning popularity of charter schools in the federal government resulted in part from the contested debate over school vouchers . . . school vouchers failed to find a home among any significant lobbying group that had the power to influence party

---

Box 5.1. Why Did the Democrats Start Supporting Charter Schools?

President Clinton's call to support charter schools in his 1999 State of the Union speech drew significant national attention to the charter schools phenomenon. In this speech, Clinton considered charter schools as a very appropriate education reform approach to promote school choice (Wong & Shen, 2002).

Existing literature does not clarify if the promotion of charter schools initiated by the Democratic-led government in the 1990s came from a profound reflection on the desirability of this policy option within the Democratic Party, or rather was the particular preference of President Clinton. As governor of Arkansas, Bill Clinton had already supported the idea of charter schools, as a concept originated with progressive educators in Minnesota in 1990. Once he became president, he was apparently very influenced by David Osborne and Ted Gaebler's theses on the use of choice competition mechanisms in public management in all type of sectors, not only education.[3] To a great extent, charter schools would allow the concrete application of Osborne and Gaebler's theses in the educational sector.

Nonetheless, some skeptical voices consider that President Clinton and the Democrats engaged with the charter program not because they considered it as an inherently desirable policy solution, but because they were "running out of viable alternatives." This is, for instance, the opinion of Clint Bolick, a long-standing advocate of school choice, according to whom:

> "For Democrats who truly believe in social justice, that presents a terrible dilemma: either forcing children to remain in schools where they have little prospect for a bright future, or enlisting private schools in a rescue mission. Democrats are increasingly unwilling to forsake the neediest children." (as cited in Boyd, 2007, pp. 11–12)

politics. In the early 1990s, moreover, Democrats in Congress drew a line in the sand with respect to vouchers, and Clinton joined the resistance. During congressional debates over the literacy and charter school bills in 1996, vouchers came under repeated attack for violating the separation of church and state and for not assuring positive student achievement. Eventually, most Republicans agreed not to fight for vouchers, because the president openly supported charter schools. With school vouchers embroiled in a fervent ideological debate, public charter schools emerged as a more practical and politically viable option. (p. 138)

Both Democrats and Republicans "have placed charter schools in a prominent position in federal education reform efforts and have granted millions of dollars to charter schools nationwide" (Bulkley, 2005, p. 528). In 1997, with Bill Clinton in the White House, a federal bill promoting charter schools was passed with bipartisan support, and substantial funding was provided to support the establishment of charter schools during the following years (Terzian & Boyd, 2004).

Another important milestone in the evolution of the privatization agenda at the federal level was the No Child Left Behind Act (NCLB), proposed by President George W. Bush (whose administration ran from 2001–2009) and passed by Congress in 2001 with bipartisan support. This law, which strongly focuses on student outcomes and exerts significant pressure on schools through yearly requirements and standardized evaluations, is considered to be highly conducive to the further advancement of charter schools. This is for two reasons: (1) the NCLB's promotion of public information on school quality through the testing regime (one of the main requests of school choice advocates); and, especially, (2) its encouragement of school autonomy and the outsourcing of failing schools (for instance, via charter school modalities) (Bulkley, 2005, 2007; DeBray-Pelot et al., 2007; Young, 2011). Another significant contribution of the Bush administration to the privatization of education can be found in the creation of the Office of Innovation and Improvement within the Department of Education, which fosters financial connections and the exchange of ideas between pro-privatization think tanks, the executive branch, and congressional staff (DeBray-Pelot et al., 2007).

The Obama administration, which began in 2009, also promoted the expansion of charter schools through the "Race to the Top" contest, which is part of the American Recovery and Reinvestment Act passed in 2009 (Young, 2011). "Race to the Top" is a competitive grant program through which states receive federal resources to implement reforms in four educational areas (standards and assessment, collection and use of data, teacher effectiveness, and distribution and reorganization of "struggling schools"). The program is considered to promote the expansion of charter schools since the absence of public charter laws (or the presence of restrictive caps to the establishment of charters) negatively affects the chances of states' applications to the fund (Burch, 2010; Young, 2011).

Legal Ambiguity and Multiple Interpretations

In the U.S. legal system, courts can interpret laws independently—and even in contradictory ways. This has important policy implications, as courts' interpretations can point in different directions when it comes to advancing (or opposing) certain policy programs. It needs to be noted that American judges go beyond the application of the law; they also make the law, in the sense that the decisions that they make establish precedent for decisions in future cases, and translate into legal rulings that often must be implemented by the executive branch.[4]

The level of ambiguity in the U.S. legal system, together with judges' ability to interpret laws, has resulted in the recurrent use of lawsuits as a core tactic in the context of the school choice debate (Boyd, 200). According to Belfield and Levin (2005), legal ambiguity means that "both advocates and opponents can infer support for their arguments from existing decisions" and "that both sides will seek to use the legal system to influence public policy" (Belfield & Levin, 2005, pp. 558–559). As a consequence, the school choice reform debate in the United States has become increasingly "judicialized" (Klitgaard, 2008). In particular, this ambivalent nature of legal dispositions seems to affect the debate around voucher programs, although charter school programs are also sometimes objects of litigation.[5]

Voucher programs are frequently challenged in the courts on the basis that they involve a violation of the First Amendment, which protects the right to freedom of religion and establishes the separation of church and state. Since vouchers frequently entail the provision of public funds to some schools controlled by religious institutions, it can be argued that this amendment prohibits the implementation of voucher programs by federal and state governments.

In some cases, however, court decisions have supported the application of voucher programs. For instance, in *Zelman v. Simmons-Harris,* the U.S. Supreme Court agreed in 2002 on the constitutionality of the use of publicly funded vouchers for religious schools and allowed the advance of the Cleveland (Ohio) voucher program (Belfield & Levin, 2005; Boyd, 2007; DeBray-Pelot et al., 2007). What the U.S. Supreme Court ruled in this case is that vouchers are not "state support" for those schools since it is the parents, not the state, who are deciding where to send the funds.

Another much older Supreme Court decision that has been used in an ambiguous way is *Pierce v. Society of Sisters* (1925). This ruling is supported by free-market advocates in that it ruled that previous legislation had "unreasonably interfered with the liberty of parents and guardians to direct the upbringing and education of children under their control" (Belfield & Levin, 2005, p. 556). At the same time, however, the *Pierce v. Society of Sisters* case has the potential to support antivoucher arguments because it can be interpreted to allow considerable state regulation to ensure social cohesion in schools. More important, this decision already raised "the concern that state entanglement with religion may create social tensions" (Belfield & Levin, 2005, p. 557).

At the state level, the so-called Blaine amendments have also intervened against the adoption of vouchers. These amendments, included in many state constitutions, prohibit the use of public funds to support religious institutions in an even more explicit and prohibitive way than the First Amendment to the U.S. Constitution. Accordingly, voucher detractors often resort to this legislation (and court decisions as well) in order to block voucher plans with the potential to benefit sectarian schools (Belfield & Levin, 2005; Boyd, 2007).

POLICY OUTCOMES: THE (UNEVEN) ADVANCEMENT OF CHARTER SCHOOLS AND VOUCHER PROGRAMS

Despite the current push for choice-oriented reforms at the federal level (notably through NCLB and Race to the Top), it is mainly through state-level legislation that these reforms are enacted in this country. The highly decentralized education system in the United States results in privatization policies being implemented to different degrees (Fitz & Beers, 2002; Kirst, 2007). At the national level, the most noticeable trend is the different degree of expansion between charter school legislation and voucher programs (see Figure 5.1).

Charter school programs were first adopted in Minnesota in 1991; since then, they have spread across the country. In 2014, charter school legislation could be found in 42 states (and the District of Columbia). In contrast, the

Figure 5.1. Number of States with Charter and Voucher Laws, 1995–2013

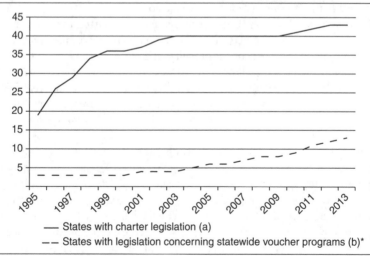

—— States with charter legislation (a)
– – States with legislation concerning statewide voucher programs (b)*

Sources: Adapted from (a) data from Center for Education Reform (2015) Rankings and Scorecard; (b) National Conference of State Legislatures (2015).

*Count based on the establishment of voucher programs in states previously lacking any arrangements. Includes the Town Tuitioning Programs, which were established in Maine and Vermont during the 19th century.

growth of publicly funded, statewide voucher schemes—despite vouchers being politically promoted much earlier than charter school programs—has been far more modest. Voucher schemes can be found in only 13 states.[6] Most important, charter schools account for an increasing share of enrollment in schooling services that are not delivered directly by the state. This trend is well captured in Figure 5.2.

The following section explains the uneven process of adoption of these two main school-choice programs. It does so by focusing on (1) the key role played by advocacy coalitions, (2) the equity dimension of charter schools, (3) the framing strategies behind these policies, (4) the importance of geographical considerations and other state characteristics, and (5) their political viability.

Advocacy Coalitions and New Alliances Around School Choice Reform

Education privatization research in the United States has paid special attention to the balance of forces between broad coalitions of supporters and opponents of promarket reforms as a way to understand the adoption and rejection of these reforms. As a consequence, it is not surprising that the advocacy coalitions framework developed by Sabatier and Jenkins-Smith (1993) is often applied in these studies. Advocacy coalitions involve people from a variety of positions who share a particular belief system (concerning both the perception of the main prevailing problems and the main solutions), and who are embarked in a certain amount of coordinated activity over time. The members of advocacy coalitions share core beliefs in relation to a particular policy issue, although they may disagree on minor matters. The wide adoption of the advocacy coalitions framework to the study of education privatization reforms in the United States reflects that this phenomenon

Figure 5.2. Students Enrolled in Private and Charter Schools, 1999–2012

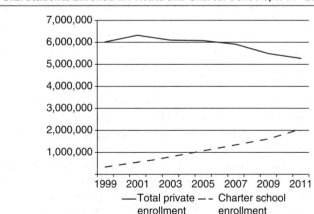

Sources: Adapted from data from Center for Education Reform (2015) and the U.S. Department of Education–National Center for Education Statistics (2015).

cannot be analyzed only by looking at the actions of conventional political institutions. Nonstate actors, including civil society organizations (CSOs), social movements and philanthropic organizations, play an increasingly central role in the processes that involve education privatization reforms (see Chapters 9 and 10 in this volume).

DeBray-Pelot et al. (2007) have studied the school choice debate in the United States through the lens of the advocacy coalitions framework. These authors observe that both the number of advocacy groups focusing on school choice reforms and their articulation in broader coalitions have increased since the mid-1990s. At the same time, the complexity of these coalitions in terms of ideological composition has increased, and is not necessarily aligned with the conventional left-right split. For instance, and as discussed next, a growing number of African-American parents and centrist and left-leaning groups have joined pro-school choice coalitions.

Nonetheless, it should be taken into account that not all the educational stakeholders align themselves equally around the same school-choice policies, and that the articulation and composition of coalitions can vary considerably in the different states and localities. Coalitions supporting vouchers and charter schools differ in their levels of strength and centrality within the educational debate, with the pro–charter school advocacy coalition being significantly stronger and more central in educational politics. The charter school advocacy coalition includes a broader range of actors, discourses, and interests. According to DeBray-Pelot et al. (2007):

> The charter movement represented the marriage of market-oriented neoliberals working from a series of state-level think tanks and progressive reformers committed to creating options within a public system. (p. 212)

This plurality prevailing in charter school advocacy coalitions has been able to challenge pro–public education ideas in many states (Kirst, 2007). In fact, according to Vergari (2007), the emergence of pro–charter school coalitions has forced the creation and crystallization of anti–charter school coalitions that aim at restricting the expansion of charter school legislation. The existence of these two major competing coalitions has generated policy dynamics that alternate moments of stability with moments of marked conflict (Kirst, 2007). The presence of anticharter movements has also meant that in some states, despite the fact that charter legislation has been approved, charter school operations are more strongly regulated or that profit generation by the charter management organizations is not allowed.

Conversely, voucher program supporters find difficulties in organizing broad coalitions that can counterbalance those well-organized groups (teachers and personnel within the school bureaucracy) that advocate keeping the public system unaltered and outside market dynamics. According to Klitgaard (2008, p. 482), this is because "the incentives for a heterogeneous voter population to organize a strong pro-voucher coalition are weak."

What Role Is There for "the Disadvantaged"?

Low-income and minority families that live in underperforming districts are increasingly interested in school-choice policies on the basis of their equity promise. Accordingly, some organizations representing minority groups have entered education reform coalitions that advocate these types of policies. Harris et al. (2007), for instance, highlight an increase in support for vouchers among the African-American population. Nevertheless, a more direct relation between the presence of minority groups and privatization trends has been observed in relation to charter school legislation. Renzulli and Roscigno (2005) observe that there is a direct connection between the percentage of nonwhite students and the likelihood of a state adopting charter school legislation. Stoddard and Corcoran (2007) observe that an increase in the Hispanic population is highly correlated with the adoption of charter school legislation at the state level.

The U.S. civil rights' movement has traditionally supported public education and actively advocated against privatization reforms. However, in the last several years, a range of organizations that support school choice policies have emerged within the movement (see Box 5.2). In contrast to more established civil rights

---

Box 5.2. School Choice and New Civil Rights Groups

The **Black Alliance for Educational Options** (BAEO) advocates the radical alteration of urban schools as a means to educate African-American students. According to Apple and Pedroni (2005), BAEO represents the most explicit African-American support for vouchers, school choice, and other conservative ideas. The organization enjoys support within black communities throughout the country, particularly in poor inner-city areas—although most of its leaders have a middle-class background—and its popularity must be understood in connection with the financial support provided by governmental and private organizations (Apple & Pedroni, 2005; DeBray-Pelot et al., 2007). BAEO "engages in activities such as state-level political organizing (i.e., providing support to legislators) and coordinating with churches located in primarily minority communities" (DeBray-Pelot et al., 2007, p. 215).

The **Hispanic Council for Reform and Educational Options** (HCREO) supports a range of choice options for parents, from public and magnet schools[7] to homeschooling and private schools. This organization has delegations in Texas, Florida, Arizona, Colorado, and New Jersey. HCREO does not work in the national policy arena, but it is involved in state-level politics by providing data, introducing its messages in the local media, or organizing rallies at the Capitol (DeBray-Pelot et al., 2007).

organizations, these new civil rights groups are more aligned with conservative or neoliberal values in education (DeBray-Pelot et al., 2007).

Proprivatization advocates have strategically articulated the *opportunities for the poor* and the *civil rights* frames to promote school-choice policies among sectors of the population that, paradoxically, are unlikely to benefit from these policies. The concept of "strange bedfellows" (cf. Apple & Pedroni, 2005; Bulkley, 2005) captures well the emergence of these counterintuitive alliances between disadvantaged population representatives and conservative groups in the context of pro–school choice advocacy coalitions. In some cases, these strange alliances are considered to be key to the advance of voucher schemes. For instance, this is the case in Milwaukee, Wisconsin, where a voucher scheme was adopted in 1990 with the support of Republican leaders, conservative philanthropic organizations, and minority leaders who were disappointed with the results of desegregation policies.

According to Apple and Pedroni (2005), the complex social configuration around pro–school choice coalitions is closely linked to the frustration generated by the failure of the desegregation movement. In 1954, the U.S. Supreme Court famously ruled against the legal racial segregation of students in the *Brown v. Board of Education* decision, an event that triggered many political reactions and policy reforms (Harris et al., 2007). However, policies enacted at the state and district levels did not meet the minority groups' expectations at times, such as when desegregation meant closing neighborhood schools in black communities and long bus journeys for black students were required. Consequently, a range of minority groups' representatives were predisposed to find alternatives, and some were found in market-based approaches (Apple & Pedroni, 2005).

Nonetheless, it should be noted that despite the presence of social organizations and minority groups in pro–school choice advocacy coalitions, these coalitions are basically in the hands of and promoted by policy elites. According to DeBray-Pelot et al. (2007):

> Choice advocacy tends to come more from policy elites than from grassroots organizing [. . .] Although there are some groups that attempt to represent wider communities, they tend to receive support from private foundations or government funding. (p. 11)

According to these same authors, the dynamics of instrumentalization of the new civil rights groups to put them at the service of the proprivatization agenda of government officials and other policy elites have been particularly obvious in the context of the NCLB (DeBray-Pelot et al., 2007).[8]

Charter Schools: The Malleability of a Policy Idea

The rhetoric of charter schools is manifestly appealing to people with divergent political viewpoints. Free-market conservatives see charter schools as the way to enhance competition and as a step toward the adoption of voucher schemes. Cultural conservatives see them as a way to increase parental control over the values taught in schools. Meanwhile, to moderate Democrats, charter schools are a means to enhance parental choice and accountability, but also a way to avoid more radical privatization measures. And even some teachers' unionists see charter schools as a way to increase the power of teachers. The charter school idea has also gained popularity among educators because they see this mode of education as a way to preserve their autonomy in the context of the education recentralization tendencies that have prevailed in the last decade (Kirst, 2007). For all these reasons, Bulkley (2005, p. 527) considers charter schools as the "all things to all people reform."

The accomodationist nature of this reform approach is consistent with the semiotic evolution of the charter school concept itself. This concept was developed and popularized by Ted Kolderie and Joe Nathan, who emphasized that charter schools "herald the end of the exclusive franchise in public education long enjoyed by school districts" (Vergari, 2007, p. 17). However, this conception of charter schools differs significantly from the early proposals of charter schooling, developed by R. Budde and A. Shanker [the latter being a former president of the American Federation of Teachers (AFT)], which were more directly connected to notions of school-site control, teacher empowerment, and educational innovation (Bulkley, 2004; Renzulli & Roscigno, 2005).

The variety of values attached to the charter school concept helps to explain the spread of charter school legislation in politically diverse states. In fact, charter school legislation in different states can have different goals and take quite different forms (Bulkley, 2005). Charter legislations diverge according to how much emphasis put on themes such as competition, innovation, incentives, deregulation, autonomy, and accountability. Another key variable to understand varieties of charter school frameworks is whether for-profit operators are allowed to operate in the context of charter school programs. Some of these variables (especially the for-profit one) explain why, in some states, the charter school reforms are more or less controversial and more or less resisted[9]—as the resistance faced by the for-profit company Edison Schools Inc. illustrates:

> Edison's attempts to form charters in New York and Philadelphia were resisted in part because of Edison's for-profit status. Political opposition is less in Michigan for a university-based charter compared to a for-profit charter conversion. (Kirst, 2007, p. 188)

The support that Democrats and Republicans have for charter schools can be predicted by the type of charter program in question. Republicans are more apt to adopt charter school legislation to promote school competition and allow for for-profit providers. In contrast, in those cases where charter schools are expected to benefit particularly disadvantaged student populations, Democrats have an ideological predisposition to support charter school legislation.

Precisely because of this ideological maze and the variety of charter school proposals on the table, the relationship between the ruling political party and the evolution of charter school legislation is less direct. Greater Democratic control of a state legislature does not seem to affect the likelihood of adopting charter school legislation, although a Democratic governor leading a Democratic legislature does affect it—negatively (Holyoke et al., 2009). Similarly, Renzulli and Roscigno (2005) highlight the lack of influence of the composition of state political bodies on the passing of charter school legislation.

In contrast, and far from the accommodationist effect generated by the charter school idea, the voucher proposal is seen as much more ideological. Passionate views on education vouchers hold sway, possibly due to their original links with the development of Milton Friedman's neoliberal doctrine (Belfield & Levin, 2005). Such an ongoing and clear ideological bias contributes to making the composition of the advocacy groups supporting vouchers more monolithic and partisan. It also contributes to the members of the coalition having a more shared and uniform understanding of the type of reform they want. As a reaction to voucher advocates, antivoucher campaigns have crystallized and actively contribute to a polarized debate on the topic, in which the role of evidence is usually secondary. As Belfield and Levin (2005) note, "ideology becomes an important driving force because there are enough persons and organized groups at the opposing ends of this spectrum to advance very strong opinions on the purpose and consequences of vouchers" (p. 558).

Spatial Diffusion and Other State Characteristics

To understand the mushrooming effect of charter schools in different localities, some authors have focused on spatial aspects, as in the effects exerted by physical adjacency or regional proximity. Renzulli and Roscigno (2005, p. 347) propose that states tend to use "similar or nearby states as a guide to help evaluate, create, and follow through on policy." A state tends to "look to its neighbors to help reduce ambiguity, garner a legislative framework, and provide legitimacy in its decision making and enactment of new educational policy" (Renzulli & Roscigno, 2005, p. 347).[10] Their study on the diffusion of charter school legislation confirms the prevalence of such mimetic dynamics between neighbor states. Thus, states that are adjacent to adopters of strong charter school legislation are nearly twice as likely to become adopters of charter schools themselves.

Holyoke, Henig, Brown, and Lacireno-Paquet (2009) also found that the evolution of charter school legislation is influenced by the behavior of neighboring states within the region. According to them, "there did seem to be a few 'catalyst' states taking the first step while others waited to see how this controversial new policy shook out" (Holyoke et al., 2009, pp. 46–47). They highlight that the policy learning between early adopters and latecomers is more frequent between neighboring states than between states in different parts of the U.S. territory. These authors are also aware of the key role of nongovernmental actors and interest groups when it comes to introducing charter school reforms in the educational agenda. However, they conclude that policy learning dynamics through active networks of legislators and administrators (which go beyond mere mimicry or isomorphism[11]) are determinant to understanding the evolution of charter school legislation.

Other scholars have focused on the mediating role of different state characteristics in the adoption of charter school legislation. For instance, a study by Stoddard and Corcoran found that "states with growing inequality, poor performance on the Scholastic Assessment Test, higher dropout rates, and low unionized teaching force are more likely to pass charter laws and to enact stronger laws" (Stoddard and Corcoran, as cited in Kirst, 2007, p. 191). This result is consistent with the fact that federal education legislation, especially since NCLB, incentivizes the chartering of underperforming public schools.

Finally, the state's political culture[12] seems to be another mediating variable in charter school legislation adoption. Kirst (2007) observes that charter school laws are stronger[13] in western states, which have a more individualistic culture, than in other states around the country that have a more traditionalistic or moralistic political culture. Anyhow, it is important to recall that, in different states, charter schools policies differ not only in the goals they pursuit, but also in the expected mechanism of change they rely on (Bulkley, 2005), what translates into a great variety of schemes in terms of financing, accountability, governance or market orientation.

The Political Advantage of Charter Schools (Versus Vouchers)

So far, this chapter has elaborated on the greater spread of charter school legislation (in relation to voucher programs), which is due to, first, the broader and more diverse advocacy coalitions behind them and, second (although strongly related to the previous point), the capacity of the charter school proposal to accommodate different discourses, ideologies, and interests, including those of the most disadvantaged population. In this section, we show that charter schools are advancing at a faster rate than voucher programs, also because of issues of political viability.

Politically, charter school programs have become a second-best option for both conservative groups, who are aware of the difficulty in passing voucher programs, and progressive groups, who see charter school programs as a means to avoid more radical market options such as vouchers (Holyoke et al., 2009; Renzulli & Roscigno, 2005).

A political factor that explains the bipartisan support for charter school legislation over vouchers is its potential electoral yield.[14] According to Renzulli and Roscigno (2005), advancing charter schools legislation is an opportunity for politicians to show their commitment to education transformation and modernization without having to introduce structural changes in the educational system. In their own words, "charter school legislation can make de jure changes to the façade of a state's educational system without de facto changes by authorizing, but not ensuring, the creation of new schools" (Renzulli & Roscigno, 2005, p. 345). Furthermore, with charter schools, policymakers can say that they support public education, which is still a popular idea in the United States. These are additional explanations of the bipartisan nature of the support for charter school reforms (see also Bulkley, 2005).

To a great extent, vouchers remain "the radical market alternative" (cf. Kirst, 2007) in the education reform debate, facing the opposition of Democrats, teachers' organizations, traditional civil rights groups, and like-minded organizations. However, it is important to point out that voucher reforms also have been rejected by factions of the Republican Party. According to DeBray-Pelot et al. (2007):

> On the federal level, the Republican Party's long-standing endorsement of federal legislation for vouchers and tuition tax-credits for private schools—reflecting an ideology of local control and a preference for market solutions—has not yet translated into the necessary support among Republican lawmakers in Congress, even after the Zelman decision. Instead, both Democrats and Republicans in Congress have settled on the legislative compromise of public school choice (including charter status) as a sanction for failing schools in No Child Left Behind. (p. 212)

The limited support that vouchers enjoy from Republican politicians is somewhat related to the preferences and interests of their own constituencies. Many Republican governors often prefer charter schools to vouchers because the proposal better suits the preferences of their voters, especially suburban ones. An important section of the Republican suburban constituency has an attitude of apathy toward vouchers, and another part perceives statewide voucher programs as a threat due to the potential negative impact of such programs in per-pupil spending, a suburb's ability to control the students' composition of schools, and real estate values (Heise, 2012). According to Moe (2001), conservative elected officials often have constituents who live in the suburbs and who are fairly satisfied with their schools. Such groups do not pressure for reform. For many Republican voters, urban or targeted voucher programs (see Box 5.3) would be more acceptable since they do not affect suburbanites, but merely offer assistance to urban students.

Overall, and beyond Republican voters, vouchers do not seem to be generating particular sympathy among the general public. In fact, when local referenda

---

Box 5.3. Targeted Versus Universal Vouchers

As happens with charter schools, targeted vouchers are more politically viable than universal voucher programs. Terry Moe (one of the most prominent education market advocates in American academia) has already predicted that the enactment of limited-choice programs (targeted to disadvantaged and urban environments) would be the most feasible strategy for advancing federal voucher legislation. According to DeBray-Pelot et al. (2007), this is due to the lack of electoral risk in targeted programs.

Nonetheless, once approved, targeted programs can be a first step toward universal programs. Boyd (2007) remarks that targeting choice for poor and disadvantaged students "trapped" in failing schools is a tactic increasingly used by choice advocates, what this author describes as "a toehold" and "nose of the camel in the tent" strategy for the long-term goal of making school choice a universal option (Boyd, 2007, p. 11; see also Heise, 2012).

Recent trends in the expansion of publicly funded voucher programs confirm the greater feasibility of targeted programs. As observed by Cierniak, Stewart, and Ruddy (2015), "most of the contemporary programs have been limited, either geographically to specific districts or metropolitan regions, or by demographics, to students with specific educational needs" (2015, p. 1). In fact, even statewide *general education* (that is, not necessarily directed at students with specific educational needs) voucher programs typically contain income eligibility requirements, targeting low-income households (and, more occasionally, directed to students attending poorly performing schools). Importantly, three of these statewide programs were initially launched as local programs and subsequently expanded. This is the case for the Wisconsin, Ohio, and Louisiana programs (which were originally restricted to Milwaukee, Cleveland, and New Orleans). In any case, this illustrates how limited (and less controversial) initiatives can work as an effective strategy that "opens the door" to a more universalistic agenda.

---

on vouchers have been held, the proposal has generated aversion and generally has been "defeated by sizeable margins" (Klitgaard, 2008, p. 488; see also Belfield & Levin, 2005; Heise, 2012; Kenny, 2005). According to Heise (2012):

> Voucher or tax-credit initiatives also appeared on a number of state ballots in the 1990s, including ones in California, Colorado, Oregon, and Washington. In each case,

voters not only rejected the proposals, but did so by wide margins [. . .] virtually every proposal to provide vouchers on a large scale has failed. (p. 1993)

However, despite voucher programs being less politically viable, the voucher proposal is far from being buried and remains central in the education reform debate in the United States. According to Lubienski et al. (2009):

Although the general idea of choice may be gaining acceptance as it proliferates in various programs, the voucher idea, first advanced by Friedman, continues to serve as the leading edge of this reform movement—as well as its most controversial manifestation. (p. 164)

In fact, while general statewide vouchers have seen only limited advancement, means-tested, local, or specific educational needs voucher programs are increasingly common (see Box 5.3). Moreover, already existing programs appear to be growing in enrollment and support, and receive more state funding accordingly. Concerning eligibility components, some states have raised the initial thresholds and now voucher schemes target lower-middle-class students (Cierniak et al., 2015). In addition, schemes largely similar to voucher programs—in the sense that they also support enrollment in private schools through public resources—can be found in an increasing number of locations, especially in urban contexts.[15] These programs illustrate how the public funding of private schooling remains a very real alternative in the school choice debate, and that vouchers (and voucher-inspired programs) continue to make a slow, but steady progress as the front line of the school choice movement.

CONCLUSION

Education privatization in the United States is a long and gradual process that has advanced through small-scale policy changes and has known different levels of impact, depending on the state and the specific policy. This process started in the early 1980s, with the crystallization of a shared public perception that public education was going through a deep crisis, which was in part manufactured by neoconservative forces through influential policy reports such as *A Nation at Risk*. These same forces skillfully reformulated the education debate by extolling the benefits of freedom of school choice and competition and had a great impact among both the general public and policymakers operating at different levels. Voucher schemes were the first policy option in which the principles of school choice and competition crystallized. However, despite the promotion of vouchers by federal governments, this policy idea did not become established and even experienced a rollback. Conversely, the charter school concept that emerged later became much more popular and enacted more widely. Since the early 1990s, charter schools have gained centrality in the political agenda and enjoy bipartisan support.

A combination of ideational and political factors has contributed to the displacement of voucher programs from the center of educational reform in the

United States. One of the most relevant of these is that voucher programs are regarded as a radical market policy solution and, accordingly, have stimulated a very ideological and polarized debate on the subject of reform. In contrast, the greater ambiguity and malleability of the charter school concept have translated into more transversal support across the ideological and political spectrum. The bipartisan agreement on the convenience of charter schools, despite its nuances, contrasts with the absence of a consensus around vouchers. In fact, voucher schemes even lack the necessary support from groups, including a faction of the Republican Party constituency, that for ideological reasons might have been expected to favor these proposals. Thus, the first conclusion to be derived from this is that those privatization policies most likely to succeed are those that appear less controversial or politically loaded.

The idea of political viability, in connection with the notion of scale, also provides some insight into the selective adoption of school choice reforms. Charter schools appear to have become a sort of common ground from the perspective of political viability and, to some extent, of administrative feasibility. Charter school legislation is seen as desirable by voucher scheme proponents, who see it as a second-best option against a backdrop of difficulty in passing vouchers, or even as a potential stepping-stone toward vouchers. At the same time, although from a very different perspective, some supporters of charter school legislation view it as a means to avoid further privatization. A similar logic translates into the adoption of targeted or universal vouchers. In this respect, electoral and political calculation explains the greater political adhesion to charter schools and to targeted (and, consequently, lower-risk) voucher programs as opposed to universal vouchers. In fact, means-tested, local, or specific educational needs voucher programs are increasingly common—which suggests that, while the charter school spread has reached a saturation point, the push for vouchers (and comparable initiatives) is still strong and working as the "vanguard" of the school-choice movement.

Another mechanism explaining the limited spread of voucher policies across the United States is related to the country's institutional architecture. The prevailing division of political power and the number of veto opportunities in the policy-making process, including the courts, have benefited voucher opponents and led to the nonadoption of voucher schemes, particularly at the federal level. Moreover, the adoption of charter school legislation, but also the implementation of targeted/urban voucher programs, point to a recurrent preference for those small-scale policies that involve limited and nonstructural change. However, the sum total of these small changes, in a context where systemwide and large-scale reforms tend to meet considerable resistance, has translated into an incremental and substantial process of educational privatization.

A final element that stands out in the education privatization process in the United States is the clear prevalence of domestic or internal drivers of change. This is due to the significant political autonomy (and lack of financial dependence) that the United States enjoys within the global polity in relation to many policy sectors, including education. However, this does not mean that education policy in this country is immune to multiscalar dynamics. Rather, it means that multiscalar dynamics of policy promotion, emulation, and imposition happen mainly within the context of the federal organization of the country. In fact, the complexity of the U.S. educational governance architecture, together with the diversity of political cultures that prevail in the different states that make up this country, definitely account for both the variety of privatization reforms and the difficulty in discerning a general, linear, and coherent privatization trend across the U.S. territory.

CHAPTER 6

Privatization by Default in Low-Income Countries

The Emergence and Expansion of Low-Fee Private Schools

In numerous low-income countries, private-sector involvement in education is growing, not because governments are actively promoting it, but because states seem to be rather passive when it comes to addressing new educational demands. This is usually the consequence of many Southern countries facing several intersecting restrictions (economic, administrative, political, etc.) in ensuring Education for All (EFA). In these contexts, private schools appear to be growing by default.

In basic education—especially at the primary level—the main privatization modality that is expanding in this way is the emergence of so-called low-fee private schools. *Low-fee private schools (LFPSs)* are defined as private schools that have been set up and are owned by an individual or group of individuals for the purpose of making a profit, and are supposed to be "affordable" for low-income families (adapted from Phillipson, 2008).

According to existing research literature, LFPSs are a growing phenomenon in sub-Saharan Africa (with Malawi, Nigeria, Kenya, and Ghana referenced most frequently), in South Asia (especially India and Pakistan), and in a number of Latin American countries such as Peru. However, there are different perspectives when it comes to determining the real size of this phenomenon, with its promoters eager to exaggerate its dimensions (see Pearson, 2015; Tooley, 2013) and skeptics downsizing it (Lewin, 2007). One of the main reasons why it is difficult to quantify the real dimension of LFPSs is that many of these schools are not registered and, consequently, the evolution of this type of school cannot be properly quantified and tracked through official data (Härma, 2011; Härma & Adefisayo, 2013; Srivastava, 2008).

Another reason why it is difficult to quantify LFPSs as a schooling sector is that it represents a relatively new phenomenon whose definition and boundaries are contentious in conceptual terms. Specifically, it is difficult to determine which private schools are included and excluded from the *low-fee* category. The meaning of *low-cost* or *low tuition fee* is especially unclear and highly subjective, and the point at which a private school stops being considered as low-fee or low-cost cannot be defined universally.[1] The determination of such a threshold will be contingent on the socioeconomic structure of the contexts in which these schools operate, as well as on the economic circumstances of particular families.

In any case, most scholars agree on the existence of a new privatization trend that, despite its heterogeneity, is different from more conventional forms of privatization. LFPSs are different from traditional elite private schools in the sense that the latter are selective by definition and generally do not target the poor. LFPSs are also different from schools run by nongovernment organizations (NGOs), communities, or churches, in that the latter also target the poor, but they are usually established on the basis of social, communitarian, or religious motivations, and not necessarily economic or for-profit ones.[2]

This chapter focuses on the reasons, agents, and other type of factors behind the growth of the LFPS sector. Among other things, this discussion shows that a phenomenon that first emerged spontaneously and at a local level is now strongly promoted by several influential international players in the education-for-development field. In fact, as will be observed, the perception of LFPSs as an appropriate solution to the challenges of achieving EFA is intensifying within the international community, and more and more governments, international organizations, and donor countries are considering integrating this type of school in public-private partnership (PPP) frameworks.

A GROWING DEMAND FOR LFPSs

According to many observers, LFPSs are "mushrooming" in developing countries (cf. CfBT, 2011; Kitaev, 2007; Tooley, 2013). Independent of the specific dimension that the LFPS phenomenon is acquiring, one of the key research questions that its emergence has generated among educationists is: *Why is this type of private school expanding* or, more specifically, *Why do poor parents choose LFPSs, and prefer them to free public schools?* (Ahmed & Sheikh, 2014). To respond to this question, the changing education demand dynamics in many developing contexts must be considered in more detail, especially the increasing interest in LFPSs from an unusual consumer of private education: poor families.

Researchers supportive of privatization consider that poor families make the economic effort to put their children in LFPSs because they perceive that these schools offer higher-quality education than public schools and, as a consequence, "will better increase their children's opportunities and potential" (Tooley, 2013, p. 460). According to these researchers, LFPSs are better managed than public schools, teachers in these schools are more highly committed and, more important in their argumentation, in LFPSs, children would learn more than in public schools. On the basis of research conducted in poor areas of India (Delhi and Hyderabad), Kenya (Nairobi), Ghana (Ga, near Accra), and Nigeria (Lagos State), James Tooley, a well-known LFPS advocate (see Box 6.1), concludes the following:

> On quality, we tested a total of 24,000 children in mathematics, English, and one other subject and found that children in the low-cost private schools significantly

Box 6.1. James Tooley: A Private-Education Champion

One of the most active and versatile players in the LFPS debate is James Tooley. He is involved in the emerging low-fee private education sector as a researcher, advocate, speaker, funder, and entrepreneur.

Tooley is the director of the E. G. West Center at Newcastle University in the United Kingdom—a research center named after Professor Edwin George West, a public-choice theorist who strongly challenged the role of the state in education delivery and funding. Tooley, on the basis of extensive empirical research in India and Nigeria, became well known for being one of the first researchers to speak about the LFPS phenomenon. In fact, in some of his publications, he likes to emphasize that he "discovered" the phenomenon (Tooley, 2013).

Tooley is far from an uninvolved and nonpartisan researcher. On the basis of his results, he passionately advocates that poor communities do not need the state intervention to access education services since they are able to enjoy better-quality education by organizing education services themselves. He also advocates that profit is a powerful incentive for school owners to deliver quality education to the poor, and that profit in education is not at odds with affordability. As a policy entrepreneur, Tooley actively promotes this solution to all types of organizations and networks that engage with education for development issues. According to Ball:

> [Tooley] clearly possesses both "strategic ability, and tenacity" [. . .]. He is a policy traveler, he animates global circuits of policy knowledge, and is a co-constructor of infrastructures that advocate, frame, package and represent policy ideas [. . .] He is a persuasive storyteller who is able to put faces and figures into the neo-liberal imaginary. (2012, pp. 39–40)

Tooley is also a guest speaker at various international events on private education, and he has received numerous awards from organizations that are well known for advocating free-market solutions, from the Templeton Foundation to the World Bank. His work has been welcomed especially by private investors due to its emphasis on the profitability of the LFPS sector.

Tooley and his team's research is generally more technical and "reveals important nuances in results on relative achievement in low-fee and state schools, concerns with equity, and education corruption at the highest levels" (Srivastava, 2014, p. 4). However, it is his more journalistic material, which contains less-nuanced observations, that has been more widely diffused across high-level policy circles (Srivastava, 2016).

Aside from being an active policy entrepreneur, he is also an edupreneur in the strict sense. Over time, Tooley has progressively moved from research to action, as a way of demonstrating that the model that he advocates is feasible. He is the creator of Empathy Schools, a chain of LFPSs in Hyderabad, India, and the cofounder and chairman of the Omega Schools, another chain of low-fee schools that started operating in Ghana in 2009 (Srivastava, 2014). Currently, the Omega chain has 38 schools and over 20,000 students,[3] and has received a multimillion-dollar investment from the Pearson Affordable Learning Fund.[4]

outperformed those in government schools, even after controlling for family background variables and possible selectivity biases. (Tooley, 2016, p. 64)

Several authors also argue that poor families are aware of and well informed about the apparent superiority of LFPSs to public schools (e.g., Dixon, Tooley, & Schagen, 2013). According to them, poor families have sufficient information to distinguish "good-quality" education and make schooling decisions accordingly. In their own words, "the choices favoring low-cost private schools made by parents in the slums are based on quality considerations, like those made by wealthier parents" (Dixon et al., 2013, p. 102).

Shailaja Fennell (2013) challenges studies that reflect on the "quality advantage" of LFPSs on the basis of parental perceptions of education quality. According to her, most poor parents lack the baseline personal experience in schooling to judge the quality of a school or teachers at the moment of choosing the school—this is why many of them would postpone their (more accurate) judgments until their children are already in school. Similarly, Balarin (2015) shows that poor Peruvian parents' discernment of school quality, when arguing about their preference for LFPSs, tends to be quite precarious. According to many of these parents, LFPSs are better than the public alternative because they give more subjects, workbooks, and homework to children. Thus, these families would perceive discipline and traditional forms of education as a proxy for the quality of education, despite current pedagogical and didactical theories clearly challenge these perceptions.

Overall, the superior quality of LFPSs is a highly contested subject in the existing literature. In fact, this theme has generated one of the most controversial debates in the "education for development" field in the last several years. A rigorous review funded by the UK Department for International Development (DFID) on the impact of private schools in developing countries recently concluded that evidence on the potential contribution of LFPSs to achieving quality EFA is still inconclusive in many aspects (see Ashley et al., 2014), The belligerent reaction of James Tooley (see Tooley & Longfield, 2015) to this report is very illustrative of the battle for evidence that surrounds this theme.[5]

Critical scholars, but also teachers' unions and civil society organizations, tend to point to teachers' qualifications and labor conditions as the main challenge of LFPSs from a quality perspective. According to them, LFPSs often hire unqualified teachers (who may receive very little training, are trained in-house, or both) and pay them very low wages (Andrabi, Das, & Khwaja, 2008; Aslam & Kingdon, 2011; Riep, 2014). Many of these schools also intensify the use of resources by increasing teacher-pupil ratios, which is a measure that has the potential to undermine education quality; on the other hand, other studies observe the opposite, with government schools having much higher teacher-pupil ratios than LFPSs (Mehrotra & Panchamukhi, 2007; Tooley, 2013). Finally, there are also those who argue that LFPSs are not better than public schools in abstract terms, but they tend to be more intensive when it comes to teaching hours, with some having classes on Saturdays, and are more strategic when it comes to teaching students how to do well on standardized tests (Riep, 2014).

The DFID review on education privatization in low-income contexts mentioned previously concluded that private schools are better than public schools in terms of more teacher presence, pupil attendance, and teaching activity. However, evidence of the superiority of the private sector in terms of learning outcomes is far from beyond question yet (Ashley et al., 2014). According to this review, even though there is a body of research showing that students from low-income countries attending private schools tend to achieve better learning results, most of this research does not "adequately account for social background differences of pupils" (Ashley et al., 2014, p. 45). This review also challenges the assumption that private schools are more accountable than public ones. Similarly, a review of this contentious academic debate by Srivastava (2014) concludes:

> Ideology aside, the evidence on issues of access, affordability, and quality of low-fee private schooling in basic and secondary education is inconclusive. Totalizing claims on the affordability, better quality, and equity leveraging potential of the low-fee private sector in developing countries should be treated with caution. (p. 2)

Unpacking LFPS Demand: Affordability

To make it easier for poor families to attend LFPSs, these schools tend to operate a daily payment system. They establish this daily fee-paying formula (which some call the "pay as you learn" model) because they are aware that poor people also earn money on a daily basis rather than having a certain weekly, monthly, or yearly income, and that their saving capacity is limited (Riep, 2014).

Nevertheless, several pieces of research challenge the idea of LFPSs being attended exclusively by the poor. Empirical research on the theme shows that, in many contexts, "the reliance on LFPSs charging school fees is likely to be prohibitive for poor households" (Härmä & Rose, 2012, p. 256; see also Ashley et al., 2014; Govinda & Bandhyopadhyay, 2008; Riep, 2014). Among other things, this means that one of the comparative advantages of LFPSs from the quality perspective could be related to the social composition of these schools. LFPSs might attract relatively poor families, but they do attract those families among the poor that have a higher level of education, more expectations for their children's education, or a combination (Akyeampong & Rolleston, 2013; Fennell & Malik, 2012; Härmä & Adefisayo, 2013). It is, therefore, no coincidence that, as mentioned earlier, many of the researchers who point to better learning outcomes in this type of private school do not properly account for students' socioeconomic status (Ashley et al., 2014).

Interestingly, the school composition factor in part explains the growing demand for LFPSs in different settings. This seems to be the case in those countries, especially in sub-Saharan Africa, that have abolished school fees in government schools in the last few decades. These countries have witnessed an increasing educational demand from the poorest sectors and have not increased the number of public schools accordingly. According to some authors, as a reaction to the massification of classrooms in government schools, but also as a way to distinguish themselves from the new (and academically less skilled) pupils entering the system, a significant number of the less-disadvantaged population have abandoned public schools and populated all types of private schools, including LFPSs (Bold, Kimenyi, Mwabu, & Sandefur, 2010). One of the results of this "exit" dynamic is that public education has become "a ghettoised option of last resort for the poorest and most marginalized in society" (Härmä, 2010, p. 38).

Other Criteria Behind LFPS Choice

Even though the evidence about the quality of private versus public education is inconclusive, there is a widespread social perception in many places that private schools are better than public schools (see Akyeampong & Rolleston, 2013). Beyond the social composition factor just mentioned, this perception is reinforced by the fact that public schools in remote or slum areas are more likely to be underresourced or poorly managed than those in better-established urban areas (Mehrotra & Panchamukhi, 2007; Rose & Adelabu, 2007). In fact, many LFPSs are emerging in remote rural areas or in new (and usually unofficial) urban settlements where public schools do not even exist yet. Thus, parents from these settings do not send their kids to LFPSs because they prefer them as a first choice, but because there are no decent free public school alternatives close enough to their homes (Heyneman & Stern, 2014).

In fact, closeness to home is one the main school choice criteria for many poor families. Choosing an LFPS that is close to home is convenient for families because it makes schooling more compatible with the parents' domestic and work duties, and because it saves money in transportation. But it is also important for security reasons. The closeness of the school to home "allows parents to be more vigilant of their children—taking them and picking them up from school—in precarious urban contexts that are perceived by their dwellers as being very high risk" (Balarin, 2015, p. 18).

Finally, religious and cultural aspects also explain the demand for LFPSs and, in particular, the demand for those LFPSs that more openly recognize and respond to the religious preferences of parents. This has been documented, for instance, in the case of the Indian Muslim community, whose education choices favor LFPSs run by Muslims because they consider that their religion is not sufficiently recognized in the predominantly Hindu public education system (Sarangapani & Winch, 2010). Something similar has been documented in the case of linguistic minorities and their schooling strategies (Walford, 2013), or in situations of internal political conflict—that is, in conflict situations, families may decide not to send their children to government schools when these families and the government have adopted different positions within the conflict (Caddell, 2006).

In a nutshell, many poor families opt for LFPSs not only because these schools are perceived as superior in terms of learning outcomes, but because the curriculum, religious option, or language of instruction in these schools is more aligned with their own cultural or political identities and preferences. In many cases, parents choose LFPSs for social distinction and security reasons as well. Nonetheless, religious, political, social and cultural aspects are variables that tend to be omitted in many of the studies advocating LFPSs, which consider that the reason behind the increasing demand for LFPSs can be reduced to education quality.

The following section reflects on the multiple forces that—beyond the demand from poor families—contribute to the growth of the LFPS phenomenon. Specifically, we focus on the role of international aid actors and education corporations in the promotion of this schooling modality.

THE GLOBAL PROMOTION OF LFPSs

Traditionally, "individual village entrepreneurs" have been considered the main agents behind the LFPS phenomenon (Walford, 2015). The owners of LFPSs tend to be described as local "edupreneurs" that have detected a business opportunity in the education sector, usually in their own community, because of an inadequate public education offering (Tooley, 2013). These edupreneurs are usually the owners of a single school that has been built with their own resources and, in some instances, even located in their own home (Härma & Adefisayo, 2013). Because of this, several authors refer to the growth of LFPSs as a sort of "grassroots privatization" phenomenon (Miller, Craven, & Tooley, 2014; Tooley, 2013).

However, in recent years, other actors, very different in nature to these local edupreneurs, have entered the LFPS sector and are promoting and offering this type of private schooling in the developing world. These include public and private organizations and individuals operating on a greater geographical scale, such as international organizations, international policy entrepreneurs, or transnational corporations.

Most of these international actors promote LFPSs with arguments of government failure and the potential efficiency gains of this education model. According to them, LFPSs need to be seen as a strategic option for both the governments of low-income countries and the international community because they facilitate more efficient access to education (at least, from the perspective of public spending). This argument especially applies to governments that are not able to plan and fund education properly due to insufficient resources or restricted administrative capacity. Furthermore, as will be revealed in the following examples, this type of argument is especially prevalent among the international aid community, whose focus is on widening education access in the context of the United Nations Millennium Development Goals (MDGs) and the EFA frameworks (Baum, 2012).

Perceiving the role of the private sector in such an instrumental way is far from a new development. Conventionally, the promotion of private schools has been seen as a cost-efficient measure because the private consumption of education (by those who can afford it) increases the total resources available for education and relieves the pressure on public budgets (Bray, 2002). In other words, by enrolling their children in private schools, middle-class families contribute to freeing up government resources that can be invested in improving public schools attended by the poor. Nevertheless, the LFPS phenomenon is altering—and somehow radicalizing—the pro–private schools discourse by proposing that poor families can also "afford" private education. In this respect, LFPSs, by enlarging the target population of those who can attend private schools, have challenged the prevailing reasoning on private school consumption.

The World Bank is, in fact, one of the global actors that have recently started to perceive LFPSs as a desirable option for the poor; to that end, it began supporting this concept through different lines of credit in Bangladesh, Pakistan, and Haiti. In the *2020 Education Sector Strategy*, released in 2011, the World Bank acknowledges and welcomes the idea of private schools as an affordable option for the poor and a method of overcoming "state failure" in education (Verger & Bonal, 2012). This report states:

> Although it is often assumed that the private sector serves mainly students who can afford to pay, private entities are important providers of education services to even the poorest communities, especially in areas that governments do not reach. (World Bank, 2011, p. 20)

For this reason, the *2020 Education Sector Strategy* considers that the International Finance Corporation (IFC), the World Bank Group agency that deals directly with the private sector, should play a bigger role in lending operations to private entrepreneurs who aim to sell basic education to the poor. In the words of the World Bank itself, the IFC has a great capacity for providing financing for "larger network providers who have the ability to invest across borders and go down-market to reach poorer populations" and "small and medium enterprises which typically target poor populations" (World Bank, 2011, p. 32). Despite the fact that the IFC has traditionally supported elite private schools in countries that are not necessarily the poorest (Mundy & Menashy, 2012), the *2020 Education Sector Strategy* seems to be having some effect, and this organization has started approving important loans for LFPS chains that operate in sub-Saharan Africa.[6]

Furthermore, as a way of promoting this line of credit and to explore how to bring private education to more people globally, every two years, the IFC organizes an international conference on private education that gathers education entrepreneurs, investors, and consultancy firms. In the recent past, the LFPS sector has been widely represented at these events.[7]

Bilateral aid agencies, such as those from Australia, Canada, the United States, and the United Kingdom, have also joined the list of international actors explicitly supporting LFPSs for the poor as part of their education development strategy (Niemerg, 2013). Of all of them, the DFID is one of the most active in LFPS promotion. Recently, this agency has clearly diversified its traditional strategy of mainly supporting and reinforcing public sector education in the South[8] and has openly stated its commitment to "expanding access to and educational outcomes for poor children, including through low-fee private schools" (DFID, 2013, p. 19). In countries like Kenya, DFID supports LFPSs as a way of bypassing a government whose corrupt practices have directly affected the operations of the British aid agency (Niemerg, 2013). Junemann, Ball, and Santori (2016) summarize the range of initiatives that the DFID is taking to promote LFPSs in the education sector:

> DFID is providing £18.5 million funding for the Developing Effective Private Educa-tion Nigeria program (2013–2018) to improve the quality of education in Lagos by sup-porting change and innovation in the private education market (DFID, 2013); DFID is also supporting the Punjab Schools Reform Roadmap in Pakistan that includes as one of its initiatives the provision of vouchers to out-of-school poor children to attend low-cost private schools (through the newly created Punjab Education Foundation) (Barber, 2013); and is funding the Center for Education Innovations (2012–2016), to document market-based education innovations that can "increase access to quality, affordable and equitable education for the world's poor" (CEI website) with the aim of "collaborating more closely with the private sector in development" (DFID, 2012). DFID is now explicitly interested in supporting private organizations, like Bridge, in the effort to achieve international development goals. Policy entrepreneurs, like James Tooley, commonly attend DFID seminars and events. (p. 544)

The increasing expansion and profit potential of the LFPS sector has contrib-uted to private corporations and finance entities stepping into the sector as well. The most well documented case in this respect is that of Pearson, a giant player in the global education industry that has created the Pearson Affordable Learning Fund (PALF) to especially target the LFPS sector. Pearson justifies this initiative, launched in July 2012 with $15 million of initial capital, with a number of arguments:

> The Pearson Affordable Learning Fund (PALF) makes minority equity investments in for-profit companies to meet a burgeoning demand for affordable education ser-vices across the developing world. Extensive market research has shaped our belief that we need both efficient public and private education actors working in tandem, if we are ever to achieve "Education For All." Across the developing world, the reality on the ground is that students are already attending low-cost private schools. (Pearson Affordable Learning program)[9]

As reflected in this quotation, private actors like Pearson are investing in these types of schools due to professed principled beliefs of making EFA a reality. How-ever, it is also doing so because of the conviction that this sector is potentially prof-itable. In an interview given to the BBC in 2012, PALF chairman Michael Barber (see Box 9.2 in Chapter 9 in this volume) emphasized this profitability concept:

> To use economic jargon, it's an immature market, so there's lots of one or two school little family companies and we think we can find some, take them to scale, get large

chains of schools that are consistent, that are higher quality and still very low-cost. . . . It's absolutely for-profit. But get this right—it's important to demonstrate profit because we want other investors to come in. (Barber, as cited in Riep, 2014, p. 264)

Similar funding initiatives to that of Pearson can be found, for example, in the Rizing Schools Program and in the Orient Global Education Fund (Srivastava, 2014). The Rizing Schools Program is a microfinance initiative for LFPS owners in Ghana launched in 2009 by the Innovation Development Progress (IDP) Foundation and the Sinapi Aba Trust. Rizing Schools' mission is "Developing innovative, scalable, and replicable programs through sustainable initiatives that move away from aid-based models and lead to greater progress in the achievement of Education for All for the most deprived."[10] Again, EFA is used as a master frame to justify further private investment in the low-fee schooling sector. So far, the Rizing Schools program is reported as "having reached 206 schools, with an aim to expand to 1,200 schools in seven regions over five years, and have an estimated impact on 350,000 students" (Srivastava, 2014, p. 3).

Elsewhere, the Orient Global Education Fund, managed by the Orient Global Foundation, the philanthropic arm of Orient Global (now Chandler Corporation), was established with a capital fund of $100 million, focusing on the market for LFPSs. Policy entrepreneur James Tooley was one of the founders of this fund (Srivastava, 2016).

In addition to these larger funds, a range of microfinance initiatives have emerged to support LFPSs. In India alone, edupreneurs can obtain financial support from a range of specialized microfunding programs provided by the Hong-Kong and Shangai Banking Corporation (HSBC), Opportunity International, and Legatum Global Development. A more complete review of these and similar funding initiatives can be found in *Global Education Inc.* (Ball, 2012).

Finally, it is important to mention that the international promoters of LFPSs, including international organizations, aid agencies, private foundations, and international consultants, regularly meet with private-school owners and other types of edupreneurs at a number of international events, conferences, and seminars held regularly in different locations, although recently they have had a bigger presence in the Gulf States. They include the IFC Private Education Conference mentioned previously, the International and Private Schools Education Forum, the Qatar Foundation's World Innovation Summit for Education (WISE), and the Global Education and Skills Conference. Interestingly, these two latter events see themselves as "the Davos of Education."[11] According to Junneman et al. (2016), conferences like these provide opportunities for "talk and touch," which produce and consolidate trust. Through the social relations that participants establish in these events, ideas are shared and borrowed, stories about "best practices" and local edupreneurs are told, and visits are organized (Santori, Ball, & Junemann, 2015). Overall, these international events contribute to expanding and strengthening networks and to closing business deals. At a more symbolic level, these spaces also contribute to entrenching a discourse in the international education arena on the desirability of including both the private-sector and for-profit motives in educational development strategies.

The Development of LFPS Chains

Due largely to the external support received from foreign investors, some LFPSs are scaling up their operations and developing into chains of schools. These LFPS organizations include Innova Schools, Bridge International Academies (BIA), LEAP Science and Maths Schools, and the Omega schools. Some of the main selling points of these school chains are that they are expected to generate economies of scale, but also to standardize their educational products and services—for example, by strongly prescribing teaching-learning content and processes. Standardization is meant to control all aspects of the education process to reduce the risk of schools not delivering "results." It is also meant to generate an identifiable chain's brand and, by doing so, help families to overcome the usual information problems that they face when choosing a school for their kids. It is quite illustrative of this standardization ambition that some of these companies state that they are creating an easily replicable, "school-in-a-box" model (Riep, 2014). In fact, by analogy to a famous hamburger chain, James Tooley concludes that:

> There is, it seems, every reason to think that a similarly "deeply understood and standardized" learning process could become part of an equally successful model of private school provision, serving huge numbers of the poor. (Tooley, 2007, p. 42)

Some LFPS chains have started internationalizing their operations or are planning to do so in the coming years. Among them, BIA, an LFPS chain based in Kenya that has expanded to Uganda and Nigeria and is preparing to expand to India, stands out. By 2025, BIA wants "to educate 10,000,000 children across a dozen countries."[12] This school chain is also convinced of the potential of standardization and, in fact, considers itself as the "Starbucks" of schools in developing countries (Srivastava, 2016).

A wide range of transnational investors has supported BIA when it came to scaling up its activity. These investors include the Omidyar Network, Pearson, the Deutsche Bank Foundation, Gray Ghost Ventures, the W. K. Kellogg Foundation (Junemann et al., 2016; Srivastava, 2016), and, more recently, the IFC. When it comes to networks and influences, BIA has connections with the U.S. charter school movement or Teach for America, with which it has common ideological commitments and modes of operation (Junemann et al., 2016).

From LFPSs to PPPs?

This chapter has outlined how the LFPS concept has influential promoters that, for a variety of reasons (economic, educational, and political), are interested in advancing this sector. National regulations—including rules that do not allow profit-making in the education system in many countries—are considered as some of the main limitations to the expansion of the sector (Patrinos, Barrera-Osorio, & Guáqueta, 2009).

Another important barrier preventing the LFPS sector from advancing more quickly is that many poor families, especially those with several children or from the lowest-income quintile, cannot afford this or any other type of private schooling. To overcome this barrier, LFPS advocates are recommending that governments adopt voucher schemes or related demand-side interventions as a way of facilitating access to these types of schools or, at least, to provide poor families with more school choices. This measure is recommended, for instance, in a recent World Bank working paper in relation to India:

> A school choice scheme using government vouchers to increase disadvantaged children's access to private schooling could bring meaningful benefits in terms of cost-effectiveness and social inclusion. This provides suggestive support to the recent Right to Education Act provision that could make India the world leader in the number of children attending private schools with government funding, and also in the inclusiveness of private schooling. (Dahal & Nguyen, 2014, p. 27)

Recommendations like this imply the establishment of formal PPPs between governments and LFPSs. In other words, they imply the establishment of a contract between the public and private sectors through which the government buys a service from a private provider for a certain period of time at a certain price, and preferably, based on results (Patrinos et al., 2009). The inclusion of LFPSs in PPP frameworks is already being discussed, piloted, and even adopted on a larger scale in low-income countries such as Uganda (Brans, 2012; Srivastava, 2016), India (Srivastava, 2010; Verger & VanderKaaij, 2012), and Pakistan (Barber, 2013). Of all of the documented cases of partnerships between the government and the LFPS sector, the case of Punjab, Pakistan, is probably the one that has become more emblematic internationally (see Box 6.2).

Using PPPs *with* LFPSs is a policy that is expected to become increasingly central in the education for development agenda because it apparently addresses, on the one hand, the efficiency criteria that many donors and financial international organizations are looking for when promoting the expansion of education and, on the other hand, the equity concerns that most privatization policies generate (in the sense that the public subsidy would provide more opportunities for the poor to choose private schools that, even if they are meant to be low-fee, the poor cannot afford). At the same time, the term *partnership* has become popular in international development discourse. This is an ambiguous enough term to predispose a broad range of local policymakers to consider engaging in processes of educational change (Verger, 2012). However, as Srivastava (2014) argues, this new trend is not without potential risks and challenges:

> The seemingly convivial mutuality of the term "partnership" obscures the fundamentally altered mode of governance under PPP arrangements, particularly with the introduction of new/non-traditional (and for-profit) private non-state actors in education. The notion of mutuality persists despite lessons emerging from countries with longer

Box 6.2. PPPs and LFPSs in Punjab

In Pakistan, there is an established tradition of PPPs in education, although the relationship between the government and the private sector in the past has been tense and volatile. A key episode in this tense relationship was seen in 1972, when the socialist government nationalized all private schools in the country and the state became the unique educational provider. Nevertheless, in 1979, the incoming government dismantled this policy and initiated a lengthy period of collaboration with the private sector.

At the beginning of the 21st century, an ambitious Education Sector Reform Plan of Action (2001–2004), which consolidated the collaboration between the public and the private sectors, was adopted. The plan started from the premise that "The government has officially recognized that the public sector on its own lacks all the necessary resources and expertise to effectively address and rectify low education indicators" (Farah & Rizvi, 2007, p. 343).

With the EFA and MDG goals as the backdrop, the government could legitimize private-sector participation in the education system. Traditionally, the government established partnerships with NGOs and other not-for-profit actors, whose number and presence in the delivery of a range of social services, including education, has increased rapidly since the 1980s (Farah & Rizvi, 2007). However, more and more often, such collaboration arrangements are established with for-profit LFPSs.

In Punjab, the most populated province in Pakistan, the role of donors like the World Bank and the DFID and the leadership of an international policy entrepreneur like Michael Barber have become key to understanding the increased public funding support to LFPSs. In 2009 and 2012, the World Bank approved two important loans to support the introduction, implementation, and impact evaluation of an innovative pilot PPP program via vouchers, per-student subsidies, and other demand-side interventions (Menashy, 2014). Thanks to these international funds, the voucher scheme expanded rapidly in Punjab and, in 2011–2012, enabled "over 140,000 largely out-of-school children to attend low-cost private schools" (Barber, 2013, p. 20).

histories of PPP-friendly institutional frameworks that large-scale PPP arrangements are not only more risky for the public sector, as there are fewer actors to bear the risk, but also that they operate with vested interests against those of the public, can lead to more complicated regulatory frameworks not less, and that they have the potential of becoming "abusive" if the stronger partner dominates. (p. 2)

CONCLUSION

The LFPS concept is a modality of private schooling that is acquiring a more central position in educational provision in many low-income countries, especially in sub-Saharan Africa and South Asia. It is portrayed as a grassroots privatization movement in the sense that these schools have been traditionally initiated by local edupreneurs who have detected a business opportunity in their communities, usually because of insufficient or inadequate public education.

Privatization advocates consider that LFPSs are expanding because they offer better quality education and achieve higher learning outcomes than public schools. Nonetheless, a significant number of scholars challenges these assumptions by arguing the following:

1. On the supply side, teachers in LFPSs are insufficiently trained and paid, and evidence on better learning outcomes in LFPSs is far from conclusive.
2. On the demand side, families choose LFPSs not only as a matter of giving more learning opportunities to their children, but also as a matter of security and control, linguistic and religious recognition, and, especially, social distinction (i.e., a way for low-income parents to distance themselves from even more disadvantaged families).

Despite its locally-situated origins, the LFPS phenomenon is being increasingly globalized, with international organizations, donors, philanthropists, and private investors further promoting and investing in them in various contexts. Thus, an initiative that was initiated by poorly resourced individuals at the community level is becoming more and more embedded in transnational networks of influence, capital, and ideas.

International players perceive LFPSs as a cost-efficient and profitable way of promoting access to education for the poor. The LFPS sector is increasingly attractive to a range of private actors because it fits neatly in the philanthrocapitalist idea (see Bishop & Green, 2008) that profit is compatible with—and can even become a driver of—more noble goals, such as EFA. As observed by Srivastava (2010, p. 523), the fact that the EFA movement has not agreed on a specific education policy or governance agenda has created an "unscrutinized space" in which different actors tactically use the globalization discourse to advance their particular agendas, including those involving further education privatization.

The international network of LFPS advocates, which tends to crystalize and meet in conferences, philanthropy encounters, award ceremonies, and other events is eager to demonstrate that this schooling modality can benefit the poor in different ways. In the context of this network, the desirability of LFPSs and, more broadly, the idea of the inherent superiority of the private sector over public education tends to be advanced via the selective use of evidence (Srivastava, 2016).

A mix of finance mechanisms, like private funds coming from international investors or voucher schemes funded by aid agencies, are some of the specific financial instruments that the international community is using to promote LFPSs.

However, the advancement of LFPSs is also benefiting from economic restrictions at the country level, which often merge with administrative challenges around planning education properly or with a lack of political will on the part of Southern countries' governments to invest more resources in public education. Thus, in many places, beyond explicit or proactive policies, the so-called politics of non-decision making (see Bonal, 2012) are an important driver of LFPS growth at the country level.

The promotion that LFPSs are witnessing, at both the international and national levels, is translating into two emerging developments in the sector. First, LFPS chains, like BIA or Omega, despite still being a minority compared to stand-alone schools, are emerging. These chains are able to standardize their education services and open similar schools in different locations (even in different countries). Second, PPPs in education increasingly include the LFPS sector as a way to give more educational choice to the poor. These new developments have generated new research questions, but also new policy concerns. For instance, the emergence of LFPS chains has created doubts about the effects of standardization on education quality and relevance. Due to their emphasis on standardization and the prescription of lesson plans, LFPS chains challenge the concept of teachers as professionals with the necessary knowledge to adapt their teaching to different situations and contexts. Finally, the biggest question that models of PPPs with LFPSs generate concerns the extent to which low-income countries will be able to persuade and regulate for-profit actors to work in the public interest, and to avoid PPPs generating further school segregation.

To sum up, the evidence presented in this chapter shows that LFPSs are moving from being considered *de facto* privatization to being a significant part of the "strategy of design" by the international development community (Srivastava, 2010, p. 3). This shift brings forward new and important challenges for the governance of education systems and the achievement of equity and learning goals in low-income contexts.

CHAPTER 7

Historical Public–Private Partnerships in Education

The Cases of the Netherlands, Belgium, and Spain

The Netherlands, Belgium, and Spain are among the few countries in the Organisation for Economic Co-operation and Development (OECD) with a high proportion of private enrollment in primary and secondary education.[1] In particular, the number of private schools financed with public funds is remarkable in these three countries.[2] However, contrary to other countries with high private-sector involvement in education, the expansion of the private sector in these countries is not the result of the "neoliberal revolution" of the 1980s. Rather, the privatization processes in these countries have a different origin and started much earlier. In the Netherlands, the significant presence of private subsidized education[3] and the principle of parental choice date back to the beginning of the 20th century. In Belgium, a system of public funding for private schools was enacted during the 1950s, whereas in Spain, publicly funded private schools emerged between the late 1970s and the early 1980s as a result of negotiations for educational expansion that followed the dictatorship of General Francisco Franco.

In the Netherlands, Belgium, and Spain, the high level of private education needs to be understood in the context of historical, political, and social contingencies and, in particular, of the prominent role that faith-based institutions, mainly Catholic and Calvinist, play in education and in other social sectors. The expansion of private provision, in these three cases, was triggered by the constitution of public-private partnerships (PPPs) in education as an institutional response to the important presence of faith-based institutions in the provision of social services.

Although the origins and institutionalization of PPPs in the education systems of the Netherlands, Belgium, and Spain were situated in different moments of the 20th century, the three cases share important features. The important role of faith-based institutions in the delivery of education, the absence of neoliberal principles behind the creation and design of the partnership between the state and the private sector, and the high levels of regulation of the private subsidized sector are some of the most important characteristics that the three countries have in common. At the same time, the number of pure private schools is relatively low in the three cases, similar to other Western countries. In fact, the PPP arrangement resulted in the emergence of a particular typology of private schools that are almost entirely subsidized by the state.

This chapter is based on the different country cases. The first section analyzes the case of the Netherlands, which has the longest tradition in the implementation of PPPs in education, specifically since the establishment of a financing arrangement between the state and the private sector dating back to the beginning of the 20th century. Then, the text explores the case of Belgium, a country with a long tradition in subsidizing private education, especially since the signature of the School Pact at the end of the 1950s. Next, the focus moves to Spain, which created and adopted a model of PPPs in education during the transition between dictatorship and democracy in the early 1980s. Finally, this chapter reflects on the similarities and differences among the three cases and draws some conclusions.

THE NETHERLANDS: *PILLARIZATION* AND RELIGIOUS SEGREGATION

Education privatization in the Netherlands is a long-term historical process that can be structured into two main stages. The first stage spans from the first emergence of the private sector in education, which can be dated roughly to the end of the 19th century, to the consolidation of a large-scale PPP in the education sector at the beginning of the 20th century. The emergence of this PPP in education needs to be contextualized within the Dutch tradition of societal pillarization (i.e., social segmentation) and religious segregation. The second stage starts with the consolidation of the PPP in education and expands until it reaches the enactment of new privatization policies in the last two decades of the 20th century. These more recent privatization measures were influenced by the spread of neoliberal ideas and principles that penetrated Dutch society in the 1980s, which were particularly conducive within an education system with a high and institutionalized private school presence. Therefore, although the creation and design of the current system of private subsidized schools is rooted in processes that took place at the beginning of the 20th century, the Dutch education system has not been immune to the globalization of neoliberal ideas during the last several decades.

Historical Origins of the Dutch PPP: The Role of Faith-Based Institutions

In the Netherlands during the 19th century, private schools dependent on faith-based institutions emerged as a result of the liberalization of the education system and the right given to private entities to establish and maintain their own schools. Nonetheless, the state maintained an important presence in the provision of education. It is important to keep in mind that at that time, schools managed by private institutions were financed by voluntary contributions, which limited their potential expansion (James, 1984).

Three main types of faith-based institutions were involved in education provision, each with different preferences in relation to how their participation within the education sector was institutionalized. Specifically, "the Dutch Reformed [preferred] a relatively secularized system of public education for everyone, the Calvinists [preferred] a public school system with a strong fundamentalist theology, and the Catholics [preferred] separate public and private systems, both with state support" (James, 1984, p. 606).

This divergence of opinions was resolved by a political alliance between Calvinists and Catholics (Vandenberghe, 1999). This coalition exerted some level of influence in the Liberal Party, which came to power in 1889, and established a state subsidy for schools managed by private institutions, although it was not equal to the level of funding for public schools. In other words, as a result of pressure from the dominant religious groups, private schools started being funded by the state, but they received fewer resources than state schools.

The elections of 1913 did not give a clear majority to the Liberal Party. To govern, the Liberals had to negotiate with more conservative forces, which forced the government to adopt a funding scheme in which private schools benefited from the same conditions as public schools. This funding arrangement was included in the new national constitution of 1917. Importantly, this constitution consolidated the principle of *pillarization*,[4] or compartmentalization of Dutch society, which included four pillars, or social groups: the Catholics, the Calvinists, the socialists, and the liberals. According to Karsten (1999):

> This compartmentalization is a peculiar form of pluralism which involves a strong vertical segmentation of all sectors of social life along religious and ideological dividing lines. Each religious or quasi-religious group has created its own social world, covering the entire life-span of an individual from nursery school, through to the sports club, trade union, university, hospital and broadcasting corporation right up to the burial association. (p. 304)

As a consequence of the pillarization of Dutch society, "separate but equal school systems became a central component in a society that was sharply segmented along religious lines during the first half of the twentieth century" (James, 1984, p. 607). Segmentation was not a specific principle in the organization of the education sector; rather, it applied to other social spheres such as trade unionism, health care, and other social services. For Karsten (1999), pillarization was the result of the dispute between those political actors who proposed a strong state (mainly liberals and socialists) and those who proposed a "facilitating" or confessional state. As Patrinos (2010) stresses, the freedom of education established in the Netherlands during this period was not based on the principles of liberalism, but rather on the principle of freedom of religion.

The right provided to private institutions to establish their own schools facilitated the conditions for the consolidation of a strong and very open system of state subsidies to private schools. The Education Act, approved in 1920, granted groups of parents the liberty to establish their own schools and established the obligation for the state to fund all initial capital costs and to cover ongoing expenses (James, 1984). As expected, Calvinists and Catholic churches, which historically provided private education, founded the majority of these new private schools. In fact, most private schools in the Netherlands are still linked to these Christian churches. Schools operated by other religious organizations (Jewish or Islamic) and nonconfessional schools remain a minority and are generally concentrated in larger cities (Dijkstra, Dronkers, & Karsten, 2004).

Thus, the constitution of 1917 and the Education Act established the same financial basis for public and private education, facilitated on the principles of pillarization and freedom of education. These legislative changes had a clear impact on the increase of private-sector involvement in the Dutch education system (see the current features of this system in Box 7.1). Figure 7.1 shows the evolution of public and private enrollment rates between 1850 and 1980 for primary and secondary education, clearly reflecting a privatization trend.

Box 7.1. Current Features of the Dutch Education System

Several education reforms have been introduced after the establishment of the Dutch PPP model at the beginning of the 20th century. Accordingly, some of the current features of the education quasi-market are:

- **School funding "follows the student."** The funding of a school is based on the number of students enrolled there. Extra funds are provided depending on the percentage of students with special educational needs of a different nature (i.e., socioeconomic academic disadvantage, immigrant background, and so on) (Nusche, Braun, Haláz, & Santiago, 2014).
- **Easy entry into the market of new educational providers.** A group of parents or teachers can propose the creation of a new school and, if they ensure a minimum number of students and certain minimum standards, the government has to provide that school with initial capital costs and ongoing expenses.
- **Freedom of school choice.** Families are free to send their children to any school they wish. There are no catchment areas within the educational system (Nusche et al., 2014).
- **Profit is not allowed.** Private subsidized schools cannot be managed by for-profit providers (Patrinos, 2013).
- **High level of autonomy at the school level.** Education governance is decentralized at the local level, and schools have an important level of responsibility for making decisions of a pedagogical or managerial nature, including the appointment of teachers. For example, in lower secondary education, more than 80% of decisions are made at the school level (OECD, 2012).

Figure 7.1. Percentage of Enrollment by Type of Institution in Primary and Secondary Education, 1850–1979

	PRIMARY		SECONDARY	
Year	Public	Private	Public	Private
1850	77	23	100	0
1900	69	31	91	9
1910	62	38	87	13
1920	55	45	75	25
1930	38	62	61	39
1938	31	69	53	47
1950	27	73	43	57
1960	27	73	35	65
1970	28	72	28	72
1979	31	69	28	72

Source: Adapted from James (1984).

Although the data presented here shows an increase of private schools between 1850 and 1910, it was after 1920 that a dramatic increase in private education institutions, principally Protestant or Catholic, took place. As a consequence of the legislative changes described in this discussion, the rate of private schools grew and, conversely, the relative weight of the public-school sector decreased. At the end of the 1970s, public schools represented only 31% of the total enrollment in primary education, and 28% of secondary education. In the last few decades, the distribution of public and private enrollments has remained pretty stable; in 2004, the enrollment in private institutions was 68% in primary education and 76% in secondary education (OECD, 2006).

The privatization of the Dutch education system is grounded on religious factors, and both Catholic and Protestant denominations have driven privatization in the Netherlands. Nonetheless, Dijkstra et al. (2004) wonder how private religious schools have maintained their importance in relative terms during the second half of the 20th century in an increasingly secular society[5] and with the arrival of immigrants with different religious backgrounds. These authors consider two main factors that explain this paradoxical situation, which are very much related to the centrality of the freedom of school choice principle in the Dutch education system (see Box 7.1), and to the more direct implications of this principle in terms of educational inequality.[6] First, in a highly segregated and competitive education system like the Dutch system, privately managed religious schools usually show better performance indicators than other types of schools; for this reason, they are the preference of middle-class families, independent of whether these families are religious or secular. The second factor that explains the survival of faith-based schools relates to the political protection that religious schools have traditionally enjoyed in the Netherlands, which goes with broad governmental support for the concept of school choice. Overall, the important role of the Christian Democratic Party in the political arena facilitated the survival of the pillarization principle and, as a consequence, the generous public subsidies to religious schools.

Recent Privatization Trends in the Dutch Education System

Since the 1980s, neoliberal ideas have penetrated the Dutch political arena. According to Karsten (1999), part of this neoliberal influence is explained by the prominent role of the OECD in the legitimization of policy reforms on the basis of scientific research and evidence. The inclusion of neoliberal principles in education policy in the Netherlands was initiated by governments ruled by conservative and liberal coalitions, and was continued by social democrats and conservative-liberals in power during the 1980s.

Karsten (1999) identifies four key elements that structured the Dutch education policy debate during the 1980s and the 1990s: freedom of choice, privatization, quality control, and school autonomy. In relation to the latter, Karsten (1999) notes that the school autonomy policies developed during that period were inspired by economic principles, not necessarily by pedagogic ones. Overall, the declared objectives of the emerging policies in this period "boiled down to the reduction of legal rules which interfere with market process" (Karsten, 1999, p. 311).

When it comes to privatization in the context of neoliberal political hegemony, Karsten (1999) affirms that, since the participation of the private sector in education is historically rooted and taken for granted by most political and social groups in the Netherlands, the further privatization of schooling services during the last decades of the 20th century was not part of the political agenda or the subject of a substantive educational debate. Rather, the introduction of neoliberal principles in education policy focused on reducing the government's share in the financing of education. An example of these related measures includes allowing parents to make financial contributions to, or privately sponsor, schools. In fact, parents' direct contributions to schools are viewed as a way to reduce the level of government bureaucracy and make schools more responsive to families' preferences, which is expected to foster diversification and education innovation.

BELGIUM: UPS AND DOWNS IN A PRIVATE SCHOOL FINANCING AGREEMENT

The development and evolution of Belgian PPPs in education can similarly be divided into two main phases. The first phase covers the period from the legal origins of the idea of freedom of instruction in the mid-19th century until the 1950s, when a crucial school pact between the public and the private sector was adopted. The second stage is more contemporary and resulted in the consolidation of the PPP framework after a period of political tension and disagreement on the legitimate role of the private sector within the education system. During this period, a process of education decentralization was also undertaken, although it did not have an important influence on the involvement of private institutions across the various Belgian communities. Rather, this was the consequence of the legal restrictions to alter the role of the private sector that were established in the new national constitution.

Historical Origins of PPPs in Belgium, and the School Pact

Belgian education politics has historically been characterized by a tense relationship between the Catholic Church and a range of political movements and organizations advocating for a state-managed education system. Many authors situate the roots of this conflict in the 1831 constitution, which stated: "Instruction is free. All restrictive measures are forbidden" (De Rynck, 2005; Dupriez & Maroy, 2003). This principle of freedom of instruction enshrined in the constitution limited the attempts of liberal governments during the 19th century to establish a unified system of state schools and to limit the role of the Catholic Church in education. Between 1884 and 1914, the Catholic Party came to power in Belgium and adopted a range of public policies that contributed to promoting the expansion of privately provided education (Kalyvas, 1998, as cited in De Rynck, 2005).

During the 1950s, in the context of a debate on how to expand secondary education, the disagreement between Catholic schools' advocates and proponents of state education resurfaced. While the Christian Democratic government (1950–1954) increased subsidies to Catholic schools and limited the expansion of state schools, the coalition between socialists and liberals (1954–1958) reduced the subsidies and promoted the expansion of state schools. During this last parliamentary term, Catholic groups organized a strong campaign and protested against the limited support for Catholic schools (De Rynck, 2005).

As an attempt to ameliorate this conflict, a School Pact was signed in 1958 among the most important political forces in the country, including the Socialists, the Liberals, and the Catholic Democrats. This pact established a system of educational funding in which the state would fund Catholic schools, as well as the right of parents to choose between state and private schools. At the same time, those private schools that benefited from the public funding scheme were obliged, by law, to meet certain requirements, such as enrolling a minimum number of students or having qualified teachers (Dupriez & Maroy, 2003). The pact also guaranteed that private school staff enjoyed the same labor conditions as staff in state-managed schools (De Rynck, 2005). In practical terms, the School Pact meant the establishment of an ambitious PPP model, in terms of scope and commitment between the public and private, in Belgian education. De Rynck defines the effects of the school pact in these terms:

> Hence, this 1950s compromise controlled the conflict by allowing both public and private schools to grow with public money. In the Pact, all parties resigned from the idea of an educational monopoly in favor of a system of "segmented pluralism." The issue of the character of state schools was settled in favor of *neutralité* (and not *laïcité*,

as in France), implying internal pluralism within schools rather than a unity of vision. Against the view of more radical statists, pupils within state schools were entitled to a choice between a course in ethics or in a recognized religion. (2005, p. 487)

During the 1960s, Belgium experienced an important expansion of secondary education as a result of the government's efforts to expand public expenditure in education. Nonetheless, public funding to private institutions, as established in the School Pact, meant that mostly Catholic schools would benefit from such an enrollment expansion and the associated funding (De Rynck, 2005).

The Communautarization of Education

The economic crisis and the corresponding public spending cuts of the 1980s triggered a range of events that signaled the end of the School Pact in Belgium. In a context of economic austerity, the Christian Democratic and Liberal coalition (1981–1988) opted to apply selective cuts in public spending, which affected public schools more than private schools (De Rynck, 2005). The Socialist Party opposed this discriminatory policy against the public sector and decided to block the deliberations of the School Pact commission. For De Rynck (2005, p. 489), this blockade heralded "the end of compromise politics as devised by the 1958 School Pact."

In the 1980s and in 1990s, enrollment in private secondary schools increased in both the Flemish and the French communities, particularly in secondary education. Figure 7.2 shows this and other trends in the evolution of enrollment in Belgium between 1980 and 2001. The increase in private enrollment is concentrated in secondary education due to the introduction of an educational reform

Figure 7.2. Percentage of Enrollment by Type of Institution, Community, and Education Level, 1982/83–2000/01

		1982–1983	1989–1990	2000–2001
Flemish community	**Primary education**			
	Regional or local government	37.46	35.23	36.06
	Private sector	62.54	64.77	63.94
	Secondary education			
	Regional or local government	29.23	25.58	24.36
	Private sector	70.77	74.42	75.64
French community	**Primary education**			
	Regional or local government	57.92	55.83	57.26
	Private sector	42.08	44.17	42.74
	Secondary education			
	Regional or local government	50.32	46.52	41.14
	Private sector	49.68	53.48	58.86

Source: Adapted from De Rynck (2005).

based on comprehensiveness, which increased the number of study options available in secondary education (De Rynck, 2005).

In addition to the cuts in state schools applied by the Christian Democratic and Liberal coalition, another important factor explains the increase in private school enrollment. According to De Rynck (2005), the organization and unity of the Catholic education community during the 1970s prevented a traditional fragmentation of local providers:

> Historically, Catholic providers had developed mostly out of local parishes, dioceses and school bodies. Stronger unity at central level emerged to cope with the 1950s' "school struggle." Organizational unity was further reinforced in the 1970s. At that time, the salience of the religious cleavage had waned considerably compared to the 1950s. The education subsidies, in contrast, which had expanded rapidly, induced and enabled Catholic actors to build up their organizational strength. (p. 489)

In the context of political disputes, the Belgian constitution was reformed in 1988, and the regional organization of the Belgian state was deeply altered.[7] The new constitution established a federal system composed of three communities (the Flemish, the French-speaking, and the German-speaking). However, at the same time, the constitution established some basic and common principles in the education sector, with the objective of reducing and preventing the discretion of communities to establish their own educational policies in key aspects of the governance of the system. The new constitution reincorporated some of the main principles of the School Pact, including the freedom to establish new schools, the right of parents to choose, and the state obligation to subsidize private educational initiatives (De Rynck & Dezeure, 2006).

In terms of financing, the new constitution defined the framework for budget allocations to private subsidized (Catholic) and state schools on an equal basis to ensure free access to both types of schools. In practice, this legal provision reduced the capacity of communities to dispute the model of publicly subsidized private schools[8] (De Rynck & Dezuere, 2006).

SPAIN: THE CONSOLIDATION OF THE PRIVATE SECTOR IN THE TRANSITION TO DEMOCRACY

In Spain, PPPs in education were established in the 1980s. Nonetheless, the private sector has historically played a prominent role within the Spanish education system, particularly schools managed by the Catholic Church. This section describes the historical origins of the current PPP model in education, as well as more recent trends and developments.

Historical Origins of the Spanish PPP System

The configuration of the current Spanish education system has been strongly conditioned by events that occurred in the last years of the military dictatorship and the beginning of the democratic period. During the dictatorship of Franco (1939–1975), the education system was characterized by high levels of inequality, which were directly influenced by the prevalence of a dual system of private and public schools (Calero & Bonal, 1999). The subsidiary role of the state in education and the limited administrative capacity and political will to strengthen the public sector facilitated a situation where Catholic schools enjoyed a privileged position and the level of social stratification in the Spanish education system inevitably increased. Bonal (2000) describes this situation as follows:

> One of the most significant features of Spanish education has been the historical retreat of the State from its provision. With some exceptions, public authorities delegated the control of education to the Catholic Church and did not make relevant efforts either to finance or regulate the education system. This withdrawal of the State from the education domain was one of the main reasons for the configuration of a dual education system, divided into an elitist private sector and a low-quality state one. (p. 203)

The first democratic government after the military dictatorship faced important challenges in terms of improving the situation of the education system. The most urgent challenge was the need for an expansion of basic education levels. Spain was lagging far behind most European countries in this respect as a result of the lack of support for public education during the dictatorship. Nonetheless, the government also had to face other educational problems, such as the shortages of school places in primary education, high levels of education inequality between social groups, and teachers with low salaries and inadequate training (Bonal, 2000).

The negotiation of the new democratic constitution, which was approved in 1978 as the result of a difficult political agreement between political parties from the left and right, established a framework that allowed the emergence of a dual education system with subsidized public and private schools (Calero & Bonal, 1999). The "school pact" (as characterized by Olmedo, 2008) resulting from the negotiations behind the 1978 constitution resulted in the legal recognition of both the principles of equality, claimed by left-wing parties, and educational freedom, claimed by right-wing parties (Bonal, 1998). An example of this tension is found in a paradoxical (or collage) article of the Spanish constitution that includes, simultaneously, the right to education and the freedom of instruction. Specifically, this article states, "Everyone has the right to education. Freedom of teaching is recognized."[9]

Thus, the new constitutional framework was characterized by a legal ambiguity that allowed the adoption of different policy options depending on the ideological orientation of each government. At the same time, it created the legal basis for the establishment of a private subsidized sector in education.

The first democratic governments (1977–1979, 1979–1982), which were right-wing-oriented, gave preference to the principle of academic freedom established in the constitution, to the detriment of the principle of equality. In 1980, the government approved the Educational Institutions Law (*Ley Orgánica del Estatuto de Centros Escolares*, LOECE) that established the institutionalization of private schools subsidized by government funds. This new law established the conditions for free school choice and reduced the role of the educational community to the benefit of the school owner (Bonal, 2000). Nonetheless, a dual education system characterized by both public and private subsidized schools would be agreed upon only when the Social Democrats came to power after 1982 (Griera, 2007). Budget restrictions, pressure from the private sector (particularly the Catholic Church), and a favorable legal framework established by the 1978 constitution were determining factors in the acceptance of PPPs in education by the left-wing government at that time (Calero & Bonal, 1999; Olmedo, 2013).

Thus, in 1985, with the Social Democrats in power and after a long political deliberation, the Right to Education Law (*Ley Orgánica del Derecho a la Educación*, LODE) was approved, establishing the current structure of the Spanish educational quasi-market. This law recognizes three types of schools: public, private, and private subsidized. At the same time, the Social Democratic government introduced high levels of regulation to ensure the equality of schooling conditions between public and private subsidized schools (Calero & Bonal, 1999). These requirements included teaching the national curriculum, avoiding the selection of students (i.e., private subsidized schools should follow the same admission rules as public schools), no fees,[10] no profit for their educational activity, and the establishment of representative bodies to foster the participation of parents and students (Olmedo, 2013; Villarroya, 2000). For Bonal (1995), these initial regulations made the establishment of new private schools difficult and restricted the expansion of private subsidized schools. However, Olmedo (2008) identifies a trend in recent years toward deregulation and reduction of public control in these institutions.

The approval of the Right to Education Law marked an important division within the coalition composed of progressive education stakeholders. The Social Democrats, parents' associations of public schools, and the movements for pedagogical renovation supported the law, whereas most teachers' unions were critical of the final text (see Box 7.2).

Recent Privatization Trends in Spain

During the first decade of the 21st century, the education policy debate in Spain is being framed as part of a broader debate on the reconfiguration of the public sector and the role of the state in the provision of public services:

> During the last decade, an apparently technical debate based on issues related to the provision of public services in Spain has been underway, however in reality what is also going on is a wider redefinition of the concept of "public service" that for the most part goes unnoticed by users, clients, and media commentators. This reconfiguration is situated in a broader context of political discussion and engineering, an intense process of administrative reforms and changes in the rules of governance. (Olmedo, 2013, p. 57)

This debate has been supported by neoliberal think tanks and other like-minded institutions[11] that, according to Olmedo and Santa Cruz (2013), have played an important role in the definition of a new and ambitious education law

---

BOX 7.2. INTEREST GROUPS IN SPANISH EDUCATION DURING THE 1980S

The coincidence in time between the restoration of democracy and the configuration of a new educational system promoted the emergence of multiple interest groups in the educational policy arena. These groups were particularly active in the first years of the democratic period. Bonal (2000) identifies two broad educational positions that allow the clustering of different interest groups: (1) a conservative position that is adopted by organizations advocating free schooling, school choice principles, and the establishment of an education market; and (2) a progressive position adopted by those groups advocating equality principles, secular education, and the promotion of education as a public good. While private schools' organizations were aligned with the conservative position and students' organizations with the progressive approach, there were teachers' unions and parents' organizations on both sides.

The above-mentioned interest groups built alliances and developed different strategies to influence the education policy decisions of the first democratic governments (including negotiation, establishment of alliances with elites, strikes, and demonstrations). However, these organizations ended up having a relatively weak impact at the time of policy adoption. This weak influence is partially explained by these organizations articulating "a set of fragmented and heterogeneous demands," primarily due to their different interests and views on education policy matters (Bonal, 2000, p. 213).

---

that has been approved by the Conservative Party, in power since 2011, and that includes a number of education privatization measures (see Box 7.3; see also Saura, 2015).

As Olmedo (2013) remarks, nowadays, the expansion of both endogenous and exogenous privatization policies differs among Spanish regions due to the existing level of decentralization of education.[12] Thus, as a result of administrative decentralization, there are important differences among regions in terms of the adoption and implementation of privatization policies. In a context marked by policy divergence, regions such as Madrid, Catalonia, and Andalusia have gone further than others in implementing measures of endogenous privatization. The autonomous region of Madrid is a clear example of education privatization expansion taking advantage of the historical PPP education model. In recent years, the regional government has extended the possibility of school choice and promoted competition between schools by eliminating catchment areas and publishing rankings of school results (Prieto & Villamor, 2012).

In Catalonia, a new regional law of education was passed in 2009 by a left-wing government coalition. This law introduced the principles of new public management into the educational system. As Verger and Curran (2014) highlight, the Catalan educational law focuses on altering the governance and organization

---

Box 7.3. The New Law on Quality Education Improvement: Deepening Privatization

In 2013, the Spanish government approved a new law on Education Quality Improvement (known as LOMCE, for its acronym in Spanish[13]). Although the LOMCE is still in the process of legal development, its application will contribute to deepening the existing levels of education privatization in Spain. Some of the most relevant and controversial legal changes included in the new law are:

- **New rules for the public subsidy of private schools.** According to the new law, the government should subsidize private schools when there is a sufficient level of demand. This represents a change from school planning based on supply to an approach informed by demand. The government also plans to expand the duration of the PPP contracts and to approve their renewal automatically.
- **Publication of school results.** Another important change is the possibility of publishing school results on standardized assessments as a way to inform school choice and to foster competition between schools.
- **Managerial approach to school autonomy.** The new regulation empowers principals in the management of schools while at the same time restricting the role of other stakeholders, such as teachers and families, by reducing the responsibilities of representative school bodies where these stakeholders participate.

---

of schools and is structured around three main pillars: school autonomy, school leadership, and external evaluation (Verger & Curran, 2014, p. 263). The legal development of this new law has focused on managerial and financial issues, not on the pedagogical components of school autonomy.

Finally, Andalusia has implemented some measures of endogenous privatization, such as standardized assessment and merit pay policies for teachers (Luengo & Saura, 2012). In the case of merit-pay measures, the regional government has implemented a voluntary program for schools. Teachers in participating schools receive a monetary incentive based on the accomplishment of educational objectives such as increased academic performance, improved school climate, or the increased participation of families.

CONCLUSION

In the Netherlands, Belgium, and Spain, PPPs in education share common characteristics in their design with other well-known experiences with public-private arrangements, such as those prevailing in the United Kingdom and Chile. However, historical and political circumstances surrounding the three cases analyzed in this chapter, together with the absence of a neoliberal inspiration in their origins, sets them apart. Probably for this reason, these three cases are rarely considered as international models of education reform by market advocates. Referring to the cases of the Netherlands and Belgium, Vandenberghe (1999) explains:

> First, "old" quasi-markets were adopted by countries confronted with a serious religious and philosophical conflict. Quasi-markets were not explicitly aimed at stimulating quality or enhancing user-oriented service delivery. Most of the time, they were simply the logical consequence of an institutional conflict between the State and particular churches. (p. 277)

In the three cases analyzed in this chapter, two main factors are influencing the adoption of PPP frameworks in education. The first is the need to have the private sector as an ally in the expansion of primary and secondary education. This was especially significant in the cases of Belgium and Spain. In Belgium, the establishment of equal levels of financing between state and private schools coincides with the expansion of secondary education. In the case of Spain, the first democratic governments after the military dictatorship had to face the challenge of a delayed educational expansion at different levels. This, together with the budgetary restrictions derived from the economic crisis, led to the creation of the current PPP model in education.

The second factor is the important and historical role played by faith-based institutions in providing education in the three countries. The presence of religious institutions in education generated continuous conflict at the time between the state and faith-based institutions and related interest groups working to establish a national education system. Furthermore, in the case of the Netherlands, conflicts among Calvinists, Catholics, and Dutch Reformed churches generated political competition among the different confessions in the struggle for control of the future national educational system. Establishing PPP frameworks was seen as an adequate policy approach to regulate and contain these conflicts in the three countries.

Another common feature in the three cases analyzed is that of a legal ambiguity resulting from the compromise between conservative and social democratic forces in agreeing on the legitimate role of the private sector in education. This legal ambiguity is manifest in the national constitutions of each of the three countries, which do not clearly invoke a market-oriented system, but do not establish the basis of an education system led by the state either. This level of legal ambiguity has allowed the discretionary application of policies that were either more or less supportive of private-sector involvement in education depending on which political party was in power. In the three cases, a legal basis exists for the development of funding schemes that allow subsidies to be given to private institutions on an equal basis with state-managed schools. Accordingly, the idea of school choice is also contemplated by the law, although school choice options are generally limited by catchment areas in the cases analyzed in this discussion, with the exception of the Netherlands.

Finally, it is important to note that although the PPPs in education established in the Netherlands, Belgium, and Spain were the consequence of political pressure exerted by faith-based institutions, this model has been maintained and even expanded with the passage of time, even after an important process of social secularization in the three countries. Many reasons of a political or demand-side nature can explain this phenomenon, but the irreversibility of the privatization process conceptualized by Carnoy (2003) in the case of Chile applies to these other cases as well (see Chapter 3 in this volume for more about the case of Chile). The presence of strong groups with contingent interests in the continuity of the PPP contracts makes any political reform to undo this model very difficult. In fact, as also happens in Chile, not only private schools and private school organizations, but also families with children enrolled in the private sector, exert significant pressure—although not necessarily in an organized way—for the maintenance of the PPP agreements.

CHAPTER 8

Along the Path of Emergency
Privatization by Way of Catastrophe

This chapter focuses on the role played by disasters as both a condition for and an enabler of education privatization. Those advocating for a market-oriented policy approach to education, including policy entrepreneurs, corporations, and think tanks, can take advantage of different catastrophic situations, including natural disasters and armed conflicts and the urgency associated with these situations, to promote the adoption of pro–private sector policies. This path toward privatization, despite it being less extensive than the other paths documented in this book, has become well established in several world locations.

This chapter reflects on the education privatization policies that have been triggered within the context of social and natural disasters of a different nature—namely, Hurricane Katrina in New Orleans, the earthquake that struck Haiti in 2010, the armed conflict in El Salvador in the 1980s and 1990s, and the war in Iraq. The chapter is organized as follows: the first section conceptualizes privatization by way of catastrophe as a distinctive path toward privatization. The second section illustrates the particularities of this path by focusing on privatization in the context of natural catastrophes, specifically in New Orleans after Katrina and Haiti after the earthquake. The third section looks at privatization processes in conflict or postwar reconstruction situations, as illustrated by El Salvador and Iraq. The fourth and final section of the chapter discusses the main findings in these areas.

EDUCATION PRIVATIZATION IN CATASTROPHE SETTINGS: IDENTIFYING CONSTANT FEATURES

Neoliberal ideas find in disasters, as well as the associated "reconstruction" efforts that occur afterward, a fertile terrain for their expansion. Catastrophes of a different nature have the potential to trigger processes of so-called *accumulation by dispossession*. This notion, which David Harvey (2003) made famous, defines a process by which resources previously belonging to one social group are transformed into capital for another group. Several education scholars, including Akers (2012), Atasay and Delavan (2012), Buras (2013), and Saltman (2006, 2007), adopt the term accumulation by dispossession as a way to conceptualize education privatization processes in postdisaster scenarios as the conversion of publicly owned and controlled services into private and restricted ones.

Despite the diversity that the episodes of privatization by way of catastrophe represent in contexts as diverse as Haiti, New Orleans, El Salvador, and Iraq, it is possible to identify common attributes in them. After synthesizing the existing literature on the topic, we have identified five of these attributes.

The first common attribute among the education privatization by way of catastrophe is that, broadly speaking, all such cases tend to pass through a two-stage mechanism: a first stage, in which public education is dismantled; and a second stage, in which the system is deregulated and opened to private providers. Saltman (2007) uses the metaphors of "back door" and "smash-and-grab" privatization to illustrate how this mechanism operates.

The second attribute refers to the socially constructed dimension of disaster episodes. While many of these episodes tend to be considered "natural catastrophes," they need to be understood as socially constructed phenomena as well. According to Atasay and Delavan (2012, p. 533), "no disaster can be simplistically detached from the problematic of sorting out its material effects from its social constructs." These authors recall that events of an undeniably material nature, such as the broken levees in New Orleans as a result of Hurricane Katrina, or the large-scale destruction that Haiti's 2010 earthquake caused, need to be interpreted through discourses that are historically in motion. Hence, even in the absence of material-ized emergencies, privatization via disaster is more likely to advance through a discursive strategy articulated by a range of political actors and the media.[1]

A third common attribute of postdisaster contexts is the legitimation and advancement of policy changes framed as relief, compensation, or reconstruc-tion interventions. In all types of disasters, a narrative centered on the idea of a "blessing in disguise" can be identified. This discursive strategy pivots around the idea of "hope after the disaster," with the disaster episode being painted as an opportunity for improving things that were not working before and as a cata-lyst of change. This was clearly observed in the case of Hurricane Katrina in New Orleans, where education privatization policies were accompanied by an array of metaphors and expressions such as "golden opportunity," "silver lining," or "bright spot" (cf. Saltman, 2007).

A fourth distinctive attribute of privatization through disasters is *amplifica-tion*. Amplification refers to the likelihood of the disaster affecting a broader geo-graphical area than the original site of the catastrophe. This would be the case, for instance, with a very localized natural disaster that ends up altering policies at the national level. International organizations and other types of external agencies that often intervene in postcatastrophe situations are key actors when it comes to activating the amplification mechanism.

A fifth and final attribute can be found in the logic of *irreversibility* that many postcatastrophe interventions involve. While many policy solutions are proffered as temporary, or contingent upon an emergency situation in the context of catas-trophes, these policy solutions tend to endure over time and, accordingly, have long term consequences. In other words, emergency measures ultimately involve a redefinition of the normalcy beyond the spatial and temporal limits of the catastrophe (Atasay & Delavan, 2012).

Overall, due to their temporal and spatial implications, both amplification and irreversibility make the "privatization by way of catastrophes" path especially relevant, despite being far less common than other paths toward privatization discussed in this book. In the next sections, we detail how these attributes were present and conformed specific processes of education privatization in the context of natural disasters and violent conflict.

NATURAL DISASTERS AS AN OPPORTUNITY TO PRIVATIZE EDUCATION

Post-Hurricane Katrina, New Orleans

Education reform in the aftermath of Hurricane Katrina, which took place in August 2005, is the most well documented case of privatization in the wake of a catastrophe. The interest of the so-called New Orleans experiment is linked to some extent to its potential impact on American education politics and policies at both the state and federal levels.

New Orleans is a model case of so-called back door privatization, as observed by Saltman (2007). According to this author, Hurricane Katrina generated the conditions for a new form of educational privatization, in which business and the political elite used a disaster to realise their ideological preferences. This instrumentalization of the catastrophe followed previously unsuccessful attempts at privatizing education by these same actors. Two years before Hurricane Katrina, in November 2003, the Louisiana legislature had passed Act 9, which impeded the advancement of a vouchers programme; and, shortly before the hurricane, the Louisiana legislature defeated a K–12 voucher bill that pro–school choice groups had strongly advocated for (Akers, 2012).

Nevertheless, Act 9 established a state-run Recovery Schools District (RSD) for failing schools, which was governed by the Board of Elementary and Secondary Education (BESE)[2] and would have Paul Vallas as its superintendent in 2007 (see Box 9.1 in Chapter 9 in this volume). Schools considered "academically unsuccessful" during four or more years were eligible to be transferred to the RSD, which usually opted for their conversion into charter schools. Only a small number of charter schools were operating in New Orleans prior to the "big storm," but the establishment of the RSD made a significant contribution to the promotion of charter schools that was about to come (Adamson, Cook-Harvey, & Darling-Hammond, 2015; Levin, Daschbach, & Perry, 2010).

Hurricane Katrina hit the Gulf Coast in August 2005, exerting a devastating human and material toll on the city of New Orleans. The majority of the city's schools suffered severe damage, and one-third of them were virtually destroyed. As reported by Levin et al. (2010), a major component in the rebirth of New Orleans was the rebuilding of its public education system, involving not only the reconstruction of facilities, but also a complete reorganization of the system. The changes in the governance of the education system described next were justified by its poor performance and financial difficulties prior to the disaster, and facilitated by the geographical displacement of key education stakeholders and the subsequent redistribution of power in the education policy sphere.

In November 2005, 3 months after Katrina hit New Orleans, the legislature passed Act 35, which expanded the definition of "failing schools"[3] and enabled the state takeover of more than 100 low-performing schools. Since the majority of the schools of the district were transferred to the RSD, the locally elected board in charge of New Orleans public schools [the so-called Orleans Parish School Board (OPSB)] was considerably weakened. Significantly, Act 35 involved the suppression of the clause that required the community acceptance for the establishment of charter schools (Adamson et al., 2015; Buras, 2015).

The new legal provisions led to higher levels of educational decentralization, with charter schools prominently featured. In fact, a combination of local authorities, state agencies, and private providers were allowed to reopen and operate schools to cope with the flow of returning students who had been displaced during the worst period of the catastrophe. In addition, this decentralization and the increased variety of education providers were expected to maximize families' school choice and, accordingly, increase the schools' overall quality and performance. As a result, the New Orleans education system became highly fragmented, with a combination of centrally managed public schools and privately managed charter schools. Charter schools served about 61% of the school population by the academic year 2009–2010. These schools were monitored by different types of state and local agencies and became increasingly subject to parental choice because of the increase in the diversity of the education made available (Levin et al., 2010). Specifically, four different types of schools can be distinguished in 2010, 5 years after Hurricane Katrina hit New Orleans[4]:

- Public schools, operated and managed by the OPSB (4 in total)
- Public schools directly operated and overseen by the RSD, governed by the BESE (33)[5]
- Privately managed charter schools, controlled by the OPSB (12)
- Privately managed charter schools controlled by the BESE (39)

Figure 8.1 reflects the decline of publicly operated schools and the rise in charter schools resulting from the post-Katrina reconfiguration of the education system.

This wide variety of providers turned New Orleans into what is probably the most diverse and complex school system in the United States, a system "teetering between a managed portfolio of educational providers and an unmanaged diverse provider system in which market decentralization and choice rule the day" (Levin et al., 2010, p. 3). Moreover, the central role played by charter schools was reinforced at the end of the 2013–2014 school year, when the few public schools directly managed by the RSD were phased out or taken over by charter management organizations (Adamson et al., 2015). As a consequence, the city constitutes

Figure 8.1. Evolution of School Management in New Orleans, 2004/05–2009/10

		2004–2005	2009–2010	Evolution
Public schools operated by	OPSB	112	4	
	RSD	0	33	−67%
	Total	112	37	
Charter schools controlled by	OPSB	2	12	
	BESE	2	2	
	BESE/RSD	4	37	+538%
	Total	8	51	

Source: Adapted from Levin et al. (2010).

a unique case in the United States and today is composed of almost all charter schools (Adamson et al., 2015). In addition to these changes, reforms included a 1-year emergency voucher program during the 2005–2006 school year. In spite of its temporary nature, this program enabled the promotion of vouchers as a legitimate reform and, most important, set a precedent for similar initiatives (Atasay & Delavan, 2012; Saltman, 2007).

Among the actors that led the education privatization reforms in post-Katrina New Orleans, organizations and policymakers operating at the federal level stand out. "Neoliberal opportunists" (cf. Akers, 2012) from the federal government and from various policy agencies came into contact with local movements in support of the implementation of measures promoting privatization. The city drew the attention of multiple privatization advocates due to the education reform opportunities that the reconstruction process offered. Interestingly, some of the actors playing an essential role in the push for the reforms were conservative think tanks that, prior to Katrina and in a context of democratic deliberation, had not seen much success in their efforts. Such organizations included the Heritage Foundation and the Urban Institute (Saltman, 2007). The media also played an important role in the reform process. An opinion piece published by Milton Friedman in the *Wall Street Journal* on May 12, 2005, boosted the strategy of the choice promoters. In this piece, Friedman stated:

> Most New Orleans schools are in ruins, as are the homes of the children who have attended them. The children are now scattered all over the country. This is a tragedy. It is also an opportunity to radically reform the educational system. (Friedman, 2005)

Friedman advocated the establishment of a voucher system that would reduce public spending, ensure freedom of choice, and increase quality, basically by means of increased competition. He argued that such a system would promote an efficient provision of schooling for families returning to the city, and pointed to teachers' unions and educational administrations as the main "enemies" of good education for all, on the grounds of their alleged monopolistic position and vested interests. These had been the usual arguments to promote school choice in other countries (see Chapter 3 in this volume), but the generalized sense of urgency and bewilderment after the hurricane hit New Orleans made many education stakeholders more receptive to such controversial proposals.

The posthurricane emergency reforms drastically altered the distribution of actors' roles, power, and responsibilities in the education policy space. Some of the key stakeholders in the pre-Katrina system, including groups of parents, members of the community and teachers' unions, were displaced in the rebuilding and redesign of the education system (se Box 8.1). The RSD, which was in charge of failing schools, grew in staff, leadership, and stature. However, community participation

---

BOX 8.1. PUBLIC EDUCATION IN POST-KATRINA NEW ORLEANS: MAIN SOURCES OF CONTROVERSY

Despite the rapid rate of change, the post-Katrina reforms encountered some resistance. In fact, since the very beginning, reformers faced important criticism from parents and grassroots organizations, who perceived the proposed reforms as an externally imposed experiment by philanthropies and other nonstate actors. According to Levin et al. (2010), the external support and funding provided by philanthropies and nongovernmental organizations (NGOs) resulted in a loss of local influence within the reform process. One of the most concerning issues was the replacement of local teachers by "outsiders" hired through organizations funded or controlled by national foundations, including Teach for America (TFA), New Teachers for New Schools, or teachNOLA, and charter management organizations offshoots. The funding from external sources, beyond issues of sustainability, was also perceived as distorting democratic accountability and local decision-making processes. Moreover, the governance of most of the new schools did not respond to locally elected bodies but to state agencies (Buras, 2015; DeBray et al., 2014; Levin et al., 2010).

In addition, the system did not guarantee the appropriate accommodation of a large and unpredictable number of students who were arriving in scattered and irregular clusters. This problem was worsened by a scarcity of qualified teaching and other staff as a result of the hurricane and the ensuing human displacement. Accordingly, "many members of the local community also felt undermined by the lack of presence of a central school authority that was able to provide overall governance, coordination, policy, and community involvement" (Levin et al., 2010, p. 1).

There were also concerns with regard to selective admissions, equity issues, and the worsening of racial segregation in post-Katrina education in New Orleans. As argued by Adamson et al. (2015), the reforms implemented in New Orleans have resulted in a highly stratified school system, which operates in a hierarchy of tiers and subtiers. According to this report, "there is a near perfect correlation between the tiered structure and average achievement, and these are, in turn, associated with highly differentiated populations of students by race, class, and disability status" (p. 48).

Similarly, DeBray, Scott, Lubienski, and Jabbar (2014) argue that schools run directly by the RSD became a sort of "second-class" schools, attended only by those rejected by charter schools, ultimately resulting in an increase in the level of segregation. Moreover, the stratification of the school system was reinforced by the promotion of school choice. In that sense, the complexity of the new enrollment procedures contributed to a concentration of poor students in the same schools since less-educated families were far less likely to be able to "navigate" within such a decentralized system (DeBray et al., 2014).

This segregation was compounded by the selective practices put in place by some schools. The new legal framework enabled schools to control their enrollment, allowing priority or selective enrollment in some cases. Many schools used different exclusionary practices in order to control their student intake, despite being designated as open enrollment. Consequently, students with a socioeconomic, academic, or behavioral profile seen as less desirable were less likely to attend high-performing schools.[6] The result was what Adamson et al. (2015, p. 49) call "a citywide ability tracking" that contributed to the reinforcement of racial segregation and stratification.

was restricted, in part because not all residents were able to return to their homes after their displacement, but also because the former decision-making structure based on school board meetings became "defunct or powerless" after the hurricane (Levin et al., 2010, p. 18). In parallel, both the entrance of new organizations and the changes in the composition of the teaching force, which we develop further in the next lines, fuelled this sense of loss of local control.

"Newcomers" of a different origin, including education entrepreneurs, land developers, venture capital and business leaders, "quickly stepped into the vacuum created in the Hurricane Karina's wake" (Buras, 2013, p. 23). Among them, New Schools for New Orleans, a sort of advocate and incubator of charter schools and charter management organizations, played a prominent role. According to Buras, the New Schools for New Orleans strategy, funded by market-oriented philanthropies[7] and by the federal government through its "Race to the Top" program, was "fivefold, as it seeks founders to start charter schools, principals to lead charter schools, teachers to teach in charter schools, members to serve on charter school boards, and investors and philanthropists to contribute to these efforts" (Buras, 2013, p. 23).

The readjustment of the teaching workforce also had a noticeable impact in the New Orleans education system (Levin et al., 2010). In the transfer of schools from the OPSB to the RSD in the wake of Katrina, more than 7,000 teachers were dismissed.[8] At the same time, charter schools expanded their recruitment net, and younger and less experienced teachers from programs such as TFA and teach-NOLA were hired (Adamson et al., 2015; Buras, 2015; DeBray et al., 2014; Levin et al., 2010). These changes resulted in the loss of local influence and the weakening of a traditional source of employment for the African-American middle class. However, such a large-scale dismissal was not without resistance, notably by a network of local actors with a tradition of political involvement and with a view to maintaining local control of the schools. Among them, the United Teachers of New Orleans, the local teachers' union, "fought vigorously against the reforms that led to the termination of teachers [through] a state-wide campaign entitled 'Refuse to Lose'" (Levin et al., 2010, p. 20). The transfer of schools to the RSD meant a significant reduction in union membership and no collective bargaining agreement. As a consequence, "the union saw its influence evaporate" (Levin et al., 2010, p. 20). The catastrophe itself became one of the main barriers to building an effective response to these drastic changes. The displacement and dispersion of those teachers affected by the takeover plan, including teachers' union leaders, weakened their organization (Akers, 2012).

Nevertheless, it also needs to be acknowledged that education privatization in New Orleans did not occur in a vacuum. In fact, the privatization process in the city began much earlier than Katrina and must be understood in connection with a long history of public disinvestment in the education of disadvantaged groups. According to Saltman (2007), per-pupil spending in New Orleans in the pre-Katrina period was about one-quarter of per-pupil spending in public school districts located in wealthy suburbs in the United States. This author considers that this type of underfunding strategy is usually a first step to undermine the quality of public services and hence legitimize their takeover by the private sector afterward. Moreover, the privatization process in post-Katrina New Orleans should be understood in the context of a more general privatization trend in the country, institutionalized and promoted at the federal level, most notably through No Child Left Behind (NCLB, discussed further in Chapter 5 in this volume). The Katrina disaster had fundamentally a catalyst effect, precipitating the adoption of a series of reforms already occupying a central place in the public debate.

In addition, it is important to understand the described education privatization process in connection to a longstanding and broader conflict involving race and poverty issues. Even before the hurricane, New Orleans was one of the poorest and least equal U.S. cities. In 2000, the poverty rate in the city was 27.9%—about twice the national average (12.4%) and well above the state mean (19.6%) (U.S. Census Bureau, 2015). Furthermore, New Orleans is affected by high levels of segregation. The city has long occupied the top positions in different indexes of residential segregation for African Americans. In 2000, it ranked 11th among the 43 large metropolitan areas included in the composite index of residential segregation for blacks,[9] and it occupied the Sixth position in the isolation index (U.S. Census Bureau, 2002). Akers (2012, p. 30), having drawn attention to the well-established class and race struggles that have characterized the state of Louisiana in the last decades, argues that "radical and sweeping change is neither sudden nor unexpected, as neoliberalization requires local organizing that often links social and cultural antagonisms with political and economic concerns." The article went on to say:

> Although seemingly sudden, the changes to the New Orleans education system had been contemplated and fought for over a 40-year period. The local school choice movement was at the forefront of this fight, working in local school districts and through the state legislature to dismantle the public education system in the city of New Orleans. (p. 34)

The post-Katrina process is an illustrative example of the abovementioned "redefinition of the normalcy," which makes some changes irreversible in moments of profound crisis. It is also illustrative of the possibilities that such a scenario offers to scale up and amplify neoliberal changes beyond the sites of crisis (Atasay & Delavan, 2012). In the words of Saltman (2007, p. 34), "not only do the Katrina federal vouchers cover far beyond the Gulf Coast region, but they take advantage of the crisis to promote the idea of vouchers and privatization generally." Thus, in spite of the short duration of the 1-year voucher program in New Orleans, the space of exception generated by Katrina would have served to spread vouchers as a legitimate school reform device far beyond the areas affected by the hurricane (Atasay & Delavan, 2012; Saltman, 2007). In fact, this emergency voucher preceded the implementation of a means-tested voucher scheme in 2008. The initiative was specifically directed to students attending failing schools and was initially limited to the RSD. However, a statewide expansion of the program was approved in 2012 (Cierniak, Stewart, & Ruddy, 2015; Cowen Institute for Public Education Initiatives, 2012).

The reforms were publicly praised by diverse senators, and even by the Secretary of Education Arne Duncan, as a successful intervention, despite a dearth of consistent evidence of their success and the concerns they generated among the education community (see Box 8.1). Similarly, national philanthropic foundations made important contributions to the campaigns of market-oriented candidates to BESE. For instance, Kira Orange Jones (a TFA alumna and executive director of TFA Louisiana) campaigned in the Louisiana BESE election of 2012 with the support of the Broad Foundation, Democrats for Education Reform, and New York City Mayor Michael Bloomberg. In fact, both the current superintendent of education in Louisiana (John White) and his predecessor (Paul Pastorek) are known for their close connections with philanthropies operating at the national level (Buras, 2015; DeBray et al., 2014). Far from being anecdotal, these examples reveal the national attention that the New Orleans experiment gained and the fact that "those with the most interest in confirming the 'success' of the reforms, or in disputing that success, are federal officials and other national actors" (DeBray et al., 2014, p. 21).

The Case of Haiti After the Earthquake

Albeit less researched than New Orleans, the Haitian case is another good example of how a natural catastrophe can be instrumentalized in favor of the advancement of privatization policies. In a context of overreliance on private education, privatization in Haiti scaled up significantly following the earthquake that devastated the country in January 2010. In view of the need to reconstruct a virtually destroyed system, and given the government's limited administrative capacity, a range of international organizations promoted the consolidation of an education system, with a heavy dependence on the private sector.

Hence, in March 2010, a few months after the earthquake, the Inter-American Development Bank (IADB) presented a diagnosis of the education system in Haiti and a proposal to redesign it to address the issues. In May of the same year, this regional bank became the main partner of the Haitian Ministry of Education. They approved a 5-year plan that established a subsidy for existing private schools through the payment of staff salaries conditional on the school's compliance with a series of requirements, including free tuition and the adoption of the national curriculum. This policy was approved with the aim of improving the quality of the private sector, which was already accommodating 90% of Haitian students before the earthquake and was characterized by strikingly low standards.

The plan was also advanced and supported by other organizations, including the World Bank, the Interim Haiti Reconstruction Commission (co-chaired by former Haitian Prime Minister Jean-Max Bellirive and former U.S. President Bill Clinton) and the Clinton-Bush Haiti Fund. The promotion of private education was also supported by Paul Vallas and The Vallas Group INC, which were contracted by the IADB as consultants in the process due to their experience in the New Orleans reconstruction (see Box 9.1 in this volume). Hence, the earthquake provided a new opportunity for the reinforcement of the leverage exerted by international organizations, as well as the consolidation and expansion of an already highly privatized education system (McNulty, 2011; O'Keefe, 2013).

EDUCATION REFORM IN POSTCONFLICT CONTEXTS

Wars and related humanmade disasters have also created opportunities for the promotion of corporate interest and transnational capital, usually under the "guise" of development aid, reconstruction, or variations thereof. As recalled by Edwards (2015), contexts affected by conflict are susceptible to becoming "blind spots" where certain kinds of reforms are tested "and then promoted by international organizations that must 'sell' policies to sustain their raison d'être" (Edwards, 2015, p. 411). The presumption is that a situation of vulnerability in conflict-affected countries makes it easier to test privatization policies, including public-private partnerships (PPPs) or charter schools. However, bringing private providers of public services into contexts where the state is weakened or divided by conflict is also seen as more legitimate (and even necessary) than ever.

El Salvador

The Salvadorian case illustrates very well how neoliberal education policies can be introduced in contexts affected by conflict. El Salvador experienced a civil war between 1980 and 1992, which served as the basis for a systemwide reform during the postwar period, in which the ambitious Program of Education with Community Participation (known as EDUCO for its acronym in Spanish[10]) was implemented (Edwards 2015). Through this program, the direct involvement of local communities in school management and the application of some market mechanisms in education were implemented in El Salvador during the last year of the civil war.

During the 1980s and early 1990s, El Salvador was immersed in a civil war between the guerrilla army of the *Frente Farabundo Martí para la Liberación Nacional* (FMLN), made up of five socialist-leaning revolutionary groups, and the armed forces and so-called death squads. International actors intervened in the conflict, with the United States providing explicit support to government forces. The conservative president Alfredo Cristiani, whose mandate started in 1989, had the explicit support of nongovernmental actors during his administration. For instance, he invited the Salvadoran Foundation for Economic and Social Development (FUSADES, for its acronym in Spanish[11]), a conservative think tank whose creation had been facilitated and largely funded by the U.S. Agency for International Development (USAID), to collaborate with the government on many different issues. Concerning education policy, the World Bank became a central partner offering financing and technical support for education reform, and the former general manager of the Business Foundation for Educational Development (FEPADE, for its acronym in Spanish[12]), which was created in 1986 also with the support of USAID, was appointed as Minister of Education (Edwards, 2015). The new education policy implemented in the country throughout the 1990s owes much to these agencies.

Initially, the World Bank, together with FUSADES and FEPADE, tried to promote privatization via support for municipalization, the involvement of nongovernment education service providers in the system, and the adoption of a voucher scheme, largely inspired by the Chilean experience. It is important to recall the indirect intervention of the Chicago Boys (for information on this topic, see Box 3.1. in Chapter 3 in this volume) and other like-minded international experts, whose contribution to the reforms was channeled through their participation in FUSADES (Edwards, 2015). However, when these policy options proved to be unfeasible, partly as a consequence of opposition by teachers' unions, the promotion of community-managed local schools emerged as a more viable option. A pilot program on community education encouraged by UNESCO and UNICEF—and very much inspired by popular community-based education models originating in FMLN-controlled areas—ended up being adopted by the government. However, the program that was finally redesigned by the government, EDUCO, distorted the community empowerment and solidarity component of the original model (Edwards, 2015). The EDUCO program, which benefited from World Bank funding for its expansion, emphasized community accountability for teacher performance, with parents legally required to manage the school budget, hire teachers (with 1-year contracts), and fire them if necessary. The community education associations, whose membership basically consisted of volunteer parents, received per-pupil financing directly from the Ministry of Education. These associations complemented public funding with their own contributions in that, in addition to paying school fees, they managed and (especially in the early years) helped to build the schools by providing labor and materials. As a consequence, this community-based decentralization was regarded and promoted as being cheaper and more cost-efficient than traditional schools (Edwards, 2015).

Despite being initially skeptical, the World Bank came to consider EDUCO as aligned with its agenda: the model was seen as an opportunity to experiment with government decentralization arrangements in education, which the World Bank considers more efficient and effective than traditional, centralized state education provision. This form of decentralization was also a way of weakening teachers' unions, which are traditionally opposed to market-based reforms. According to Edwards and Klees (2012):

> The EDUCO strategy was meant simultaneously to legitimise (and hence control) the community schools in rural areas, delegitimise education provision by the state (by shifting responsibility to the community), and subvert the teachers' union (by requiring that the teachers hired be non-union). (p. 66)

The provision of financial and technical support on the part of the World Bank contributed greatly to the expansion of the EDUCO program (Edwards, 2015). In fact, over the last several decades, the program has come to account for slightly more than half of the rural public schools in the country (Gillies, Crouch, & Flórez, 2010). EDUCO is a particular privatization strategy, since not-for-profit parents' associations are contracted and given the legal responsibility for managing state-financed schools, and since unpaid parent labor ends up playing a very important role in the governance of schools (Cuéllar-Marchélli, 2003). EDUCO also involves a form of market accountability in the sense that it promotes client pressure on the schools (Edwards & Klees, 2012).

The privatization via disaster pattern can be observed clearly in the Salvadorian case. Significantly, the first World Bank loan to support the EDUCO program was agreed upon in 1991. This was before the Peace Accords of January 1992, and hence before there was a real chance for the reform to be democratically and openly discussed. Since the reform strategy was privately defined before the official end of the war, this case illustrates the political opportunities that contexts of conflict offer to advance education privatization (Edwards, 2015). As recalled by Poppema (2012), school-based management programs such as EDUCO are particularly likely to be implemented in conflict or postconflict countries since these areas represent one of the scenarios where international organizations enjoy more noticeable leverage.

The Salvadorian case also illustrates how international organizations can use conflict areas to experiment with education reforms prior to their global promotion. In fact, the World Bank promoted the community management model, represented by EDUCO, during the 1990s and 2000s through a series of technical support initiatives, workshops, and conferences. As reported by Edwards (2013,

2016), the World Bank also funded and disseminated a series of studies that emphasized the positive impact of EDUCO on student achievement (see, for instance, Jimenez & Sawada, 2003; Sawada, 2000). This gave the EDUCO program a sort of global status, and, ultimately, the program was accepted as an international "good practice" not only by the World Bank, but also by institutions such as UNESCO and the Global Partnership for Education. EDUCO has also inspired or been invoked in relation to educational reforms in a variety of contexts, such as Guatemala, Honduras, Nepal, and Uganda (Edwards, 2015).

The Case of Postwar Iraq

The Iraq war (2003–2011) is another scenario where privatization by way of catastrophe can be observed.[13] The conflict began with the invasion of Iraq by U.S. and UK troops (jointly with contingents from other countries) on the grounds of a violation of a disarmament resolution of the United Nations (which Iraq denied had been committed). An initial period of armed conflict (March–April 2003) was followed by an occupation of the country and the establishment of a provisional administration, opposed by successive waves of insurgency. It was during this phase of U.S.-led invasion that Iraq encountered the use of disaster as means to advance privatization.

The for-profit corporation, Creative Associates International (CAI), is one of the international corporations that got more actively involved in postwar Iraqi education. The company was contracted by USAID to rebuild schools, plan curricula, develop teacher training, and provide educational supplies after the invasion of Iraq. Significantly, its second contract (signed in April 2004) set the stage for privatization of the Iraqi education system on a wider scale. Through this contract, CAI was put in charge of the design of the decentralization of the education system, where charter schools and other forms of privatization were a central component.

The Iraqi case reflects the "smash and grab" idea (Saltman, 2007) lying behind the path toward education privatization via catastrophe. The education infrastructure of the country was first devastated through sanctions and conflict; afterward, two simultaneous processes of privatization and decentralization were introduced. The privatization agenda, hence, was advanced through consecutive stages of military destruction and reconstruction that, according to Saltman (2006), were embedded within a broader process of neocolonization in the country.

The Iraqi case also illustrates how relief-centered discourses can be deployed to legitimize education privatization processes. The "promotion of democracy" frame behind CAI's projects in Iraq, but also in other parts of the world affected by conflict and war,[14] represented the intervention as a matter of progressive encouragement of civic participation, individual rights, and constitutional rule of law. Nonetheless, the underlying objective of the intervention was the encouragement of a free-market liberal democracy, with an education system modeled on privatization ideas originating from the United States (Saltman, 2006, 2007). As in post-Katrina New Orleans, the significance of the Iraqi case lies in its potential effects in other contexts, thus becoming a sort of tentative experiment. The invasion of the country and the subsequent education privatization turned the plan into both a financial and an ideological investment:

> As Naomi Klein, Christian Parenti, Pratap Chatterjee, and others have argued, the Iraq war has been a radical experiment in widescale neoliberal privatization—an attempt to essentially hand a nation over to corporations. . . . Education is, on the one hand, just another business opportunity provided for by war and, on the other hand, an experiment with the conservative U.S. domestic policy agenda of educational privatization that includes vouchers, charter schools, performance contracting, for-profit remediation, and the broad spectrum of educational reforms designed to set the stage for these initiatives including performance-based assessment, standardization of curriculum, recourse to so-called "scientific-based" educational research. But CAI, USAID, and the Department of Defense do not openly admit that their projects are foremost a matter of promoting a U.S. brand of capitalism. Rather, these projects are defined through "democracy promotion." (Saltman, 2006, p. 28)

CONCLUSION

The privatization via disaster path emerges as a particular sequence of changes in which the variation, selection, and retention mechanisms (see Chapter 2 in this volume) overlap more clearly than those of other privatization paths analyzed in this book. Catastrophe works as a material catalyst of change, opening up opportunities for privatization advocates to question the current state of education. The catastrophe also makes education stakeholders more receptive to the messages of privatization advocates. Due to the destruction and the sense of urgency that catastrophes generate, policymakers and other educational actors are more open to considering drastic policy changes, especially if such changes are framed and perceived as inherent to the reconstruction process. More important, catastrophes, including conflict situations, lead to the selection and retention stages running (virtually) in parallel, since contestation and resistance to reform are often very scarce or penalized in these situations.

In catastrophic situations, deliberation and veto opportunities are reduced to a minimum, usually under the pretext of emergency and need for quick action. In fact, disasters tend to signal the simultaneous reconfiguration of the policy and power fields. In the cases analyzed in this chapter, this has translated into a drastic marginalization of traditional stakeholders and potential veto players (including teachers' unions), the elimination of institutional or regulatory obstacles to the private sector, and an intense effort to reframe public opinion. Combined, these factors make the advancement of education privatization possible in places where previous privatization attempts usually have had little or no success. All in all, it is important to take into account that such processes do not take place in a vacuum, nor are they built from scratch. The transformative power of a catastrophe should not be underestimated, but neither should it be treated as the single driver of privatization reform. A catastrophe tends to be an additional, albeit often accelerated, stage in a longer process of the dismantling of the public education system.

In spite of the clear material condition of the disasters discussed here and the reconstruction processes that came after, semiosis and meaning-making also play a key role within these scenarios. This is because disasters must be socially constructed and recognized as such and, more important, the need for relief or humanitarian support, along with the convenience of adopting certain policies, requires a noticeable persuasion and legitimation effort that usually involves elaborated rhetorical constructions and metaphors. We have also observed that disasters provide external agents (including international organizations, aid agencies, and private corporations) with an opportunity to step into domestic reform processes and use these interventions as a way to experiment with, scale up, and bring privatization to other locations. As both the Salvadorian and the New Orleans cases show, emergencies provide an opportunity for the coopting and instrumentalization of local-level initiatives. These projects are likely to be amplified and institutionalized by actors operating at higher scales, whose interests intersect with those of local actors in different (and not necessarily corresponding) ways.

In conclusion, despite existing evidence on this theme remains scarce, the singularity of the privatization via catastrophe path, the long-term effects that it has (beyond the catastrophe scenario), and its potential amplification (i.e., the expansion of "emergency" interventions beyond the territory affected by a catastrophe) make this path especially relevant from a political economy perspective.

Part III

ACTORS FOR AND AGAINST PRIVATIZATION

The Emerging Role of Nonstate Actors in the Promotion of Educational Privatization

A range of nongovernmental actors, including private corporations, private foundations, philanthropists, think tanks, and the media are increasingly active in the promotion of different forms of education privatization worldwide. Indeed, a state-centered approach is no longer appropriate to understand education privatization reforms, not only due to the globalization of educational politics, but also because nonstate actors are increasingly active in multiple policy domains, including education policy. Recent transformations in the organization of the state and the emergence of forms of *governance by networks* have contributed to an increasing presence of private actors and private interests within public policy processes. It is no coincidence that in the different education policy spaces where they participate, these private actors tend to be eager to advocate education privatization and marketization.

The emerging role of private actors in education policymaking processes prompts Ball and Youdell (2008) to identify a new form of educational privatization (which goes beyond the conventional forms of privatization *in* and *of* education)—namely, privatization *through* education policy:

> It is not simply education and education services that are subject to privatization tendencies, but education policy itself—through advice, consultation, research, evaluations and forms of influence—is being privatised. Private sector organizations and NGOs are increasingly involved in both policy formation and policy implementation. (p. 105)

This chapter analyzes the strategies and actions of an array of nonstate actors, other than official decision makers, as proponents of market-oriented reforms in the context of an increasingly privatized education policy arena. To a great extent, the chapter is structured according to the different types of private actors that go beyond the traditional private schools associations and that, as reported by existing literature, are increasingly intervening in the education privatization debate. The first section looks at think tanks and similar organizations whose activity focuses on the production, management, and dissemination of education privatization ideas. The second section focuses on the promotion of education privatization policies by the media. The third section explores the role played by a range of so-called policy entrepreneurs, who are usually well connected and prestigious individual policy actors, in the context of education privatization reforms. The fourth section deals with the increasing involvement of the business sector in the promotion of different forms of education privatization as advocates, consultants, and philanthropists. The chapter finishes by synthesizing the main strategies and mechanisms of influence deployed by these nonstate actors within the education privatization debate.

THINK TANKS: PRODUCING PRO-PRIVATIZATION IDEAS

In contemporary politics, think tanks play a distinctive role in the advancement of education privatization reforms. Despite varying levels of presence and relevance across different contexts, think tanks tend to influence educational reform processes through their active engagement in the politics of knowledge production.

According to Rich (2004, p. 11), think tanks can be defined as "independent, non-interest-based, non-profit organizations that produce and principally rely on expertise and ideas to obtain support and influence the policy-making process." Existing literature suggests that these institutions exert a noticeable influence on both agenda-setting processes and the reframing of educational debates by identifying key problems and promoting particular policies as appropriate solutions. Think tanks cultivate their authority through the publication of research studies, a high media profile, and connections with key political actors and policy networks. They also invest significant time and resources on building a well-preserved public image since this ensures the legitimacy of their activity and aims.

These organizations are especially active in the United States, where they are at the center of many policy debates and, especially in the field of education, seem to be generously financed (Boyd, 2007). U.S. think tanks, drawing on a remarkable array of material and intellectual resources, have played a key role in the promotion of market-based reforms (Kirst, 2007). According to Bulkley (2004), think tanks such as the Mackinac Center and the Goldwater Institute (linked to the Heritage Foundation) have contributed to the advance of a competitive model of charter schools in different states. According to her, the power of conservative think tanks in the educational field relies mostly on their close relationships with like-minded politicians.

The proliferation of think tanks in the United States dates back to the late 1970s and early 1980s. Their emergence was triggered by the disengagement between the academic and the policy worlds, with many politicians reluctant to inform their policy decisions on scholarly work that they perceived as too complex and biased to the left (Lubienski, Scott, & DeBray, 2014; Rich, 2004). The number of think tanks drastically increased during the 1980s with the Republican Party in power. Conservative think tanks emerged at twice the rate of growth of progressive ones, partly because they benefited from important levels of funding from conservative private foundations (DeBray-Pelot, Lubienski, & Scott, 2007; Rich, 2004).

After the United States, the United Kingdom is probably the country where the relevance of promarket think tanks is better documented. Here, the influence of the think tanks was especially notable in the 1980s, during the government of Margaret Thatcher, although the creation of right-wing organizations such as the Center for Policy Studies (CPS), the Adam Smith Institute, and the Institute of Economic Affairs (IEA) dates back to the 1970s (Exley, 2012; Fourcade-Gourinchas & Babb, 2002). The determinant participation of CPS in the introduction of the City Technology Colleges (CTC), the precursor of Academies, in 1986 (West & Bailey, 2013) exemplifies well the policy influence of think tanks in British educational politics. Remarkably, the expansion of the Academies program in 2007 owes much to the advocacy work conducted by Policy Exchange, a think tank close to the Conservative Party (Exley, 2012; West & Bailey, 2013). However, think tanks close to Prime Minister Tony Blair's Third Way ideology also proliferated from the mid-1990s onward, "driven by and driving" the rise of the so-called New Labour (Ball & Exley, 2010; Exley, 2012).

It is important to note that think tanks usually exert their influence through connections with insiders (including government officials and decision makers) and the media. Windle (2014) analyzes the influence exerted by think tanks from the early 1980s onward in Australian education politics and highlights the fact that their role in school choice advocacy has been greatly channeled through the media. Hence, the Center for Independent Studies popularized arguments supporting choice through articles in major Australian newspapers and interviews on radio. Elsewhere, the Chilean think tank *Libertad y Desarrollo (LyD)* provides an illustrative example of the importance of the connections with political elites as a way to achieve certain aims. Established during the transition to democracy by three recognized architects of promarket reforms during the military dictatorship, LyD solidified its influence on legislators and government officials through technical assistance, building networks with business and religious institutions, and securing the reproduction of engaged intellectuals and professionals (Corbalan Pössel & Corbalan Carrera, 2012).

Nonetheless, it can be considered that think tanks have lost their monopoly in the mobilization of knowledge for policy purposes. Charity organizations, grassroots coalitions, advocacy groups, civil rights organizations, parents' associations, lobbyists, research consortia, teachers' unions, and philanthropies are increasingly involved in the management and production of knowledge oriented toward policymaking (DeBray, Scott, Lubienski, & Jabbar, 2014; Lubienski et al., 2014; Scott & Jabbar, 2014). The notion of an *intermediary organization* aims to capture this broad array of agents involved in the management and mobilization of research in policymaking settings. The increasing number of knowledge intermediary organizations has made the knowledge producer-to-consumer relationships more complex and multidirectional. Traditionally, policymakers were seen as the passive consumers and receivers of think tank actions. However, currently, policymakers can take advantage of this wider array of knowledge actors to cherry-pick the knowledge products that fit best within their policy preferences and agendas. According to DeBray et al. (2014):

> On the supply side, university researchers and traditional think-tank scholars must compete with new organizations that are created to advance particular agendas and are highly adept at (and well-resourced for) packaging and marketing a defined message to policymakers. On the demand side, policymakers appear to be embracing evidence that is concise, slickly produced, timely and accessible—and aligned with their policy positions or from sources they trust (p. 3).

THE MEDIA: MEANS OR AGENTS IN EDUCATION PRIVATIZATION?

Media actors—and especially big media groups—can contribute directly to the promotion of promarket education reforms in several ways. They might do so by predisposing public opinion favorably to these reforms, by continuously representing public education negatively, or by prioritizing individual and consumerist values in education over considerations on social equity (see Santa Cruz & Olmedo, 2012).

Media influence in education privatization processes has been documented in a variety of contexts. In Chile, for instance, the two mainstream newspapers have traditionally played a key role in the defense of the quasi-market education model. These newspapers, *La Tercera* and *El Mercurio,* are some of the most loyal advocates of the need to continue and extend the voucher model. They argue that the voucher system has generated some levels of dissatisfaction only as a consequence of its imperfect implementation and uncompleted decentralization, the insufficient levels of competition between schools, and the fact that teachers' unions would have captured public education (Santa Cruz & Olmedo, 2012).

Media coverage, particularly among neoliberal newspapers, is also contributing to the rapid dissemination of James Tooley's ideas on the advantages and benefits of low-fee private schools (LFPSs) in India (Nambissan & Ball, 2010; see Box 6.1 in Chapter 6 in this volume). Likewise, mass media in countries like Australia and Spain have been key to the dissemination of competitive testing results and in the promotion of a culture of consumerism and competitiveness (Connell, 2013; Olmedo, 2013).

More examples are found in the United States, where conservative media outlets are essential in the strategy of school-choice advocates (Boyd, 2007). More recently, school-choice campaigners have resorted to nonconventional media such as documentaries and films as a way to popularize their message and "to trigger an emotional reaction in people" (Cave & Rowell, 2014, p. 237). *The Cartel, The Lottery, Waiting for Superman,* and *Won't Back Down* have been produced for this purpose. The production of these movies "represents a new approach to informing and moving the opinions of a broader audience to help inform policymaking" (Lubienski et al., 2014, p. 139), hence contributing to an important shift in the politics of research use.

Frequently, the mainstream media favor education privatization options for reasons of ideological alignment or social class affinity with privatization advocates. However, it needs to be noted that some media conglomerates have direct links with the education industry and, accordingly, support education privatization due to their vested interests in the sector. Well-known examples of such linkages are Pearson and the *Financial Times*, the *Washington Post* and Kaplan, or *News Corporation* and several education companies. According to Cave and Rowell (2014), these relationships between the media and education businesses generate a conflict of interest that alters the way that these media players report on school reform and the role of the private sector.

POLICY ENTREPRENEURS

Policy entrepreneurs are political actors that aim to promote new policy solutions among practice communities (Kingdon, 1995). Unlike think tanks, they do not necessarily have a very high public profile. Their focus is to articulate innovative ideas and to influence political and legislative agendas, usually in the shadow of public scrutiny (Mintrom & Vergari, 1996). For policy entrepreneurs, policy expertise and scientific arguments are essential sources of credibility and legitimacy for them as they face all kinds of practitioners and decision makers.

Some of the main functions that policy entrepreneurs perform in the context of educational reform include identifying unsatisfied needs and suggesting innovative means to fulfill them; managing the reputational, financial, and emotional risks inherent in actions with uncertain consequences; and solving collective problems through the coordination of networks of individuals and collectivities with key resources for the achievement of change (Mintrom & Vergari, 1996).

Despite policy entrepreneurs usually being conceived as individual actors, they tend to work in close connection with broader policy networks and may be members of consultancy firms, international organizations, or other types of knowledge organizations. These networks and spaces offer policy entrepreneurs a conducive environment in which to forge and promote their policy innovations (Verger, 2012). This is well illustrated by the U.S. case:

> Chester Finn leads the Thomas B. Fordham Foundation, Tom Loveless and Diane Ravitch lead the Brookings Institution's education policy efforts, Rick Hess directs the American Enterprise Institute's education policy activities, the Hoover Institution at Stanford University sponsors the *Education Next* magazine and hosts the Koret Task Force of K-12 Education, and Paul E. Peterson directs Harvard University's Program on Education Policy and Governance, where he has trained and inspired a whole cohort of bright young scholars and policy analysts dedicated to choice and market-based approaches in education. (Mezzacappa, as cited in Boyd, 2007, p. 9)

Policy entrepreneurs have been able to advance and disseminate school-choice policies, charter schools, and other proprivatization policy ideas across different

U.S. states (Boyd, 2007; Mintrom, 2000). According to Bulkley (2004), the adoption of charter school legislation in Arizona, Michigan, and Georgia owes much to the role of policy entrepreneurs. By adopting a counterfactual approach, this author notes that, without the role of a number of policy entrepreneurs in each of these states, "it is unclear whether charter legislation would have been passed" (Bulkley, 2004, p. 23). She adds that for policy entrepreneurs to succeed, they had to establish alliances with key political players and legislators and, more important, they had to adapt the concept of charter schools to their particular contexts. In other words, for the charter school concept to become politically viable, it needed to be adapted to the specific administrative, institutional, and cultural context in which the idea was being promoted.

Some of the most renowned policy entrepreneurs in the dissemination of charter schools in the United States are Ted Kolderie and Joe Nathan. Kolderie and Nathan are well known for having promoted the enactment of the very first charter school law in Minnesota in 1991, but also for having helped to galvanize a charter school "issue network" at the national level (Boyd, 2007; Kirst, 2007). However, currently, Paul Vallas is probably the best-known advocate and entrepreneur of the charter school idea (see Box 9.1).

Policy entrepreneurs also play a relevant role in the promotion of privatization policies in low-income countries. The best-known case is that of James Tooley, whose involvement as a researcher, advocate, speaker, funder, and entrepreneur of private schooling has made him the most active individual in the promotion and advancement of the so-called LFPSs (covered in detail in Box 6.1, in Chapter 6 of this volume). According to Nambissan and Ball (2010, p. 326), Tooley scores well in those personal assets that policy entrepreneurs are considered to need, such as "intellectual ability, knowledge of policy matters, leadership and team-building skills, reputation and contacts, strategic ability, and tenacity."

Since the end of the 1990s, Tooley has been a very active player within a broader network of education experts who have promoted pro–private sector ideas within the education-for-development domain. As reported by Verger (2012), most of the participants in this network are strategically placed in well-resourced and prestigious international organizations, transnational education consultancy

---

BOX 9.1. PAUL VALLAS: CHARISMATIC AUTHORITY AND EDUCATION POLICY

Having played a central role in education reforms within and outside the United States, former businessman Paul Vallas has become a sort of ubiquitous "privatization specialist." His case exemplifies perfectly the notable impact that some individual experts can have in the advancement of education privatization processes.

Vallas's trajectory in education began as chief executive officer (CEO) of the Chicago Public Schools, where he guided a reform that included the establishment of community and charter schools (Levin, Daschbach, & Perry, 2010). This reform, along with his reputation as a "strong manager" (Maranto, 2005), fed into his next appointment as CEO of the School District of Philadelphia. There, Vallas constituted a narrow governing coalition with little engagement with traditional education stakeholders. Initially focused on discipline, standardized curricula, improving teacher recruitment, and reducing the size of the schools, Vallas also indicated his willingness to work with private operators and implemented a multiple-provider model. To this end, he helped to establish contracts with for-profit and not-for-profit organizations to operate an important section of Philadelphia's schools. Vallas's networking abilities became apparent during that time. In the early days of the reform, he worked hard to develop a positive relationship with the two main education unions in the country. Similarly, he attempted to build ties with parents, public stakeholders, and community groups. However, it is worth noting that these efforts were more oriented to building support for the reform than to genuinely engaging these groups in the decision-making process (Bulkley, 2007; Levin et al., 2010; Maranto, 2005).

In 2007, 2 years after Katrina hit the Gulf Coast, Vallas became the superintendent of the state-run Recovery School District (RSD) of Louisiana, where he arrived as a "turnaround specialist" (Levin et al., 2010, p. 29). Hired by the state superintendent, Paul Pastorek, Vallas was responsible for the operation of 33 public schools in New Orleans, enjoying important room for maneuvering in defining the city's educational policy. During his time in New Orleans, he was accountable to the Board of Elementary and Secondary Education (BESE), headquartered in the state capital, Baton Rouge, but not to any local governance body. Jointly with Pastorek, Vallas advocated converting the remaining conventional public schools to charter schools, as well as minimizing the size of central authority in the district (Levin et al., 2010).

Vallas's main source of authority comes from his charisma and capacity to build public confidence. When the Inter-American Development Bank (IADB) chose him to be part of the redesign of the postearthquake Haitian education system, the bank's chief of education said "[we have chosen Vallas] not because there were so many parallels between the cities or situations [referring to New Orleans] but because we needed an example of a disaster and a leader" (McNulty, 2011, p. 116).

Paul Vallas, who has been defined as a "man of action" and as "the ultimate pragmatist" (Bulkley, 2007), has built on this international prestige and political clout to establish The Vallas Group Inc., a consulting firm whose main clients are school districts in such states as Connecticut, Texas, and Indiana (O'Keefe, 2013).

firms, and global universities, such as the World Bank, the Asian Development Bank (ADB), the International Finance Corporation (IFC), the Center for British Teachers (CfBT), and Harvard University. This network was forged in the context of the World Bank's Economics of Education Thematic Group, which promoted research and discussion on alternative forms of education provision (initially focused on sub-Saharan Africa). Their discussions were geared around the concept of public-private partnerships (PPPs), which they conceived as a more appropriate frame to promote the role of the private sector in education at a time when the privatization agenda was stigmatized due to its linkages with Structural Adjustment Programs (SAPs), which had been highly contested in developing countries.

The launching of a handbook for policymakers on how to implement PPPs in education in 2001 (International Finance Corporation, 2001) was the first tangible outcome generated by this network. This handbook was followed by numerous reports, policy briefs, and toolkits on PPPs in education, as well as the organization of a series of events that were well attended by policymakers, donor agencies, academics, and representatives of international organizations. The network also contributed to the global promotion of PPPs in education through technical assistance to governments, especially in the context of lending processes from the World Bank and the ADB (Robertson & Verger, 2012; Verger, 2012).

PRIVATE CORPORATIONS AND NEW FORMS OF PHILANTHROPY

The corporate sector is increasingly active in the education policy arena. Traditionally, private corporations have participated in education systems by selling a range of services, information and communications technologies (ICT) and other learning materials to governments, private schools, and families. However, today, more and more private corporations are also active in the policymaking process. In many instances, the participation of private corporations in governance structures focuses on the promotion of business-friendly principles, content, and standards in education systems, although they also do this by packaging a range of education policy solutions and school improvement services for governments.

As developed in this section, corporations are increasingly active in the promotion of education privatization policies by following various channels (namely, corporate advocacy, philanthropy, and consultancy), which are discussed next.

Corporate Advocacy

The potential profitability of the education market appears to be one of the key drivers of the increasing participation of corporations and private firms in policymaking processes. As Cave and Rowell (2014) recall:

> Corporations invest in lobbying for government policies that will benefit their bottom line, with the money and effort invested often scaled to the market potential . . . public

education systems around the world are now seen by many as the next big commercial opportunity. (p. 232)

With a focus on the United States, Belfield and Levin (2005) report that private firms support voucher initiatives in the hope of landing possible lucrative contracts for providing education services to a potential clientele of 60 million students. Similarly, Nambissan and Ball (2010) report that school-choice and private-schooling advocacy networks in India increasingly include investment companies and venture capitalists that are eager for new market opportunities. Nevertheless, beyond direct profit and financial gain, other authors suggest that corporate actors promote market and managerial education reforms because they see these reforms as a way to strengthen the education system and, by doing so, favor their competitiveness in an increasingly globalized economic environment (Fusarelli & Johnson, 2004).

The involvement and influence of corporate advocacy in education policymaking varies widely in different countries. In some settings, the participation of the business sector in advocacy frameworks is taken for granted. This is the case in the United States, where business communities have long advocated market-driven education policies as a way to improve education performance, empower parents, and, ultimately, stimulate economic development (Holyoke, Henig, Brown, & Lacireno-Paquet, 2009; see also Fitz & Beers, 2002; Fusarelli & Johnson, 2004). There, the business community exerts an influence through an overtly recognized lobbying activity. According to Cave and Rowell (2014, p. 247), this is due to "commercial lobbying in America being better resourced, more aggressive and more willing to engage in debate," but also to the fact that "U.S. lobbyists are subject to transparency rules" which makes their presence and activities more visible to the public.

In the United States, private providers of education have their own lobby, the Education Industry Association, which is strongly engaged in U.S. education politics at multiple levels (Bulkley & Burch, 2011). On the other hand, in the United Kingdom, there is the Private Sector Education Group (PSEG), a lobby group made of 14 top private education companies that enjoys a great deal of access to key education policymakers such as ministers and top civil servants (Fitz & Hafid, 2007). In the British case, however, the channels of influence of these types of nonstate actors are not visible to most citizens, precisely because of the lack of a formal structure and the informal spaces and relations through which they operate (Fitz & Hafid, 2007).

In Brazil, a national business coalition called *Todos Pela Educaçao (TPE)* has developed and acquired a high public profile in educational politics. According to Martins (2013), this coalition has contributed to the construction of a new hegemonic educational project for the Brazilian nation, with a focus on promarket policy ideas. To advance its proposals, TPE has relied on a powerful communications strategy, solid technical support, and good connections with all three branches of the state apparatus. According to Oppenheimer (2010):

In 2010, the TPE was already a consolidated movement, well-known, and with a concrete impact on the Brazilian political agenda. They had 5000 radio stations mobilized, the six major television networks in the country and 350 journalists actively involved in their activities. (p. 226)

TPE has become a model for other education business coalitions in Latin America. In fact, in this region, business coalitions have their own network called Latin American Network of Civil Society Organizations for Education (known as REDUCA for its acronym in Spanish[1]), which was created with the support of the IADB and is composed of 14 national coalitions (Martins & Krawczyk, 2016).

A final example of an international corporate coalition involved in educational affairs is the Global Business Coalition for Education, established in 2012 and supported by the leaders of 20 powerful global companies (including Accenture, Intel, LEGO, Microsoft, and Pearson, to name a few). This coalition aims to smooth the connections between corporations and other sectors, conduct research, and highlight the role of business actors as partners in providing and funding quality education for children all over the world (Bhanji, 2016).

Philanthropy and CSR

Philanthropic institutions are organizations aimed at promoting others' welfare through donations. As with other types of actors explored in this chapter, the relevance of these organizations, as well as their funding capacity, strategies, and impact, vary territorially. Existing literature mainly focuses on their role in two different settings—first, in the United States, and, second, in developing countries generally. As we will see, in both contexts, these organizations are among the most active advocates of education privatization.

Philanthropy in the United States: Toward Venture Philanthropy. In the United States, philanthropic organizations have a direct impact in the setup and direction of the privatization debate. These organizations are behind some of the most important campaigns and think tanks that promote privatization policies, including charter schools, vouchers, and pay-for-performance schemes. Nonetheless, on occasion, part of the funding of philanthropic organizations goes to support concrete private initiatives and experiences, such as specific charter school chains, as a way to demonstrate that these modalities of provision work and are a desirable policy option.

The philanthropic field has experienced significant changes in the last few decades in the United States, which directly affects how philanthropies intervene in the educational sector. To start, more and more private foundations embrace a venture philanthropy approach, which can be considered a new paradigm in the philanthropic field in the sense that introduces substantive changes in both the instruments and the goals of the philanthropic activity. One of the main differences between traditional and venture philanthropy is that the latter operates through more entrepreneurial and donor-driven funding programs and treats donations as investments from which significant returns are expected (Scott, 2009; Scott & Jabbar, 2014). Venture philanthropists are inclined to adopt a market language whereby "grants become investments, programs are ventures, and measures of impact generally involve the ability to scale up an initiative" (Scott, 2009, p. 115).

Furthermore, where traditional philanthropy tends to make donations to support specific programs and interventions, the aim of venture philanthropies is more ambitious: it is oriented toward promoting more macroeducational transformations, including market-based reforms, through which they expect to improve the learning outcomes of the most disadvantaged students. A number of relatively recent philanthropies, including the Gates, Broad, Lumina, and Joyce foundations, have embraced this new philanthropy paradigm and are investing heavily in transforming education systems through the promotion of school choice and private provision expansion (Scott, 2009; Scott & Jabbar, 2014; see Box 9.2).[2] Many philanthropists belief in the potential of market solutions in education by analogy with their successful careers in the business world. As Scott (2009, p. 107) observes, new philanthropists "often believe that educational reform could greatly benefit from the strategies and principles that contributed their financial successes in the private sector." Accordingly, "they tend to favor market-based hallmarks such as competition, standardization, and high-stakes accountability."

BOX 9.2. THE BILL AND MELINDA GATES FOUNDATION: A PRIME MOVER OF EDUCATION REFORM

As the largest philanthropic organization in the field of education, the Bill and Melinda Gates Foundation is also the most visible one promoting education privatization (Robertson, 2012). This foundation was established in 2000 and has Bill and Melinda Gates and Warren Buffett as the main donors. An important part of its efforts focus on the promotion of charter schools, the scaling-up of charter management organizations, and the promotion of school choice in general (Scott, 2009). In fact, it is often referred to as one of the "big three" philanthropies in education reform, in view of its sustained ideological and economic commitment to charter school advocacy (Au & Ferrare, 2015). With this aim in mind, the Bill and Melinda Gates Foundation has made donations to a variety of recipients, including Teach for America, Knowledge Is Power Program (KIPP), New Leaders for New Schools, Black Alliance for Educational Options (BAEO), the National Alliance for Public Charter Schools, and the NewSchools Venture Fund (Scott, 2009). The fact that the Gates Foundation is funding other foundations makes it particularly difficult to track its financial contributions properly. The foundation also invests in school reform projects or programs, regarded as "experiments in education" (including the privatization undertaken in the wake of Hurricane Katrina—see Chapter 8 in this volume), as well as in education reform advocacy (by funding political lobbying and public relations campaigns aimed at shifting public opinion) (Cave & Rowell, 2014).

The contribution of the Gates Foundation to the education sector goes beyond its economic dimension. Hence, Bill Gates exerts a noticeable ideational leverage among policymakers and is portrayed as "the nation's true schools superintendent" (Ravitch, 2006). A survey distributed among key education stakeholders in 2006 reflected that Bill Gates is considered the most influential person in American education, even more than the president and the secretary of education at that time.[3] In this regard, the individual influence of Bill Gates makes him something of a policy entrepreneur. According to Cave and Rowell (2014), Bill Gates has long been advocating and funding school reform, and has adopted a highly critical stance on the U.S. public education system that has attracted an attentive audience. He has been a central player in the Billionaire Boys Club, a group of wealthy CEOs galvanized by the incentivist reforms proposed by New York City Mayor Michael Bloomberg and the schools chancellor, Joel Klein. In a speech to the National Governors' Association in February 2005, Gates declared publicly his support for Bloomberg and Klein's proposals, claiming that high schools had become "obsolete" and were "limiting—even-ruining—the lives of millions of Americans every year" (Cave & Rowell, 2014, p. 236).

In sum, among the array of organizations providing financial and intellectual support to privatization reforms, the Bill and Melinda Gates Foundation seems particularly salient not only as a consequence of the size of its investments or material power, but also because of its visibility and the high profile in education reform debates of Bill Gates himself.

The instruments that venture philanthropists use to achieve their education reform ambitions are very diverse and include knowledge production, support for advocacy groups and campaigns, and the generation of best models and good practices. The production and dissemination of evidence on education reforms conducted by philanthropist organizations tends to target academic, media, and policy audiences. On occasions, foundations produce their own research, although they tend to contribute to knowledge production more indirectly via support for like-minded think tanks and policy research institutes.[4] The dissemination of ideas on the advantages of privatization in the United States owes much to the funding provided by philanthropists or foundations such as Eli and Edythe Broad, Dell, Bill and Melinda Gates, Heritage, Hewlett-Packard, or the Walton family.

These and other American foundations are also active in supporting pro–school choice advocacy groups and new civil rights movements supporting the school choice idea, such as the National Alliance for Public Charter Schools, the Center for Education Reform, the BAEO, and the Hispanic Council for Reform and Educational Options (Scott, 2009). In fact, the "racial achievement gap" seems to be a recurrent theme in the discourse of many philanthropic foundations, and is behind their policy option favoring vouchers and other pro–school choice measures (Apple & Pedroni, 2005; DeBray-Pelot et al., 2007; Scott, 2009).

Wealthy individuals and their philanthropic organizations also sponsor pro–charter school and provoucher campaigns, especially in the U.S. context. The Gates Foundation and other donors connected with Gates generously donated a total of $8.32 million to the Yes on 1240 campaign, organized by the Washington Coalition for Public Charter Schools, to convince the citizens of Washington State to vote in favor of the Charter Schools Initiative (I-1240). This amount, which represented around 80% of the campaign's total budget, became key to understanding why, after losing three previous popular referenda, the Charter Schools Initiative became state law in December 2012 (Au & Ferrare, 2015; Au & Lubienski, 2016).

Finally, venture philanthropists provide the financial backbone for specific charter schools and charter management organizations such as Green Dot Public Schools, the KIPP network, or Uncommon Schools. By converting these schools into models of excellence and best practice, philanthropies aim to demonstrate that their educational reform approach works, as well as to encourage governments to scale it up. However, this type of donations to specific schools or school chains has raised questions about the distortion, inequalities, and other types of tensions that philanthropies generate within the educational system (Bulkley & Burch, 2011; DeBray-Pelot et al., 2007; Scott, 2009).

Philanthropy and CSR in Developing Countries: Doing Well by Doing Good?

In the Global South, transnational corporations tend to use their foundations or corporate social responsibility (CSR) policies not only "to do good," but also as a way to promote self-interest. For instance, for transnational corporations, philanthropy is a way to penetrate emerging markets (Bhanji, 2008), and to promote social peace in contexts where they have a controversial impact in social or environmental terms, as tends to be the case with many energy companies (Van Fleet, 2012). However, as also happens in the U.S. context, many philanthropic organizations aspire to become key policy players in the education-for-development field and, when doing so, education privatization tends to be high on their policy agenda.

Srivastava and Baur (2016) show that in the Global South, similar to the U.S. scenario, philanthropic actors adopt an approach to education policy that is market-oriented, results-oriented, and metric-based. Among other forms of privatization, philanthropic organizations in the South prioritize policies to promote voucher schemes and LFPSs. Importantly, the increasing power of these actors in education policymaking is legitimized through a series of claims about the altruistic, results-oriented, and neutral (not state, not commercial) nature of their activity.

India has become a sort of laboratory where many philanthropists actively promote privatization in different ways. To start with, several private foundations, such as the Azim Premji Foundation (APF) and Pratham [with the support of the Indian IT company Wipro and the Industrial Credit and Investment Corporation of India (ICICI) Bank, respectively], are part of an Indian transnational advocacy network that pushes for school choice and private education. These organizations try to achieve this goal by establishing connections between different actors such as think tanks, policy entrepreneurs, and other education stakeholders. They are also enthusiastic disseminators of James Tooley's work on LFPSs among Indian practitioners and the Indian public. Most philanthropic foundations operating in developing contexts (and in India in particular) are set up by private corporations. Nevertheless, the nonprofit nature of these foundations seems to have contributed to them being contracted by the Indian government to run underperforming schools. One example is the Bharti Foundation, funded by telecommunications company Airtel, which is in charge of 50 government schools in Rajasthan. Another example is the nongovernmental organization (NGO) established by the wife of the CEO of Infosys, which runs schools for the poor in Bangalore (Nambissan & Ball, 2010).

Overall, CSR has become a new global norm that legitimizes the increasing presence of the business sector in education networks globally, and especially in the Global South (Bhanji, 2008; Nambissan & Ball, 2010). Nevertheless, this is still an underexplored research area. According to Bhanji (2008), more research is necessary to distinguish between foundations with genuine philanthropic interests and foundations that consider that philanthropic and business aims are compatible and reinforce each other, so that they can "do good and have their profit, too" (Strom, as cited in Santori, Ball, & Junemann, 2015, p. 39).

Consultancy

Global consultancy and law firms, such as KPMG, PricewaterhouseCoopers, and McKinsey, constitute an emerging education industry player that is also very active in the promotion of privatization and PPP solutions among policymakers (Robertson, 2012). In many countries, consultants have an increasing power in education policy processes. They are in charge of some tasks that were traditionally carried out by public servants, such as research, policy analysis, creation of policy texts, and evaluation of programs and policies (see, for instance, Pinto, 2012). In some cases, the delegation by governments to consultancy firms is so strong that these firms even draft education legislation (Ball, 2012). Some authors use the concept of policy outsourcing to refer to this phenomenon. The term *consultocracy* has also been widely used in policy research because it captures well the increasing power of consultants rather than democratically elected institutions in educational governance structures, a shift which raises issues of conflict of interest and democratic control. Among other reasons, this is because "the interests of profit-maximizing management consultants may become the key determinants of managerialist policies" (Hodge, as cited in Robertson, 2012).

External consultants tend to be perceived as neutral actors by domestic stakeholders. Because of this, it is quite common that governments turn to the services of consultancy firms as a tiebreaker in moments of polarization in education reform processes. According to Steiner-Khamsi (2012b), when education reform processes get trapped in highly politicized public debates, domestic actors may invoke an external source of authority, such as a consultant who can work as a coalition builder or as the provider of a third-best solution to unblock a certain situation. In Ontario, Canada, for instance, the government (when in the hands of the Progressive Conservative Party) relied on external consultants to develop its curriculum policy. According to Pinto (2012), the government resorted to consultants to develop this core element of the educational system in order to address a staffing shortfall, but also as a better way to carry out its agenda without political interference.

Countries with high levels of decentralization and school competition, such as the United Kingdom or Chile, have witnessed an explosion in the number of educational consultants. In these countries, as well as large-scale global consultancy firms, many small consulting companies, and one-person consultancies have emerged (Gunter & Mills, 2016). These consultants offer their services not only to national, regional, and local governments, but also to public and private schools directly.

In the UK context, the role of external advisors and consultants has been also determinant in contemporary processes of educational reform. Interestingly, the number of advisers and consultants underwent noticeable growth under the New Labour government, something that, as in a zero-sum game, resulted in a decline in the authority of senior civil servants in education reform. For example, specialist school reform was mainly conducted by a small group of ministerial advisers who devised ideas and documentation in an informal manner (and, apparently, without engaging in broader consultations with key stakeholders). This policy informality was legitimized by a narrative about the urgency for reform and, in fact, through a critique of tame policy created by bureaucratic civil servants (Ball, 2008a; Exley, 2012). In the United Kingdom, the members of this informal policy network appear to be linked by friendship and a common background in journalism, Third Way think tanks, and elite universities (Exley, 2012; Junemann, Ball, & Santori, 2016). Sir Michael Barber (see Box 9.3) is probably one of the most emblematic examples of the influence that this type of policy expert has exerted in the United Kingdom and beyond.

ADVOCATING PRIVATIZATION:
FREQUENT STRATEGIES OF INFLUENCE

In this final section, we outline two of the most common strategies that private interests and actors, including think tanks, policy entrepreneurs, and private foundations, use to promote privatization in education. They are (1) the politicization of research and (2) networking and the revolving doors mechanism.

The Politicization of Research

The politicization of research (i.e., the instrumentalization of research and research results for political aims) is a common practice among those think tanks

BOX 9.3. SIR MICHAEL BARBER:
A PROVEN RECORD IN EDUCATION PRIVATIZATION

As with many other policy entrepreneurs, Sir Michael Barber is a multi-faceted figure. A former teacher in President Robert Mugabe's Zimbabwe, where he befriended James Tooley, a professor at the Institute of Education (University College London) and collaborator of the National Union of Teachers (Exley, 2012; Srivastava, 2014), he ended up a key agent in the promotion of promarket education policies.

Barber participated actively in the education reform promoted by the New Labour government in the United Kingdom during the 1990s, both as a direct advisor in education of Prime Minister Tony Blair's and as part of the New Labour administration. In 1997, Barber became head of the Standards and Effectiveness Unit, and between 2001 and 2005, he directed the Delivery Unit. Barber's work and trajectory in these two units earned him recognition as a "visionary" by Michael Gove, later the Conservative Education Secretary from 2010 to 2015. The market-oriented nature of the New Labour reforms cannot be understood without referring to Barber, who promoted a complete turnabout of the education system, claiming that only the private sector and market competition are capable of guaranteeing innovation in education (Cave & Rowell, 2014; Exley, 2012; Fitz & Hafid, 2007; Hatcher, 2006; Srivastava, 2014).

Upon leaving office in 2005, Barber was appointed as a consultant with McKinsey. There, he became one of the advisers of the school reform undertaken by New York City Mayor Michael Bloomberg and produced the well-known 2007 report, *How the World's Best-Performing Schools Come Out on Top* (Ball, 2008a; Cave & Rowell, 2014). More recently, he was hired by the Pearson corporation as a chief education adviser, becoming a key agent in the promotion of private schooling for the poor and advocating the scaling-up of LFPSs (Härmä, 2013; Hogan, Sellar, & Lingard., 2015; Riep, 2014; Srivastava, 2014; see also Chapter 6 in this volume). Given Barber's connections to different government and academic agents in the education field, his appointment has conferred more legitimacy on Pearson as a policy actor (Hogan et al., 2015).

His capacity to operate at multiple scales and his expertise in reform processes undertaken in very different contexts makes Barber an education reform "all-rounder." Empowered by personal contacts and by his strategic situation as a broker and nodal player within different networks, Barber has been able to create both the ideational and material conditions for the advancement of different forms of privatization in multiple settings.

and policy entrepreneurs that advocate controversial reforms, including charter schools, vouchers, and pay-for-performance schemes. As argued by Rich (2004):

> Far from maintaining a detached neutrality, policy experts are frequently aggressive advocates for ideas and ideologies; they even become brokers of political compromise. Many of these most aggressive experts are based at think tanks; think tanks have become an infrastructure and an engine for their efforts. (p. 6)

In many countries, the education policy debate no longer occurs exclusively in academic or government settings, and is no longer informed by traditional and peer-reviewed sources either. Rather, evidence informing such a debate is increasingly based on the knowledge produced, funded, gathered, and interpreted by intermediary and advocacy groups, which usually have a particular political agenda (DeBray et al., 2014; Goldie, Linick, Jabbar, & Lubienski, 2014; Lubienski et al., 2014; Reid, 2013). Through research funding policies, some of these organizations, especially private foundations, have a significant capacity to frame the research agenda of university scholars and the consequent dissemination of research results (Henig, 2008; see also Box 8.3 in Chapter 8 of this volume).

Of course, policymakers might also make a tactical use of research, either to arrive at or imprint empirical legitimacy to a previous position. They might do so by selecting those sources that support their policy preferences or perspectives, and excluding from the policy process those researchers who are less favorable to the administration's agenda. All in all, it is worth noting that this process of cherry-picking evidence is not necessarily intentional or deliberate. From a bounded rationality perspective, policymakers often should be seen as ill equipped to assess complex research domains or conflicting evidence, turning to other broker organizations such as think tanks or international organizations to interpret evidence for them.

The instrumentalization of research is more frequent in relation to issues that generate uncertainty and around which the evidence is inconclusive, as is clearly the case with most forms of education privatization. As recalled by Lubienski, Weitzel, and Lubienski (2009):

> In these types of policy sectors where there are both real demands for empirical evidence of effectiveness and widespread consumption of non-empirical "evidence," the use of research evidence may be more susceptible to politicization. (p. 135)

The case for vouchers and school-reform policies in the United States constitute a good example of these tensions around knowledge production and use. Here, evidence is often employed by political groups to provide an academic appearance to their ideological preferences (Belfield & Levin, 2005; see also Goldie et al., 2014). Furthermore, as a consequence of the political charge of the debates around vouchers and charters, relatively neutral research on these themes is usually insufficient, and significant difficulties arise when it comes to resorting to reliable sources (Belfield & Levin, 2005; Boyd, 2007; Kirst, 2007; Vergari, 2007). Overall, research framing the policy agenda on privatization themes lacks the necessary rigor, while university-based, referenced, peer-reviewed research is sidelined or misused (see Box 9.4).

BOX 9.4. "THERE IS A BROAD CONSENSUS ..."
THE ECHO-CHAMBER EFFECT AND SELF-REFERENTIALITY

Researchers and think tanks backing privatization have been questioned for citing a limited number of usually low-quality (i.e., not peer-reviewed) studies, often produced by like-minded organizations, as a way of creating an illusion of a general consensus around the advantages of quasi-markets and free-choice policies in education. This is what Lubienski et al. (2009) characterize as an "echo-chamber effect" in the use of research.

Existing research on school-choice programs in the United States offers mixed or modest results at best. However, school-choice advocates insist that there is a broad research consensus on the benefits and greater efficacy of school-choice programs, and demonstrate this by cherry-picking the most convenient sources among the available evidence. Despite their insufficient rigor, these assertions tie in with a range of common beliefs and public values that prevail in American society and, accordingly, tend to attract media attention and frame policy debates. As Lubienski et al. (2009, p. 184) observe, "[T]he strategy of making consensus claims based on a limited body of research appears to have been rather successful from an advocacy perspective." The echo-chamber effect is not only visible in policy papers and reports, but is more and more visible in social media such as Twitter (Goldie et al., 2014).

In the United States, concern about the political use of research is so strong that there are initiatives to counteract it. One example is the Think Tank Review Project, created by the National Education Policy Center of the University of Colorado, Boulder, which uses academic standards to challenge the main assumptions and recommendations included in the reports of the most politically influential American think tanks. Education privatization is one of the key themes of this project. So far, the researchers and associate researchers of the Think Tank Review Project have reviewed 23 think tank reports on vouchers, 58 reports on school choice, and 39 reports on charter schools.[5]

In relation to low-income countries, Robertson and Verger (2012) note that the members of the international network of experts promoting PPPs in education quote and refer to each other's work very frequently, and mutually reinforce each other's messages through repetition. At the same time, they use evidence selectively and ignore or misrepresent research pointing to the negative or neutral effects of PPP policies (Verger, 2012).

The selective use of evidence is also an issue in education politics in the United Kingdom. Exley (2012) reports that prevailing policy networks in Britain turn out to be self-referential and work through like-minded individuals endowed with policy responsibilities. The World Bank is also well known for managing knowledge on education policy in this tactical way. In its promotion of the privatization agenda, the World Bank creates a virtuous circle between policy, research, and evidence. Robertson (2012) uses the metaphor of "knowledge ventriloquism" to refer to the way the World Bank draws evidence from a limited group of studies that have been produced by its own researchers or commissioned to a reduced and closed group of policy entrepreneurs and economists of education.

Changing Places: The Revolving Doors Mechanism

The demarcation between state and nonstate advocates of privatization is far from being clear cut. As outlined in this chapter, both the notions of policy entrepreneurs and of policy networks and the consequent blurring between the public and private spheres are key to explaining the functioning of policy influence within the education privatization debate. The revolving doors mechanism is probably the most obvious illustration of the permeability between the public and the private sectors in the education policy field.

Various academics have documented the flow of privatization advocates between different public institutions and private advocacy or research organizations, which is a flow that goes in multiple directions. In the United States, for example, private foundation and think tank staff have moved in and out of the federal government (DeBray et al., 2014; Scott & Jabbar, 2014). For instance, Andy Rotherham, a former education advisor to Bill Clinton and a well-known supporter of charter schools, became director of the 21st-Century Schools Project at the Progressive Policy Institute (in association with the Leadership Council). Likewise, the G. W. Bush administration recruited privatization advocates (such as Nina Shokraii Rees from the Heritage Foundation and the Institute for Justice, or Michael Petrilli from the Thomas B. Fordham Institute) into the Office for Innovation and Improvement (an administrative division within the Department of Education created to promote choice and charter schools and inform families about the choices they have under the No Child Left Behind Act (NCLB; DeBray-Pelot et al., 2007).

In the United Kingdom, key figures within Conservative governments were responsible for the establishment of influential think tanks in several cases. One example of this is the case of the Center for Policy Studies, which was set up by Margaret Thatcher and Keith Joseph, then a central figure in the Conservative party (Exley, 2012). In Britain, movements between public administration and the education industry also have been frequent. As reported by Ball (2008a):

> Some LEA [Local Education Authority] Officers who were made redundant as a result of ERA [Education Reform Act, adopted in 1988] and others who gained experience, as a result of ERA, of the commercialization of LEA services saw the possibility of new challenges and career opportunities in setting themselves up as private providers of education services (p. 187).

The revolving doors between McKinsey and the Tony Blair administration also became quite evident. In 2005, for instance, David Bennett (a former McKinsey executive) was appointed as a senior adviser to Prime Minister Blair, and Sir Michael Barber (policy adviser and then-head of the Delivery Unit) joined McKinsey (Ball, 2008a).

This circulation of personnel also can be identified between national governments and international organizations. In New Zealand, the chief executive of the Ministry of Education (who had a relevant role in the design and implementation of new public management reforms in the country) was appointed director of the Education Sector of the Human Development Network at the World Bank (Dale, 2001). This is a mechanism that, despite its apparent micro and anecdotal dimension, has contributed to the international dissemination and promotion of a range of managerialist and market ideas in education that first were experimented with in New Zealand (Dale, 2001).

CONCLUSION

Even though the role of the private sector in education policymaking is still an emerging and somewhat underresearched field in most contexts, some general conclusions can be drawn from the data presented in this chapter. First, it can be observed that nonstate actors play an increasingly central role in agenda-setting processes and the framing of educational debates. Some of these actors are even directly behind the selection of specific education privatization policy solutions in different countries. Corporate actors try to influence educational reform processes in a promarket direction, usually due to ideological reasons (since they believe in market mechanisms as effective regulators and distributors of incentives in all types of policy sectors). Nonetheless, they also do so because they are concerned with the low quality and reduced relevance of the educational systems of their countries. Specifically, they consider that the disconnection between education systems and the needs of the economy is affecting—or has the potential to affect in the near future—their economic competitiveness.

Second, in most contexts, privatization advocates invest a significant amount of resources in attempting to influence the decisions of politicians, legislators, and key decision makers, while also aiming to shape broader public opinion simultaneously. To this end, they are producing and commissioning research to like-minded think tanks and research institutes, and are disseminating their results proactively through different channels, including the mass media.

Third, some private actors have also directly contributed to the development of an education industry that is behind certain levels of educational privatization in different countries. This emerging education industry benefits from governments outsourcing an increasing number of activities that have been conventionally delivered by the public sector directly (including the provision of education services, the drafting of education policy texts, or the evaluation of policies and programs). This emerging industry also promotes governments and schools buying into their ICT and certification products, testing preparation services and other types of so-called school improvement services.

These different roles as knowledge producers, advisors, advocates, and service providers are on occasion carried out by the same type of private actors or by a range of actors that are closely and even organically networked. Among other political implications, this generates issues of conflict of interest and undermines democratic control in education policymaking processes.

Without going any further, the evidence presented in this chapter highlights the emergence of a very strategic and well-resourced network of nonstate actors that is behind the advancement of privatization reforms in many different contexts. Despite the increasing number of case studies and publications on the theme, this phenomenon will require more attention from education researchers in the near future.

CHAPTER 10

Resisting Privatization

The Strategies and Influence of Teachers' Unions in Educational Reform

Education privatization reforms usually meet some form of resistance, which can range from overt hostility to more subtle forms of opposition (Giles, 2006). Resistance tends to come from groups that are most likely to be affected by privatization directly or that, from a more principled standpoint, think of education as a public good that should not be undermined by the presence of private players or market dynamics. Among the groups opposing educational privatization, the role of teachers' unions (TUs) stands out. TUs have consistently opposed market-oriented reforms in most of the cases and trajectories reviewed in this book. Of course, TUs are not alone in this struggle. The composition of the opposing forces to education privatization varies across countries, on occasion including grassroots organizations, parents' and students' associations, social movements, civil rights' groups, and teachers' organizations that are not necessarily unions.[1] Nonetheless, in the existing research literature, the resistance against privatization by TUs is much better documented than that of other education stakeholders.

This chapter focuses on the diversity of TUs' positions, strategies, and impact within education privatization reforms. The chapter is organized as follows: the first section highlights the fragile and contested conception of TUs as legitimate stakeholders during policymaking processes and identifies the main arrangements, schemes of involvement, and forms of relationships between governments and TUs. The second section explores the general approaches or positions maintained by TUs around current privatization trends, as well as TUs' main strategies and repertoires of action in the context of privatization reforms, with an emphasis on their evolution over time. The third and last part explores those factors that restrict or enhance the scope of TUs' influence in the context of education reform processes, focusing on those involving some level of educational privatization.

TEACHERS' UNIONS PARTICIPATION IN POLICY PROCESSES: DIFFERENT MODELS OF ENGAGEMENT

Quite often, TUs are portrayed as vested interests whose main function is negotiating better salaries and better working conditions for their members. Nonetheless, in most contexts, a broader and more complex political connection between TUs and education policy prevails. In the educational arena, TUs are political actors that tend to be recognized by governments as key stakeholders in different education policy processes.

The inclusion of TUs in the discussion of education reforms is significantly linked to the likelihood of the TUs supporting and contributing to these reforms and, consequently, to a more successful implementation. Vaillant (2005), for instance, argues that much of the resistance to education reforms by Latin American TUs is due to a lack of consultation. Similarly, Gindin and Finger (2013), after conducting an exhaustive literature review on the role of TUs in Latin America, observe that TUs have been more open to supporting incentive schemes for teachers when governments have been "willing to compromise." According to them, having a voice in the design of incentive schemes contributes to TUs supporting new policies, but also to these policies being less harmful and more constructive from the quality education and labor rights' perspectives. Gindin and Finger (2013) compare the cases of Mexico and Chile, where the TUs were active players in the definition of teacher evaluation and incentive policies to the cases of Peru and Ecuador, where TUs were excluded from negotiations and organized massive strikes against teacher evaluation policies. In the latter cases, these policies ended up being adopted in a way that did not take into account teachers' needs and priorities and their implementation was contentious (see also Tuin & Verger, 2012).

TUs' involvement and inclusion in education policy varies substantially in different countries and at different times. In fact, TUs' participation is not legislatively guaranteed in all countries, and in many instances, they are systematically excluded from educational decision-making processes (Bascia & Osmond, 2013). In most cases, the presence of an institutional infrastructure or formal negotiation arrangement between the government and TUs is rather precarious. TU involvement seems to be somewhat dependent on the political will of the government in office. In Quebec, Canada, for instance, the coming to power of a Liberal government in 2003 (jointly with the establishment of a results-based management policy, inspired by new public management principles) contributed to undermine TU participation in consultative spaces and resulted in a return to confrontation dynamics (Maroy & Vaillancourt, 2013). Similarly, in the United Kingdom, periods of conflict alternated with periods of cooperation in the education policy arena due to the unstable character of the union-administration connection (Bascia & Osmond, 2013; Stevenson & Carter, 2009). The Nova Scotia Teachers Union (NSTU) in Canada is another example of a TU that, having traditionally played a relatively central role in the province's education policy, has been subsequently circumvented by more recent governments:

> For NSTU . . . deliberate exclusion from the policy formulation process is a new phenomenon that emerged during the 1990s. Traditionally, NSTU representatives have served on a number of advisory committees to the minister of education, and NSTU received advance drafts of policy, regulations, and guidelines for its reaction. The Cameron and Savage governments of the early and mid-1990s, however, bypassed the

union on policy issues; under these governments, NSTU received copies of proposed legislation as they were introduced to the legislature and copies of regulations as they were implemented. The change was sudden and unexpected according to participants. (Poole, 2001, p. 183)

TUs tend to be consulted when forthcoming policy changes have the potential to alter the working conditions of the profession, including issues related to class size, staffing levels and ratios, calendar and hours of instruction, contractual agreements, and limitations to the right to strike. However, this is not always the case for all types of TUs. For instance, it has been documented that in British Columbia and in the United Kingdom, under New Labour, the consultation with government in relation to teachers' labor matters was a privilege reserved for those unions with a more "cooperative attitude" (Exley, 2012; Poole, 2007).

Moreover, it is also worth taking into account that TUs may be circumvented in spite of their rhetoric inclusion in government discourse. In Israel, for instance, the government endorsed the *Dovrat Report,* which recommended the application of market-oriented measures in education, but publicly agreed not to implement its contents until negotiations with TUs, which had rejected the report from the start, had concluded. However, real negotiations never happened, and most of the report's measures ended up being implemented in spite of TU opposition (Zilbersheid, 2008).

There is a wide spectrum of models of union-government relationships. At one end of the spectrum lies a *negotiation model,* where a nonimposing attitude by different stakeholders and the existence of a regular forum for negotiation between governments and TUs are conducive to the adoption of consensual reforms. At the other end, the *confrontational model* is characterized by overt conflict, the lack or absence of dialogue, and the hostility of standpoints.

Of course, models of engagement can vary in the same country with the passage of time and according to the ideology of the ruling government. Nonetheless, these models usually enjoy of some level of continuity that goes beyond particular political junctures. For instance, traditionally, the negotiation approach predominates in central and northern European countries such as Norway, Finland, Belgium, Sweden and, to some extent, Ireland. In these countries, a sort of collaborative working arrangement, as labeled by Bascia and Osmond (2013), prevails, consisting of frequent contact between the TUs and the executive and a certain degree of discursive convergence about education priorities. The post-Pinochet era in Chile is also representative of this orientation. In this country, between 1992 and 2010, there was a succession of negotiations to discuss a range of teachers' related policies, including the introduction of teacher evaluation policies and incentives. The initial rejection by TUs of these types of measures evolved into a consensual acceptance. This is partially explained by a negotiation approach adopted by both parties, which evolved into successive bargaining rounds and into the substantial influence of TUs in the final design of the policy (see Box 10.1).

**Box 10.1. Ongoing Negotiations:
The Case of Incentive Pay in Chile**

In Chile, persistent government initiatives to introduce pay incentives for teachers by the center-left government in the first decade of the 21st century ended up in the establishment of a collective and individual teacher evaluation system associated with an incentive pay scheme. Interestingly, this reform ended up being broadly accepted by the main stakeholders, including teachers and their unions, despite the firm opposition of the main TU, the *Colegio de Profesores*, to this reform in its initial stages.

One of the key factors in understanding the *Colegio de Profesores'* reconsideration of its initial position is related to the open and successive rounds of negotiations that surrounded the incentivist reform (Mizala & Schneider, 2014). The union was predisposed to negotiate about merit pay because the debate on teachers' working conditions and pay has a long history in Chile and has a significant presence in the public domain (Vaillant, 2005). Furthermore, there is a certain routinization of education reform in Chile and a deeply rooted tradition of dialogue between the government and the TU since democracy was reestablished. In fact, it is very common for the Chilean government and unions to deliberate about reform ideas before they are debated in Congress (Mizala & Schneider, 2014). All these factors contributed to predisposing the union to discuss sensitive issues, such as merit pay, on behalf of their constituents.

The particular sequencing and pace of the reforms played an important role as well. Two main aspects deserve attention. First, the fact that the reform was initiated by a government that had increased teachers' salaries and reestablished the teacher labor code (or Teachers' Statute) contributed to building confidence among the union in the face of the reform. Second, the introduction of collective incentives in the 1990s as a prior step to the introduction of individual incentives in the subsequent decade ensured a smooth habituation process and reduced the levels of controversy generated by the incentivist policies.

Of course, the fact that the *Colegio de Profesores* had the opportunity to actively participate in the definition of the standards and the design of the evaluation and incentives schemes was a determining factor in understanding the union's acceptance of the reform. In this respect, the quality of the professional teams at the Ministry of Education, the TU, and the Association of Municipalities can be seen as another key factor that facilitated the acceptance by teachers of the new system of teacher evaluation passed in 2004, in spite of their initial rejection (Avalos & Assael, 2006).

More confrontational relations are documented in countries such as Argentina, Ecuador, and Peru, where TUs are well known for strongly opposing educational reforms, especially when these reforms alter the regulation of teaching staff and are unilaterally advanced by the governments (Gindin & Finger, 2013). In Australia, confrontation seems to be the norm in the education policy domain. According to Connell (2013), since the 1970s, the Australian public sector TUs have been very assertive toward the government as a consequence of their systematic exclusion from education policymaking.

Nevertheless, most of the existing TU-participation models are located some-where between the confrontational and negotiation styles. In England, a collective agreement called Raising Standards and Tackling Workload (known as the "social partnership"), in place from 2002 until the end of the Labour government in 2010, is a good example of this intermediate model. There, some TUs contributed to building a dialogue framework with the government and local-authority employers as a way to overcome the antagonistic style of discussions that had predominated since the eighties. In fact, this initiative resulted in the first agreement since the removal of teachers' national negotiating rights following the 1984–1986 strikes. However, the agreement was limited in its implementation since only some of the British TUs were involved in it. Specifically, the National Union of Teachers opposed some key elements of the education reform agenda advanced through the social partnership and stood outside this initiative, whereas the National Association of Head Teachers had a more ambivalent attitude toward the reforms. Nonetheless, the establishment of the social partnership allowed the creation of stable structures for dialogue, to rebuild relations of trust between government and TUs, and to the common definition of educational priorities (Bascia & Osmond, 2013; Stevenson, 2007).[2] Significantly, this case shows that the creation of formal spaces for negotiation does not automatically lead to unconditional acceptance of the government's agenda. In fact, in England, TUs have retained an oppositional attitude against privatization in spite of the new relationship established through the social partnership (Bascia, 2014; Stevenson, 2007).

UNIONS' STRATEGIES AND REPERTOIRES OF ACTION

Carter, Stevenson, and Passy (2010) identify three possible approaches that TUs might use in response to the governmental announcement of neoliberal education reforms (namely, rapprochement, renewal and resistance):

- **Rapprochement** strategies are those that "go with the grain on the new educational agenda and seek to maximise gains for their members within that" (Carter et al., 2010, p. 14). They are a form of pragmatic acceptance that does not challenge the neoliberal basis of the reforms. By adopting this approach, TUs attempt to include professional issues in the bargaining agenda or to discuss implementation aspects, but they do not attempt to challenge the direction of the policies under discussion.

- The **renewal** approach means that the TUs take advantage of the context generated by the neoliberal reform to strengthen their organization or to achieve some other gains. Many governments have promoted education decentralization as a way to fragment and reduce the influence of TUs. However, some TUs have conceived decentralization reforms as an opportunity for renewal and revitalization. According to Fairbrother (1996), the centralized and bureaucratic model of organization limits TUs' capacity for action—a reason why decentralization processes are likely to bring conflicts into the workplace and increase TU influence instead of reducing it. For Carter et al. (2010), the renewal strategy would involve the adoption of more flexible, participatory, and "rank-and-file" forms of organization.
- **Resistance** approaches are those actively seeking to alter or oppose the trajectory of neoliberal restructuring in education, on the grounds of its impact on teachers' pay and conditions, as well as on other dimensions (pedagogy, education quality, and so on). Unlike the rapprochement approach, resistance strategies are more likely to reject forms of interest-based bargaining in favor of more conventional forms of collective bargaining.

Bascia (2014) provides numerous examples of the development of these different strategies in specific contexts and demonstrates their possible coexistence. For instance, in England, in the context of an aggressive policy of *academization* adopted by the government, which altered teachers' pay and working conditions (see Chapter 3 in this volume), TUs undertook a twofold strategy. On the one hand, they organized actions of public resistance (including industrial action) to government reforms and a public relations campaign (in order to fight the negative government press alleging teachers' lack of professionalism). On the other hand, TUs adopted a less publicly visible renewal strategy, involving the support and organization of teachers at the school level, since the focus on collective bargaining at a national level no longer applied to those teaching in Academies.

The response of the largest Swedish TU, *Lärarförbundet,* to the adoption of the vouchers scheme (see Chapter 4 in this volume) illustrates quite well what the rapprochement approach means. In the beginning of the voucher reform, instead of directly opposing it, the Swedish TU focused its attention on possible areas of compromise with the government, such as the improvement of the professional status of teachers. Moreover, and in spite of the concerns about government funding for private and for-profit education, these differences of opinion were not a primary issue, but an issue to be discussed separately through direct contact between the TU and the government. As Bascia (2014) states, "While privatization was a concern to teacher unions, the approach they took was to negotiate quietly with government officials rather than engaging in overt action" (p. 7). However, Klitgaard (2008) notices that, at some point, during voucher reform in Sweden, the traditional corporatism in decision making changed: TUs had few opportunities of gaining access to the policy process and ended up organizing an unusual demonstration outside the Parliament on the day that the reform was approved (Klitgaard, 2008).

Of course, the prevalence of any particular approach is very much contingent upon the existing connections between TUs and the government in office in a given context. As mentioned earlier, this is not always a question of juncture since it also depends on the prevailing administrative traditions, political cultures, and other factors of a more historical nature. Both a long confrontational stage or, on the contrary, a deeply rooted dynamic of ongoing negotiations generate some levels of path-dependence and condition the behavior of the TU and the government in the future, independent of the particular party and people who are in office. For instance, *Lärarförbundet*'s renewal approach in Sweden cannot be disentangled from a long history of (and legal basis for) dialogue between the government and "all interested parties" at any level. This, together with a long tradition of unionization, generally contribute to a compromise-oriented form of negotiation.

Traditional and New Repertoires of Action

This section focuses on the specific action repertoires articulated by TUs in the context of privatization reforms. Action repertoires involve the contestation tools and collective actions that are available to TUs when raising a range of demands and influencing decision-making processes. Some action repertoires are more disruptive than others, although the same TU might opt to articulate more or less disruptive actions according to the political juncture and to the nature of the education reform being discussed.

Civil disobedience (understood in the context of this discussion to refer to the simple refusal to implement reforms that are perceived as harmful or illegitimate, without further agitation or rebellion) is a recurrent repertoire in the face of privatization reforms or other education reforms drastically affecting teachers' labor. It is a disruptive response that tends to be adopted when the government closes the doors to negotiation or dialogue. This repertoire can be observed in British Columbia in 2001, in the face of the adoption of new legislation that reduced teachers' labor rights. Specifically, this included limitations to the teachers' right to strike, the dissolution of the College (the self-regulatory body for licensed K–12 educators) and its replacement by a government-appointed member, the imposition of a contract, and the removal of several items subject to bargaining. In this context, the TU engaged in illegal strike action, encouraging teachers to withdraw from extracurricular activities and to submit their annual College fee to the union rather than to the College (Poole, 2007).

Judicial challenge is another possible strategy for TUs. As described in Chapter 5, this is a common strategy for blocking the implementation of voucher reforms in the United States. It is also common for TUs to resort to the courts (although with more uneven results) when attempting to block or revoke charter school legislation or at least introduce caps on the number of charter schools (Young, 2011).

(Legal) industrial action, including strikes and demonstrations, are also common protest repertoires articulated by TUs. In Spain, since the transition of the

country to democracy, teachers' collective action and their capacity to paralyze the system through strikes and demonstrations have contributed to important improvements in teachers' labor conditions, which were seriously decimated during the Franco dictatorship (Bonal, 2000). In the early 2000s, in Catalonia, an autonomous community in Spain, TUs organized four general strikes against the approval of a new education act in a period of eight months. These actions forced the regional government, in the hands of the Social Democrats at that time, to eliminate charter school provisions from the first draft of the act. Nevertheless, the law that was finally approved had a marked managerialist and school-based management approach to educational reform, which is something that TUs could not alter despite their efforts (Verger & Curran, 2014).

A Less Confrontational Approaches

The repertoires of action described so far are quite disruptive in nature and are the type of repertoires used as part of confrontational social movements. However, TUs also articulate less confrontational strategies as a way to influence the direction of educational policies in their countries. For instance, in the United States, it is common that all types of trade unions, including TUs, contribute substantially to the electoral campaigns of the main political parties as an insurance that their needs will be taken into account following elections. Hartney and Flavin (2011) observe that the greater the percentage of campaign contributions to candidates for state office coming from TUs, the less likely it is that the states approve reforms favoring vouchers, public school choice, charter schools, or teachers' merit pay policies. According to these authors, TUs' contributions to electoral campaigns predict the tone of educational policies better than other factors, such as the proportion of main union members among state residents or the overall public sector union density.

Poole (2001), on the basis of his study of TUs in Nova Scotia and Connecticut, identifies a range of strategies among unionism, which are not necessarily reactive or confrontational, but are effective when it comes to enhancing the TUs' influence in policy making. Among these strategies, the author highlights the potential of innovative *framing*, including the articulation of demands that are more centered on improving public education and not exclusively on labor issues, and the *building of strategic alliances and public relations campaigns*, which enables the TUs to influence and establish new themes in the political agenda.

Research production and management is another strategy available to TUs to raise their claims and alter education policy decisions. In Nova Scotia, the NSTU used the specialized expertise of union members by commissioning a study of eight pilot site-based management schools that had not been previously evaluated by the Department of Education. The new knowledge generated through this study became "a value-added competency that the union can use to its advantage and to the benefit of quality public education" (Poole, 2001, p. 188). In the United States, teachers' organizations and civil society organizations published a critical range of evaluations of privatization initiatives to show that evidence on the benefits of privatization policies is not as conclusive as many think (Fitz & Beers, 2002). In the context of the delegitimization campaign that American unions face, Young (2011) notes that this is a strategy with a potential political gain:

> The unions' best defense appeared to be the release of reports that did not provide convincing evidence that certain reforms were effective, their undeviating and relentless talking point—for the good of the children—and critical assessments of media portrayals of educational reforms and reformers (for an example, see Diane Ravitch's, 2010, review of Waiting for "Superman"). (p. 346)

Finally, it is worth mentioning that TUs do not always proactively strategize against privatization. In fact, it has been documented how privatization reforms have occasionally been consciously coopted by TUs. Cooptation can be seen as a strategy that, within the bounds of possibility, allows TUs (and other nonstate actors) to influence education policy processes that have been externally settled and driven. Cooptation, in the case of education privatization reforms, involves the proactive participation by unions in processes that have not necessarily been defined by them and are somehow "a radical departure from normative union behaviour" (Poole, 2001, p. 188). For example, in Connecticut, the Connecticut Education Association supported charter school reform and worked to ensure that teachers in this type of school were qualified and enjoyed a minimum level of labor rights. The TU even encouraged teachers to start their own charter schools and sponsored one of the first 12 charter schools that opened in Connecticut in 1997. The comments of the local president of the union at the time illustrate this rationale: "We are not going to stop [charter schools and for-profit companies]. We better get on the train. You can't always keep criticizing" (quoted in Poole, 2001, p. 189).

Generally speaking, TUs in the United States, as a consequence of their continuous reversals in the context of conservative and neoliberal reforms, have been pushed to adopt a less confrontational strategy on a range of policy issues, including charter schools. The combination of resistance, cooptation, and leadership in relation to charter schools is what has helped American TUs to maintain their memberships, their financial base, and their legitimacy (Young, 2011):

> Teachers unions are no longer just simply fighting reforms; they are also adapting to some of the reforms that seem to persist (e.g., unionizing charter schools) and collaborating to reshape others (e.g., merit pay for teaching in hard-to-staff schools). These changes in strategy allow the unions to maintain the different resource dimensions of their niche and, in doing so, survive. (p. 349)

In a way, cooptation or adaptation strategies seem to be closely connected to the rapprochement approach described by Carter et al. (2010), as well as to the collaborative approach identified by other academics, since they involve nonconfrontational behavior by the TUs (see Maroy & Vaillancourt, 2013). As part of these strategies, TUs proactively try to identify a common-interest agenda with governments and to pursue forms of integrative bargaining as a way to advance possible mutual advantages.

CONDITIONS OF INFLUENCE:
OPPORTUNITIES, RISKS, AND THREATS FOR UNIONS

According to Young (2011), there are five resource dimensions that work as necessary conditions to understand the survival and policy influence of TUs: (1) membership; (2) selective benefits to members (including professional, purposive, solidary, and material benefits); (3) proposed government action on issues of interest (i.e., "something to lobby for"); (4) a sufficient level of finances; and (5) access to policy processes on relevant issues. The last aspect depends, in turn, on the nature of the conflict within the education policy arena; the existence of government allies, and the tradition of government-TU collaboration; the level of issue expertise on the part of the TU; and the ideological credibility of the lobbying activity and the way it resonates within public opinion. According to existing literature, some of these mentioned elements are key not only to understanding the variable impact of TUs in the context of proprivatization education reforms, but also how privatization reforms alter the resources available for TUs in education politics. In this section, we focus on the most relevant of them.

It has been documented that privatization policies such as charter schools or pay-for-performance negatively affect TUs' membership (Young, 2011). Charter schools and other public-private partnership (PPP) arrangements segment and introduce heterogeneity and selective benefits into the teachers' force, which represents a challenge in terms of collective bargaining. For unions, losing members means a reduction in financial resources and representational legitimacy, and this ultimately translates into a reduction in mobilization capacity and political influence.

Privatization policies also affect trade union participation at different levels, including diminished access for teachers to legal support from their unions on issues like salary levels, job security, or working conditions (Bascia, 2014). In fact, on many occasions, the arrangements between governments and private school owners tend to reduce or eliminate teachers' access to union representation. The privatization agenda goes in concert with a displacement of the decision-making centers from the national, regional, or local level to the school level, which is something that also happens at the expense of TUs' presence and relevance. According to Bascia (2014):

> Teacher unions thus face a dual challenge: teachers need organized representation more than ever, but at the same time teacher unions' ability to represent teachers is compromised. In fact, reducing the authoritative role teacher unions have played in public education is one of the often explicit goals of educational privatization. (p. 2)

When it comes to resisting or negotiating privatization policies, the reviewed literature provides us with multiple examples of the importance of TUs establishing *governmental allies*. Nonetheless, the presence or absence of these allies tends to be contingent on the ideological orientation of the government in power. In the case of the United States, Holyoke, Henig, Brown, and Lacireno-Paquet (2009) explain that the National Education Association, in the presence of legislative allies (through whom they could influence the lawmaking process), became more active and effective in placing restrictions on charter school activity.

In Denmark, a historically rooted alliance between the government and the trade unions is central to explaining the absence of a "neoliberal revolution" in the education system in the 1980s. According to Wiborg (2013), the power and legitimacy of public-sector unions is a crucial factor for understanding the limited expansion of market-oriented reforms in the country. In fact, even Denmark's Conservative Party "defined itself as a social-liberal party and committed itself to cooperate with the powerful trade unions, which limited them from turning their anti-welfare rhetoric into concrete policy reforms" (Wiborg, 2013, p. 413).

The way TUs frame their messages and demands is also important for understanding the level of public support that they receive and, accordingly, the effectiveness of their campaigns against privatization. Poole (2001) notes that drawing attention to the potential threats to public education or equity issues that privatization policies generate—instead of focusing exclusively on teachers' welfare—is key for earning public support. This relationship is dialectical in the sense that being aware of having public support also encourages teachers to join collective action initiatives. The cycle of strikes that the NSTU promoted in the 1990s provides a particularly illustrative example of the importance of framing strategies. In 1995, a strike vote received approval from 89% of the membership in Nova Scotia. This was an important level of backing given the illegal status of the strike, and considering that, 18 months earlier, a similar vote garnered little support. What changed in this short period in the union? According to Poole (2001), the way the union reframed its message became key to understanding the change in the support base to the strike:

> Participants explained that the issues in 1994 and 1995 were different. Significant issues in 1994 pertained to teachers' economic welfare, and the public was nonsympathetic. In 1995, however, the issues included governance of the education system, equity in education, and union security. The public supported the teachers' cause in 1995, participants believed, because the issues went beyond teachers' economic welfare. (p. 186)

Johnston (2014) reached a similar conclusion when comparing the resistance to charter schools in Kentucky and Washington. On the basis of these two cases, this author argued that the TUs' ability to use and mobilize their discursive resources made a significant difference in the final outcome of the reform. While in Washington, charter school proponents succeeded in portraying public schools as low-quality institutions (and charter school legislation was finally adopted as a result), the Kentucky's teachers' union neutralized the generalizations of the privatization advocates. In Kentucky, the union emphasized the need for public solutions by articulating a language of achievement and diversity and, in the end, impeding the advancement of charter school bills. This premise on the importance of framing strategies against privatization reforms applies to TUs, but also to other education stakeholders such as students' movements (see Box 10.2).

Box 10.2. The Chilean Students' Movement: Communication Strategies and Social Support

The Chilean students' movement is behind one of the most emblematic and influential mobilizations against education privatization of the last few decades. This movement emerged for the first time in 2006, with the so-called Penguin Revolution in secondary education (the *penguin* concept comes from the black-and-white uniforms worn by secondary students in Chile). In 2011, the students' movement took to the streets again, this time under the lead of university students.

The Chilean education system is one of the most market-oriented in the world. Despite the great educational expansion experienced in Chile during the last few decades of the 20th century, the education reforms implemented by the military dictatorship and their later consolidation during the democracy have led to an education system with high levels of inequalities and quality deficiencies (see Chapter 3 in this volume).

In 2006, the secondary students initiated a campaign, principally based on demonstrations, to obtain free transportation and the removal of fees for the university admission exam. However, the students gradually increased their demands, with the support of TUs and university students, and started focusing on quality and equity issues at all educational levels. Bellei and Cabalin (2013) categorize the demands of secondary students into four main themes: free education, defense of public education, the abolition of for-profit providers, and the abolition of schools' discriminatory practices. The secondary students' mobilization combined two traditions of Chilean students' movements: "it articulated a solid ideology on educational issues and it brought a significant list of concrete demands to the negotiating table" (Bellei & Cabalin, 2013, p. 114). At the same time, Cabalin (2012) highlights the capacity of secondary students to change the political agenda through attracting media attention and the sympathy of Chilean citizens. As a result of this first students' mobilization, the Chilean government approved in 2009 a new Education Law that, despite representing only a limited victory for the students in terms of policy changes, had great symbolic value and an empowering effect, as it demonstrated the potential for collective action to influence the political agenda.

Some years after the Penguin Revolution, in 2011, university students staged the most important student protest in Chilean history. In this case, the university student organizations gathered under the umbrella of the

Confederación de Estudiantes de Chile (CONFECH), whose charismatic and media-friendly leaders played an important role in conveying the message of the movement to society. As happened with the 2006 protests, the demands of the university students gradually increased, from more resources for public education and free access to university for socially disadvantaged and middle-class students to free postsecondary education for all students and the removal of profit motives from the whole education system (Bellei & Cabalin, 2013). In addition to carrying out street protests, students' organization developed a strategy based on the creation of networks with other education stakeholders (e.g., TUs and civil society organizations). The publication of policy documents and position papers were extensively disseminated by the media.

Salinas and Fraser (2012) say that the 2011 student movement succeeded for a number of reasons:

> . . . inequalities in education that were an outcome of three decades of neoliberal economic and educational policies; the discursive agency and communication tactics of student organizations that provided meaning to a collective challenge to current policy; the opportunities opened by long-term (i.e., democratization) and short-term (i.e., the Piñera administration and the "year of higher education") changes in the national political context; and, finally, the new conditions created by economic development and educational expansion in Chile for a young generation with increased capabilities and critical attitudes readily available to channel into political action. (p .39)

Bellei and Cabalin (2013) highlight how the students were able to frame their demands in a way that challenged the traditional problem-solving approach of Chilean political parties and, at the same time, contributed to students becoming recognized as relevant education stakeholders. In this sense, "student movements not only highlighted 'new problems,' but also new interpretations of those problems. Such interpretations implied the need for systemic changes in education, which were outside the frame of reference for Chilean policy makers" (Bellei & Cabalin, 2013, p. 118). Thus, the student protests organized between 2006 and 2011 are key to understanding not only the education reforms, but also noneducation sector reforms, such as the taxation reforms that are discussed nowadays in Chile.

The reviewed research also shows that the legitimacy and popularity of TUs in society is key to understanding their policy influence. These elements positively condition the TUs' capacity to exert pressure on policymakers in different spheres. Mizala and Schneider (2014), drawing on the Chilean case, report that

TUs in the 1990s were empowered by their previous actions during the dictatorship period:

> The Colegio [the teachers' union] had earned a lot of popularity and legitimacy in its participation in the struggle to end the military dictatorship, and the subsequent democratic government feared its ability to call disruptive strikes. So, the union managed in the first round of negotiation to get its preferred labor regime despite opposition within the government, including by some of the more technocratic factions. (p. 90)

One of the major threats faced by TUs comes from the difficulties associated with their public image and their perceived illegitimacy as relevant actors in society. It is worth taking into account that black-and-white views of TUs tend to prevail in many places. In Latin America, as Gindin and Finger (2013) note, the media has extensively covered the actions of public-sector TUs and has contributed to the politicization and polarization of perspectives on the TUs' role in education politics. These authors also note that policymakers have tended to label TUs as hindrances to an increase in quality, as a consequence of their policy preferences and their strike activities. For example, in a country like Argentina, there is almost an assumption that constant and massive teachers' strikes would lead to the withdrawal of families from public education sector in favor of private education. Nevertheless, it has not been empirically tested whether teachers' industrial action explains the increased demand for private education in this country (Narodowski et al., 2013).

As Bascia and Osmond (2013) report, in many countries, TUs are portrayed as illegitimate, unprofessional, simplistic, and selfish by both the media and the government. They point out that an increasing vocal criticism of teachers runs parallel to a growing criticism of their unions. In Chile, the two main conservative newspapers portray teachers' organizations as groups intending to secure first and foremost their own private interests, rather than the public interest (Santa Cruz & Olmedo, 2012). Similarly, during the neoliberal reforms adopted in New Zealand in the 1980s, teachers were seen and portrayed as "motivated by self-interest, with propensities for opportunism and 'provider capture'" (Codd, 2005, p. 195). In the United Kingdom, the sidelining of TUs was advanced to some extent by the media. Other stakeholders systematically labeled them as a *vested producer interest*. According to this narrative, the vested interests of teachers slowed down education reforms that the government perceived as necessary, such as the specialist schools program (Exley, 2012) (see Box 10.3).

According to Young (2011), in the U.S. context, criticism of TUs dates back to the emergence of teacher unionization in the 1960s and continues today. Here, critics tend to blame TUs for their "adamant opposition to change" and attribute the ineffective and inefficient practices in education that still prevail to their "unwillingness to alter their bottom line" (p. 338). The 2010 documentary *Waiting for Superman* is a recent example of the survival of these prejudices against TUs and their role in education. "Overall, the media and government officials' bashing of teachers' unions have led many citizens to view teachers' unions as obstacles to

---

BOX 10.3. MOTIVATIONS FOR ACTION:
EDUCATIONAL PRINCIPLES OR VESTED INTERESTS?

Existing research on the role of TUs in education policy portrays them in a dichotomic way: as "special interests pursuing a self-interested agenda" or as "encompassing social movements advocating for public education" (Gindin & Finger, 2013, p. 3). This box reflects on how such divergent constructions about TUs are drawn.

The vested interest approach owes much to Terry Moe's work, where TUs seem to be invariably disposed to block reforms through activism, lobbying, and campaign donations to protect their interests. Hartney and Flavin (2011) conceive public-sector employee unions as explicitly advantaged interest groups, which benefit from collective bargaining laws that encourage government employees to join unions. Belfield and Levin (2005) consider TUs as agencies inclined to "maintaining and promoting the continued employment and economic conditions of their members" (p. 560)—something that ultimately contributes to the make the debate on vouchers and similar privatization reforms more ideological than evidence-based.

According to the second view, TUs are "social movements with an important contribution to education policy." This view is quite prevalent in the education literature produced in Latin America:

> This literature sees [TUs] as the promoters of the value of public education, not narrow-minded, self-interested lobbyists and campaigners. They are vehicles of social justice, motivated by the right to a quality public education and democracy and delegitimizing regressive policies. Moreover, this literature sees teachers as proactive, not just reactive; scholars have emphasized unions' role in promoting positive change in education, such as through increases to the education budget targeted toward the public sector. (Gindin & Finger, 2013, p. 5)

In the context of the United Kingdom, Hatcher and Jones (2006) analyzed how the campaigns against Academies reflect that TUs articulate with other civil society groups and join a broader social movement whose main priority is the defense of public education and the right to education.

All in all, it may not be appropriate to adopt vested interests and principled based-action as fixed categories or in an exclusionary way. In fact, TUs can simultaneously be principled and self-interested actors, or they can behave according to one dimension or the other in specific moments or political junctures (Mizala & Schneider, 2014). According to Maroy and Vaillancourt (2013), those political actors that produce policy discourse, such as TUs, are simultaneously holders of ideological visions and professional and social interests:

> The actor, whether in an individual or collective sense, is simultaneously a strategist and a conveyor of meaning, in arenas where not only negotiations

and interest transactions are at play, but also the definition of the (social or school) reality or the definition of the political action under construction" (Boltanski, as cited in Maroy & Vaillancourt, 2013, p. 99, and translated by us)

Overall, as reported by Carter et al. (2010), there is a difficult balance between the image of the teacher as a professional and as a worker. This dichotomy is to some extent rooted in a historical tension in teacher unionism between conceiving TUs as professional associations or as labor unions:

> Almost everywhere it is possible to see a struggle as teacher unions have sought to reconcile a commitment to "professional" concerns with a similar commitment to so-called "bread and butter" concerns of pay and conditions. The history of teacher unionism in many different contexts can often be presented as a struggle between these agendas—frequently manifested as inseparable and complementary, but in reality often in conflict and difficult to reconcile. (p. 12)

Finally, it is also feasible to consider that, in the same geographical territory, TUs with different orientations coexist—some of them more self-interested than others. For instance, in Spain, which has a highly diverse and decentralized education system, the diversity of TUs in terms of both their political orientation and the nature of their social bases is very high (Bonal, 2000).

education reform at best and obsolete at worst" (p. 346). Likewise, Brogan (2013), drawing on a case-study analysis of education reforms in Chicago, reports a sustained assault on teachers and their unions. Brogan explains the prominence attached to this attack as a consequence of TUs' potential resistance to neoliberal reforms (particularly when considering that teachers are the largest sector of unionized workers in the United States), but also as a result of opportunities that teachers' deprofessionalization itself offers to the expansion of marketization and the reduction of public expenditure on education.

One of the most common demonization strategies by policymakers, academics, and the media against TUs is the dissociation of unions from the teachers themselves. In other words, a common way to delegitimize TUs is to propose that these organizations do not really represent the views of the majority of teachers. Rather, the claim is that TUs use teachers' interests as a way to advance their political and corporate agenda. Poole reports:

> In accordance with neo-liberal philosophy, unions are viewed as obstructions to achieving economic prosperity. TUs are not exceptions. Critics of teachers' unions blame unions, but not necessarily teachers, for problems in public education. Typically, teachers' unions are viewed by neo-liberals as third parties, separate from

teachers, interfering in the relationship between teachers and their employers. Often, teachers are characterized as victims who are simply being used by unions. (Poole, 2007, unnumbered)

Internal unity and cohesion make a major contribution to the political and policy influence of unions. One of the common sources of internal cohesion issues occurs when there is a base of teachers who want the union to focus on short-term interests, as opposed to union officials, who are usually more oriented toward long-term and strategic challenges. Bascia and Osmond (2013, p. 13) argue that, especially in those contexts where TUs are strong partners in education decision making, "[TUs] must walk a fine line between a focus on relationship maintenance and support for jointly agreed policies and advocacy work on the part of their members." In the case of the social partnership in England, for instance, these authors report how difficult it was for the TUs to have a positive relationship with partnership members and, at the same time, pay attention to the different needs, concerns, and values of their constituency.

This trade-off between the long- and the short-term needs of teachers might condition the reorientation strategies and internal power dynamics of TUs. In this respect, Poole (2001, p. 194) finds that "teachers, dealing with the everyday challenges of the classroom, often do not see the broader challenges confronting the profession and insist that the union focus on the short-term needs of teachers." In Chile, such divergent priorities between the leadership and the affiliates have led to important changes within the main TU, the *Colegio de Profesores*. In 2007, the then-union president, Jorge Pavez, lost the election to a more leftist candidate as a consequence of Pavez's support of compulsory evaluations for teachers in public schools (Mizala & Schneider, 2014).

Furthermore, it is worth considering that the same difficulties associated with long processes of negotiations with governments also contribute to competing conceptions of education, which in turn could be conducive to internal schisms within a TU. This is precisely what happened in Quebec, where difficulties during the negotiation of public management-oriented reform in the mid-2000s, combined with preexisting internal divergences on education conceptions, led to the division of the Centrale des Syndicats du Québec and to the creation of the Fédération Autonome de l'Enseignement (Maroy & Vaillancourt, 2013).

The number of TUs involved in the education policy field in a particular context is also important for understanding the TUs' sphere of influence. Vaillant (2005), after reviewing a range of case studies on the role of TUs in educational reforms, concludes that dialogue with the government is more likely to be successful when only a few TUs take part in the negotiations or when TUs participate in the dialogue cohesively. In contrast, a divided TU camp weakens the ability of TUs to negotiate. In this respect, Vaillant (2005) notes that rivalries between TUs, but also internal divisions within the same TU, diminish their ability to oppose or influence government decisions.

Finally, the level of issue expertise is increasingly considered as a condition for TUs' access to the policy process. In the context of increasingly networked forms of governance, TUs compete against a growing number of interest groups, foundations, and research institutions when it comes to accessing legislators or political officials (see Chapter 9 in this volume). In countries without an established negotiation tradition, like the United States, this has meant that the TUs' influence on policymakers has diminished against that of other stakeholders (Young, 2011). However, as discussed previously, many TUs have adopted strategies connected to the promotion and production of expert knowledge and, accordingly, have started to address some of these threats.

CONCLUSION

This chapter has explored how TUs are political actors that tend to be recognized by governments as a key stakeholder in education policy processes. However, the scheme of engagement between TUs and governments in the education policy arena is variable and can be influenced by many circumstances. The participation of TUs can be more or less collaborative (or more or less tense) according to the political regime and participative culture that prevails in a country or region, as well as a particular political juncture. Furthermore, the relationship between TUs and governments depends on the content and nature of the education reforms being discussed, with privatization reform being one of the reforms that generates the most tension between these actors.

TUs have been involved in one way or another in most of the processes of educational privatization reviewed in this book. The relevance of TUs in these processes is, in fact, evidenced by the considerable attention that they receive from privatization advocates, who tend to consider TUs as one of the most important barriers to the advance of privatization reforms.

Overall, it can be observed that, in the context of education privatization reforms, the role of TUs tends to be restricted to the retention stage (see Chapter 2 in this volume)—that is, the period when reform discussions are in their final phase. In relation to privatization reforms, TUs seem less able to condition agenda-setting processes than other more powerful state and nonstate actors, which tends to relegate them to a reactive or antagonistic role. Being pervasively perceived as an antagonistic actor affects the legitimacy and popularity of TUs in the general public and, therefore, their influence in education policy processes. It should be taken into account that a range of political groups, international organizations, and media sources are contributing to this social perception of TUs as actors that always resist change and are inevitably located at the barricades. However, TUs' recent adoption of evidence-based advocacy and knowledge-production approaches to educational politics represents a strategic reorientation that may contribute to reversing this stigma. This is a positive move for TUs since a positive public image is one of the key conditions for ensuring that governments hear their voices.

In general, privatization has resulted both in the need for a redefinition of the TUs' role in educational systems, forcing them to assume new functions such as research production, and the introduction of additional difficulties for collective action due to the potential impact of privatization on membership, resource availability, and access to decision-making centers. Nevertheless, the existence of some success stories, and particularly the experiences of several TUs engaging with knowledge-production processes and other agents in the struggle against education privatization, suggest that the organization of an effective and constructive resistance against privatization is possible.

CHAPTER 11

Conclusions
A Cultural Political Economy
of Education Privatization

THE MULTIPLE TRAJECTORIES OF EDUCATION PRIVATIZATION

Education privatization is a global trend. Existing data show that there is a worldwide tendency toward privatization in relation to key educational indicators such as provision and financing.[1] Debates on the benefits, challenges, and costs of education privatization are currently taking place in the academic, political, and international aid fields, and across a broad range of scales, from local to global.

Increasingly, governments, international organizations (IOs), donors, and philanthropic entities are converging around the idea that the involvement of the private sector in education systems is inevitable and, to some extent, desirable. Various rationales contribute to this idea: namely, efficiency (privatization as a cost-effective way to expand education), effectiveness (the private sector as a source of competition and improvement in school performance), diversification (the private sector as a promoter of pluralism in educational systems), and innovation (the private sector as a transmitter of new educational ideas and know-how in the public sector).

Thus, the assumption that the private sector can contribute to the positive development of education systems has become a sort of global norm that, for different reasons, is being increasingly embraced by key education stakeholders. This is an important normative change with significant implications for the way that education systems are governed worldwide. Even nonstate actors, such as several nongovernmental organizations (NGOs) and trade unions that previously opposed the role of the private sector in education, now consider that the privatization trend is irreversible and the focus should be on how to regulate and make the private sector more accountable. The fact that evidence on the potential benefits of privatization in different dimensions and world locations is far from conclusive yet,[2] makes more relevant trying to understand the reasons behind such a global, and apparently counter-intuitive, normative change.

However, the emergence of norms in global agendas does not automatically translate into specific, homogeneous, and even substantive changes on the ground (Martinsson, 2011). In fact, the strong presence of education privatization debates and ideas in the global education agenda has not led to a trend toward policy convergence and to education systems looking more like one another globally. What we witness so far is that both the policy outcomes and the processes constituting the education privatization phenomenon can be extremely diverse in nature.

Regarding policy outcomes, the education privatization agenda translates into policy manifestations with very different objectives, instruments, and designs, including voucher schemes, charter schools, outsourcing private provision incentives to private school consumption, and so on. On many occasions, these education policies translate into the increasing participation of the private sector in education delivery and financing, referred to as *exoprivatization* by Ball and Youdell (2008). On other occasions, it means the promotion of school choice and school competition dynamics and, accordingly, the public sector emulating the values and the way that the private sector operates in the education field, or *endoprivatization* in Ball and Youdell (2008)'s terms. These trends tend to go together with the increasing participation of private actors in education governance activities that go beyond schooling. In numerous cases reviewed in this book, privatization in education also manifests in the state outsourcing a broad range of services to private agencies, such as testing, curriculum development, teachers' training or inspection services. Essentially, the advance of the private-sector participation in a range of education governance activities happens through a broad range of policy measures and types of private agents.

In relation to policy processes—and more important for the objectives of this book—education privatization is far from advancing as a monolithic policy trajectory. Education privatization is driven by very different rationales, political and economic factors, and agents' strategies. These elements, as this book shows, frequently associate with each other in clusters of contextual dispositions, agents' strategies, and social mechanisms, constituting different education privatization trajectories in different locations. Specifically, following a thorough and systematic literature review on the political economy of education privatization, this book has identified six paths toward education privatization, described next.

1. Education privatization resulting from a drastic restructuring of the state's role in the delivery of public services (see Chapter 3 in this volume). This path refers to the advance of education privatization policies and programs as part of a broader strategy of structural state reform under market principles. This privatization trajectory, which began to be enacted in the early 1980s in the context of the so-called neoliberal revolution, has been especially evident in countries such as the United Kingdom, Chile, and New Zealand. The privatization policies utilized in these contexts are voucher schemes and other competitive funding formulas that aim to introduce market logic, rules, and mechanisms within the education sector.

These policies were adopted for ideological reasons and, in the cases of the United Kingdom and Chile, by conservative governments that strongly subscribed to a neoliberal ideology. Accordingly, beyond promoting private-sector participation, these policies aimed to introduce competition and choice within the education system. The structural nature of the proprivatization reforms adopted was so profound at the regulatory, institutional, and discursive levels that these reforms became a strong source of path dependence. This happened to such a degree that the social democratic (or center-left) governments that arrived later in the 1990s did not challenge the privatization trend, but rather consolidated and even deepened it.

2. The Nordic path toward privatization (see Chapter 4 in this volume). This path mainly focuses on the education reform processes that have prevailed in Nordic social democratic welfare state regimes. These are countries that have historically enjoyed highly redistributive welfare states and been very active in the provision of public goods. However, they have engaged with some aspects of the education privatization agenda since the beginning of the 1990s. To a large extent, the social democratic parties have led this transformation as a way to address the legitimacy crisis of the welfare state and to promote diversification within the education system (since they perceived choice and diversification in public services as one of the key demands of their middle-class voters).

Despite similar rationales and causal factors for engaging with the education privatization agenda, the Nordic countries' policy outcomes were rather dissimilar. In most cases, many elements of the endoprivatization agenda were adopted. However, exoprivatization measures were much less evenly adopted. On one extreme of the exoprivatization spectrum is the case of Sweden, where this path resulted in the adoption of a very ambitious voucher system. This voucher system, which even allows for-profit schools to benefit from public subsidies, has contributed to a substantive increase of private sector enrollment in the last years. However, Finland sits at the other extreme of the privatization trend within the region. At the end of the 1990s, this country also considered the adoption of market reforms. However, the release of the Program for International Student Assessment (PISA) 2000 results, in which Finland excelled, discouraged the adoption of these types of polices and encouraged the continuation of strong public intervention in education.

3. Scaling up privatization (see Chapter 5 in this volume). This path is characterized by conflict and to-and-fro attitudes toward education privatization. We have illustrated this path by focusing on the United States, a country where the expansion of voucher programs and, especially, charter school legislation is an uneven, although gradual, privatization process. This process has prevailed despite it being the object of tense disputes among a range of state and nonstate actors at the local, state, and federal levels. It has progressively altered a long-standing model of educational governance traditionally characterized by public and uniform provision. Despite the fact that the United States is the birthplace of the school voucher proposal, this idea has not taken off at the federal level. This is for a variety of reasons—namely, ideological (vouchers are perceived as a radical market proposal), political (a lack of support from the most important faction of the Democrats, the presence of other veto players, etc.), and institutional (the U.S. education system's high level of fragmentation and decentralization, legal ambiguity concerning the role that religious organizations can play in education provision, etc.).

In contrast, charter schools, which represent a more ideologically malleable policy program and carries a much lower political risk than universal voucher schemes, has been more acceptable to a broader constituency. Consequently, charter schools have become the main track along which education privatization has advanced in this country.[3] In the United States, but also in other countries where the charter school model has been implemented, this schooling modality works as a sort of second-best approach (or a stepping stone toward more radical privatization measures) for market advocates.

4. De facto privatization (see Chapter 6 in this volume). This type of privatization prevails in numerous low-income countries and operates, to a large extent, through the expansion of the so-called low-fee private schools (LFPSs). LFPSs are an emerging type of private schooling that is driven by profit and, at the same time (and somewhat paradoxically), targets poor families. The emergence of LFPSs is conceived as a spontaneous phenomenon in its origins, with local *edupreneurs* creating this type of school in poor communities to respond to insufficient public education offerings. Despite this bottom-up origin, both international aid agencies and private-sector investment groups, such as the International Finance Corporation (IFC), the UK Department for International Development (DfID), and Pearson, have increasingly backed the LFPS sector, both materially and discursively, as a way to scale it up. For their international promoters, LFPSs are an example of how the achievement of noble global development goals is compatible with the expansion of businesses' activities in social sectors such as education. As a consequence of this strong international promotion, chains of LFPSs are emerging, and more and more countries are including (or considering the inclusion of) LFPSs within educational public-private partnership (PPP) frameworks.

5. The constitution of historical PPPs in the education sector (see Chapter 7 in this volume). PPPs represent the core privatization model in countries with a long tradition of religious schooling, such as the Netherlands, Belgium, and Spain. In these countries, both the historical role in the education sector and the political influence of faith-based institutions strongly conditioned the design and architecture of the education systems during the educational expansion of the 20th century. The origin of these types of PPPs is not related to the emergence of neoliberalism in education in the 1980s since these partnerships with the private sector were enacted much earlier, and for different reasons. At that time, the reasons were rather pragmatic (namely, taking advantage of an existing resource) and political (namely, the historical political compromises between the state and the church). The main advocates of the PPP model—including the private sector itself, the families attending it, and some political parties—defend its continuity by articulating the freedom of education discursive frame.

More recently, countries with historical PPPs have experimented with new public management (NPM) measures in education as a way to promote the public sector emulating the private one and, to some extent, competition between the two sectors.

6. Privatization by way of catastrophe (see Chapter 8 of this volume). This path toward privatization reflects how natural disasters or violent conflicts set the stage for a sudden and radical advancement of market-oriented policies in education. In several locations that have been affected by this type of catastrophes, such as Haiti, El Salvador, and New Orleans, the relief and reconstruction interventions have turned into a clear political opportunity for privatization advocates. A group of IOs, philanthropies, and policy entrepreneurs have taken advantage of the urgency to restore normalcy as a way to advance their policy ideas more rapidly. In such periods of *democratic exceptionality*, privatization efforts face less opposition than they otherwise would in situations of greater stability.

The privatization by way of catastrophe path is far less common than the other paths discussed in this book. However, the long-term implications of this path, together with the fact that privatization experiments in postcatastrophe situations are usually scaled up and exported to other contexts, make this sixth path toward privatization especially relevant from a political economy perspective.

Figure 11.1 presents the main characteristics of the different paths toward privatization identified in this book.

These paths toward privatization need to be seen as *ideal types*[4] that contribute to systematize and group different (real) cases of education privatization, but do not necessarily correspond to empirical situations directly. Thus, in some countries, only a few of the constitutive elements of one of the paths toward privatization have occurred at a time. In other countries, in contrast, elements from more than one path have converged in the same period and location. Chile is a good example of the latter. In this book, we have discussed how Chile illustrates the path of privatization as state reform, but this country is also a good example of privatization via disaster. The violent coup d'état in 1973 and the subsequent lengthy period of political repression (see Klein, 2007) ensued a political environment that facilitated the country's far-reaching promarket reform in the beginning of the 1980s.

For the purposes of the elaboration of this book, the systematic literature review (SLR) methodology has enabled the organization of a huge volume and diversity of literature and research, across different theoretical, methodological, and thematic perspectives. The identification of the six paths toward privatization has made it possible to organize this vast amount of information in an intelligible and meaningful way and to participate in broader theoretical debates on the political economy of educational reforms. Nonetheless, as with any other methodological approach, SLR has some limitations, significantly that the knowledge to be created is conditioned by the existing gaps in the literature of the field in question (see Box 11.1).

Figure 11.1. Different Paths Toward Education Privatization

Path (Countries)	Drivers of Educational Privatization	Origins	Active Actors	Policy Outputs
Reshaping the role of the state in education (United Kingdom, Chile, New Zealand)	• Neoliberal orientation of conservative governments • Authoritarian forms of governing • Explanatory frames to legitimate the reform: "public education in crisis," "public sector monopoly" or "market advantage." • Mechanisms explaining continuity: ➢ Difficult institutional reversibility ➢ Political pressure from parents and private education providers ➢ Unfavorable political timing and political bargaining ➢ Ideological evolution of the social-democratic/center-left parties (an "equity" frame is used to legitimate private-sector involvement) ➢ Aid conditionality from the World Bank (Chile)	1980s	Conservative governments Center-left governments Think tanks Parents Private providers	Per-capita funding and other mechanisms of school competition Liberalization (i.e., easier access to the education system for the private sector) Generation of a quasi-market model with high levels of freedom of school choice More recently, focus on endoprivatization reforms
Education privatization in Social-Democratic Welfare States (Sweden, Denmark, Norway, Finland)	• Economic crisis and global hegemony of neoliberal policy ideas. • Legitimacy crisis of welfare state and reformulation of social democratic parties' agenda concerning the role of the public sector in welfare provision. This meant a push for decentralization of and diversification in public services. • Reform pressures resulting from international organization membership, and participation in international assessments.	Sweden: Early 1990s Denmark: Mid-2000s Norway: Early 2000s Finland: Late 1990s	Conservative parties, like-minded think tanks Social democratic parties European Union, Organisation for Economic Co-operation and Development	Sweden: Ambitious voucher program, liberalization of the education sector Denmark: Pro-school choice legislation Norway: Subsidies to private schools are allowed Finland: The success of PISA prevented major market reforms

Scaling up privatization (United States, Canada, Colombia)	• Frame alignment between school choice and "freedom" ideas; generation of a new common sense around school choice • Mechanisms explaining the charter school policy adoption (over vouchers): ➤ Malleability and ambiguity of the charter school idea ➤ Federal legislation has been able to promote charter school provisions at the state level ➤ Judicialization of the voucher debate ➤ Lower political risk of charter reforms (versus vouchers) ➤ Influential philanthropic organizations supporting the charters idea	1980s	Nonstate actors: think tanks, grassroots' movements, philanthropies, loose advocacy coalitions Republican and Democratic Parties	Charter school legislation in almost all the states Voucher programs at a smaller scale and of limited duration (although more recently, voucher policies rebound upward)
De facto privatization in low-income countries (Malawi, Nigeria, Kenya, Ghana, India, Pakistan, Peru)	• Increasing educational access demand inadequately addressed by the state • Unattended demands of religious or linguistic minorities • Discursive and financial promotion of LFPSs by a range of global actors • Legitimating effect of the education for all (EFA) and the Millennium Development Goal (MDG) frameworks	2000s	Village entrepreneurs or edupreneurs Demand-side forces External actors: IOs, international consultants, policy entrepreneurs, transnational corporations	Increasing presence of LFPSs More recently, development of LFPS chains; incorporation on LFPSs in PPPs

(Continued)

183

Figure 11.1. Different Paths Toward Education Privatization (*Continued*)

Path (Countries)	Drivers of Educational Privatization	Origins	Active Actors	Policy Outputs
Historical PPPs (The Netherlands, Belgium, Spain, France, Argentina)	• Historical centrality of faith-based institutions in educational provision • Conflict/compromises between state and faith-based institutions • Pressures for expansion of primary and secondary education • Legal ambiguity concerning the role of the private sector in education • Emphasis on choice and freedom of education/instruction as legitimating frames	The Netherlands: Beginning of the 20th century Belgium: Late 1960s Spain: Early 1980s	Religious education providers and related communities and families, acting as interest groups	Public subsidies for private schools within long-term contracts (PPPs) More recently, endoprivatization reforms
Privatization by way of catastrophes (New Orleans [United States], Haiti, El Salvador, Iraq)	• Catalytic effect of natural disasters or armed conflicts; crises as political opportunities for privatization advocates • Lack of scope for a democratic or open debate as a result of a situation of exception • Narratives emphasizing relief and reconstruction cover and legitimate controversial reforms • Loss of local control, vulnerability of the state and elimination of institutional obstacles for the entrance of new/external agents • Reduction of veto opportunities and heavy penalization of resistance	Posthurricane New Orleans: 2005 Postearthquake Haiti: 2010 Postwar El Salvador: Early 1990s Postwar Iraq: Mid-2000s	External actors: IOs, market-oriented think tanks, foundations and philanthropic organizations, edubusinesses	New Orleans: Rise of charter schools, decentralization, maximized school choice Haiti: Consolidation and expansion of the central role of subsidized private education via vouchers El Salvador: Expansion of school-based management Iraq: Decentralization and promotion of PPP schemes

---

BOX 11.1. RESEARCH GAPS ON EDUCATION PRIVATIZATION

In the case of education privatization literature, three content gaps stand out. First, existing literature systematically omits some important aspects of the political economy of education privatization reforms. This is especially true for episodes of resistance to these reforms and the role played by teachers' unions (TUs). This gap makes it challenging to capture a full and complex account of the opposition faced by privatization reforms. Overall, the specific role and influence of TUs in educational reforms is still an understudied topic, rarely addressed in empirical research. As recalled by Carter, Stevenson, and Passy (2010):

> Too often, teachers' unions are omitted from studies of education policy, and their influence on the processes of change are underestimated or ignored, even by authors with little sympathy for the managerial orientation of the Government. (p. 2)

Second, certain countries and regions are underrepresented in the education privatization literature, while others are overrepresented. Among the overrepresented countries, Anglo-Saxon countries (especially the United States, followed by the United Kingdom) stand out. The underrepresented group includes Eastern European countries, French-speaking countries, emerging countries (such as India and China), and, more generally, Southern countries. Education privatization trends in these countries are not only understudied, but the research produced remains relatively outside mainstream channels of research distribution. In this study, some of these limitations were partially addressed by resorting to key informants and experts from the countries in question, but certain regions remain underrepresented nevertheless. Ultimately, these absences reveal an important divide between central and peripheral regions in relation to research production and knowledge dissemination.

Third, some emerging themes in the education privatization field—such as new developments with LFPSs or the recent expansion of voucher schemes in the United States—are not yet sufficiently well covered in the literature. In this case, this is not due to scholars ignoring such themes, but because they are too incipient. Relying on the systematic literature methodology for data gathering, instead of directly collecting the necessary data in the field, means that there will always be a temporary gap between the phenomenon being studied and the available evidence.

THE POLITICAL, ECONOMIC, AND CULTURAL FORCES BEHIND EDUCATION PRIVATIZATION

Today's expansion of educational privatization is explained by a combination of global forces and more contingent and locally situated forces. In terms of the forces structuring the global education reform agenda, drivers of both an *ideational* and *economic* nature stand out. Ideational drivers include the increasing acceptance of the potential role of private schooling in education systems among key education stakeholders, as well as the widespread conception of education as a consumable good. In recent decades, more and more people globally are embracing the idea of education as a privatized, individual, and positional good. Many families compete to enroll their children in what they perceive as better schools in terms of education quality, but also in terms of social composition, since they know that both school quality and composition will have positional effects for their children in the labor market and society. Accordingly, these parents are increasingly receptive to (and on occasion advocate for) school choice and other pro–private sector policies, since they perceive them as policies that work to their own advantage to achieve their individual/family goals (Labaree, 2007).

Of course, this type of normative or ideational changes on the demand side responds to more materially inscribed changes within the global political economy. To begin with, in an increasingly globalized economy, competition between economic actors and territories intensifies, and education is treated as a key instrument of competitiveness by governments, companies, and, as just mentioned, by families and students. At the same time, the fact that education is becoming in itself an increasingly profitable global industry[5] is contributing to crystalize a range of corporate interests that aim at opening new education markets and, accordingly, put significant pressure on governments to adopt private sector-friendly policies in education (Verger, Lubienski, & Steiner-Khamsi, 2016).

Overall, the globalization of the economy lies behind the re-organization of the state and the changing role of the state in the economy and in society. In an environment of increasing economic competition and interdependences, the welfare state has been transformed into what some call a competition state (Cerny, 2010), a Schumpeterian workfare state (Jessop, 1993) or, more simply, a neoliberal state (Harvey, 2007). According to Jessop (1993), who was one of the first authors to notice this transformation, this new globalized state, more than in the distribution of welfare, focuses on:

> The promotion of product, process, organizational, and market innovation; the enhancement of the structural competitiveness of open economies mainly through supply-side intervention; and the subordination of social policy to the demands of labor market flexibility and structural competitiveness. (p. 19)

In this new scenario, education privatization and deregulation are at the center of the state reform agenda, and the creation of new market opportunities in all type of areas becomes a high state priority. In addition, the macroeconomic conditions required by a more liberalized global economy predispose the competition state to outsource public assets and services, especially in periods of economic recession and/or increasing demand of these services. Nonetheless, despite its economic focus, or precisely because of it, the competition state also needs to intervene strategically in education and in other extra-economic institutions.

For the competition state, education is not only a potential market sector; it is also a crucial device to improve economic growth and competitiveness. As a result of this complex, and to some extent paradoxical, relationship between education and the state, education and other welfare institutions are not privatized as drastically as other services were privatized before (water, energy, telecommunications, and so on). Instead, quasi-market forms with strong public funding and regulation tend to prevail.

The global transformations described so far are highly conducive to the adoption of some level of education privatization measures. In the face of such structural forces, national politicians and policymakers may appear to be losing influence about whether they should privatize education. Nonetheless, in most cases, national and local decision makers still have an important say in choices regarding the extent and nature of privatization. Thus, the structural factors mentioned earlier, despite partially explaining education privatization, do not determine education privatization processes globally and their concrete policy manifestations. Institutional and more contextually inscribed drivers are also important for explaining why and how education privatization happens in particular scenarios. In fact, focusing on more locally situated factors is key to understanding why education privatization, far from being a monolithic process, translates into different policy outcomes and paths, such as those identified in this book.

The *cultural political economy* approach is particularly useful for capturing the abovementioned multiscalar and multifactorial interplay. As shown in Chapter 2 in this volume, this approach pushes us to observe how agentic and structural, global and local, material, and ideational drivers interact in the production of educational reforms. These interactions occur through the mechanisms of *variation* (i.e., the contingent emergence of new policies), *selection* (i.e., the subsequent privileging of these policies), and *retention* (i.e., the ongoing realization of the policies in question) (Jessop, 2010). The following section applies this approach to the education privatization cases reviewed in this book as a way to systematize and discuss some of the main results of the review.

Variation: The Key Role of Crises

There is always a more or less explicit trigger or turning point in education privatization processes, for instance, an economic or fiscal crisis, the continuous social dissatisfaction with public education, mediocre results in international standardized tests, or a natural catastrophe. When these elements (many of which are externally initiated) emerge, they tend to generate uncertainty within the education policy field and contribute to politicians considering educational reform and, in particular, the adoption of different forms of pro–private sector measures in education as an appropriate policy response.

In terms of education privatization processes, the beginning of the 1990s represented a key moment of variation in many places. In that period, the so-called end of history (after the collapse of the Soviet Union), the economic recession of 1990–1992, and the structural adjustment programs of the international financial institutions set both the normative and the material conditions to advance processes of education privatization in many locations globally, especially in developing and transitional economies.

The path in which the mechanism of variation becomes more tangible and, somehow, empirically observable is privatization via catastrophe. Within this path, an external shock (whether in the form of a natural disaster or a violent conflict) triggers a rapid chain of reforms in the educational system. As documented in Chapter 8, education privatization via catastrophe has crystallized in post-Katrina New Orleans, postearthquake Haiti, and postwar Iraq and El Salvador. Nonetheless, in many other cases presented in this book, periods of economic crises have had a similar shock effect to the one identified in the privatization via catastrophe path. Quite often, economic and financial crises end up becoming a "moment of decisive intervention" (Hay, 1999, p. 317) in the restructuring of different public sectors, including education. The global economic crisis at the beginning of the 1990s, for instance, is behind many Nordic governments contemplating the adoption of market reforms in education. Similarly, the financial crisis that imploded in 2007 is behind deep budget cuts in education, the degradation of public education, and the *de facto* promotion of private schooling in numerous southern European countries (Bonal & Verger, 2017-forthcoming).

Some authors consider that the "catastrophism" generated around poor results in international large-scale assessments, such as PISA, have been used by privatization advocates to advance their pro–private sector ideas in a way very similar to what can transpire following an economic shock or natural catastrophe (Saltman, 2007). Furthermore, global development programs, such as education for all (EFA), have also represented a political opportunity for privatization advocates. In contexts of insufficient resources, privatization advocates persuasively portray the private sector and, in particular, LFPSs as key allies to achieve the EFA goals (Srivastava, 2010; see Chapter 6).

In a nutshell, moments of crises (economic, political, or humanitarian) and the urgency to achieve global educational goals or better results in international assessments tend to be used as a window of political opportunity by policy entrepreneurs and advocates who promote education privatization as an appropriate and suitable policy option to strengthen the performance of educational systems.

Selection: Bridging the Ideological Divide

Most of the cases reviewed in this book reveal that government party ideologies are not a reliable predictor of education privatization policies. Despite the logical disposition of right-wing governments to opt for private provision and market reforms, and left-wing governments to promote public provision and state intervention in education (Elinder & Jordahl, 2013), such ideological boundaries have blurred in recent decades.

In the 1980s, education privatization was, almost exclusively, part of the agenda of neoconservative governments. These governments opted for pro–private sector policies on the basis of ideological convictions (i.e., a strong belief in market mechanisms and competition as drivers of positive educational change), rather than for pragmatic or evidence-based reasons. Nonetheless, in the 1990s, social democratic governments selected some elements of the privatization agenda, although they did not do so necessarily for the same reasons than conservative governments did. This was the case with the Democratic Party in the United States promoting charter schools, the center-left governments in the United Kingdom and Chile consolidating market reforms, and the Swedish social democrats promoting school choice reforms and facilitating the establishment of a voucher system. These progressive political forces did not support pro–private sector educational reforms in their respective countries as a way to (at least explicitly) undermine public education or the role of the state in education, but rather to modernize and promote diversification within public education and, to some extent, to provide new educational opportunities to the most vulnerable population.

Instead of simply a question of the "left acting right" (Wiborg, 2015, p. 480), the described change in social democratic parties' decisions concerning the role of the private sector in education needs to be seen as part of a broader and worldwide ideological shift in the social democratic doctrine that was given in the 1990s and that has come to be known as the Third Way (see Giddens, 1998, and Chapter 3 in this volume). As part of this international movement to rethink the Keynesian policy paradigm, social democrats have transformed the traditional way that they think about welfare and public services.

Nonetheless, the fact that the left-wing versus right-wing divide is not so clear cut in relation to education privatization policy decisions does not mean that both the right and the left select the same policy tools from the education privatization toolkit. Nor does it mean that the reasons for these two ideological groups to embrace education privatization are the same. As mentioned, conservatives opt for proprivatization reforms for ideological reasons, especially when efficiency and competition are the salient values of the reforms. In contrast, progressive governments select pro–private sector polices that have less of a market connotation, but rather have equity and diversification as the core values.

Beyond political ideologies, neoinstitutionalist scholars would predict that education privatization policies diffuse between countries with similar institutional arrangements (Lejano & Shankar, 2013). As seen in Chapter 7, the adoption of PPP schemes is more intensive in countries with a well-established tradition of private schools (usually run by faith-based institutions). In countries like Belgium, the Netherlands, and Spain, the adoption of a PPP model responds neither to a particular situation of shock and crisis nor to neoliberal hegemony, but rather to a more logical development of the education system in which the private sector was already rooted and accepted among the political elites and an important part of the population.

It is also evident that policymakers and politicians are increasingly inclined to select policies that appear to be supported by evidence. Privatization advocates are aware of this trend and try to frame the desirability of their preferred solutions in a scientific, evidence-based way. Nonetheless, as observed in Chapter 9, such advocates tend to use evidence in a selective manner. For instance, several

U.S. foundations and think tanks, as a way to create momentum around privatization reform, produce a sort of *echo-chamber effect* around a small, usually low-quality and unrepresentative sample of studies produced by like-minded research centers (Lubienski, Scott, & DeBray, 2014). A similar phenomenon has been observed by other scholars in Australia and Spain, where neoliberal think tanks use evidence selectively to advance pro–school choice legislation (Olmedo & Santa Cruz, 2013; Windle, 2014).

The presence and weight of private actors influencing the selection of education policies varies by context and in relation to the different paths toward privatization identified in the book. As Junemann, Ball, and Santori (2016) state, the influence of private actors in public policy is contingent upon different administrative traditions and on the disposition and capacity of the state to act as a *market maker* in education. The centrality of nonstate actors within the education privatization debate turns out to be particularly salient in countries with a tradition of openness to advocacy coalitions and private interests in their political system, such as the United States, the United Kingdom, Canada, and Australia. As recalled by Béland (2005), the *parapolitical sphere* differs importantly from one country to another, with Anglo-Saxon political systems being known for their pluralist tradition and openness to interest groups. Nevertheless, the special relevance of think tanks and policy entrepreneurs in the United States and United Kingdom is also related to the ground-breaking role of these countries as policy laboratories in the global education arena. According to Nambissan and Ball (2010):

> In general, the U.K. and USA are probably the most active sites of both axes of reform [choice and private schooling], and are reform laboratories from which experiments are exported around the world. They are also important sites for the articulation and export of the rhetoric and discourses of reform. (p. 324)

In low-income countries, the presence of external actors in education policymaking is also particularly salient. In these countries, IOs, aid agencies, philanthropic foundations and, increasingly, consultants are ever-present in the design, funding, and implementation of educational programs, including those that involve some level of educational privatization (Fennell & Malik, 2016).[6] The administrative and economic shortcomings that most low-income countries face when it comes to managing their education systems make these countries particularly vulnerable and open to external agents advocating global education policy solutions. As shown in this book, external actors have been especially active when it comes to imposing their promarket preferences in postcatastrophe contexts and in the context of the LFPS debate.

Retention: Institutions and Frames Matter

Public opinion and societal values are expected to intermediate in the selection and retention of privatization policies (Boyd, 2007). Policy proposals that promote school choice and competition resonate more in societies that have strongly embraced consumerist values or tolerate better the existence of socioeconomic inequalities. These policies are less resonant in societies where education is traditionally conceived as a public good or equity is high in the hierarchy of values.

Similarly, welfare states theory says that the form and core values of the welfare state system will condition education reform processes and the main policy outcomes of such processes. Accordingly, liberal welfare states should be more receptive to market reforms in public education, whereas social democratic welfare states would be expected to strengthen public education and citizen influence in educational reforms (Klitgaard, 2008). Both welfare states and socially shared values have a path-dependent character and strongly condition the retention or rejection of market ideas in public systems. For instance, as observed by Møller and Skedsmo (2013):

> [In Norway,] the comprehensive education system is still strongly rooted in ideologies and norms, emphasizing various aspects of equity that are linked to social-democratic values and participation and the importance of providing equal access to education regardless of geographic location, gender, social or cultural background or ability is stressed. These norms and values are in contrast to some elements emphasised in NPM reforms, such as privatization, competition and the market. (pp. 346–347)

However, just as governmental ideology does not predict the selection of privatization reforms, welfare regimes and societal values do not predict the retention of this type of reforms. Counterintuitively, a country with a social democratic welfare state, like Sweden, has gone much further than a liberal and more consumerist country, such as the United States in the adoption of market reforms in education. So, welfare regimes predispose governments to select a particular educational reform approach, but they do not explain their final retention in concrete regulatory frameworks. Other factors of an institutional and political nature can intervene here, such as a high presence of veto players, high levels of administrative and political decentralization, or a significant division of powers within the political system. All these elements, which clearly converge in the U.S. political system, have not facilitated the approval and enactment of complex and drastic market reforms in this country (Klitgaard, 2008).

Nonetheless, the democratic rules of the game have made the adoption of voucher schemes difficult in countries other than the United States. For instance, at the end of the 1990s, the Colombian government considered the possibility of adopting a voucher scheme similar to the Chilean one, but it ended up adopting a charter school program. The main architect of this program, when interviewed about the history of charter schools in the country, admitted:

> We were not able to do such a risky thing as Chile. . . . Even though we are moving closer toward a more market scheme, we still have many restrictions. Chile could do it because they had a dictatorship; in a democracy, you cannot implement a scheme like Chile did. (Interview with the former education secretary in Bogotá, in Termes, Bonal, Verger, & Zancajo, 2015, p. 18)

As this quotation implies, situations of democratic exceptionality (such as those generated after the coupe d'état in Chile and in post-catastrophe reconstruction scenarios) are those more conducive to extreme privatization reforms. Nevertheless, in most cases reviewed in this book, education privatization happens through a more gradual and path-dependent type of institutional transformation. One of the reasons for this to happen is that, in democratic settings, education privatization reforms tend to be the object of heated deliberations.

Of course, some education privatization policies generate much more debate and face more opposition than others. Vouchers in education are very present in global policy and academic discourse, as well as in the agendas of important IOs, such as the World Bank, but are rarely adopted and retained in educational systems worldwide. In contrast, charter schools, but also other forms of PPPs seem to face less resistance and are better perceived by a broader range of educational stakeholders (see more details in Chapter 5 in this volume).

Teachers' unions (TUs) are the most persistent opponents to privatization reforms in most of the cases analyzed in this book. As shown in Chapter 10 in this volume, their strategies for resisting privatization reforms have been most effective when TUs combine conventional industrial action with evidence-based advocacy and knowledge-production approaches. However, their influence on the educational debate and decision-making processes is contingent upon the scheme of engagement between unions and governments, which is more collaborative in some countries and regions than in others.

Generally speaking, social democrats (or center-left political forces) have more legitimacy than the right when it comes to reforming public services. As a consequence, their reform proposals tend to face less resistance from TUs and other educational stakeholders, even when these proposals mean the introduction of promarket measures. As observed by Klitgaard, "social democratic governments engaging in unpopular social policy retrenchment may be more acceptable to the voters because they enjoy more credibility in protecting the system than right-wing market reformers" (2007, p. 174). In fact, several chapters of this book have shown that when the left or center-left is in power, pro–private sector reforms face less resistance.

Given their awareness of the resistance that privatization reforms usually face, those IOs, governments, and other actors promoting education privatization are paying more and more attention to how to frame their proposals. This is evident, for instance, in how they attach their pro–private education programs to noble aims, such as the achievement of global development goals or the promotion of education opportunities for the disadvantaged. An analogous strategy consists of repackaging old concepts from the privatization agenda to make them appear more credible and appealing to a broader audience. For instance, these days, the World Bank is rebranding Friedman's voucher proposals by using more friendly and, apparently, more neutral concepts such as PPPs (Verger, 2012). For similar reasons, education market advocates in the United States, instead of talking about vouchers, have started using the term *opportunity scholarships*.[7]

Concepts like partnerships, but also school autonomy and accountability, are politically persuasive due to "their vague and euphemistic qualities, their capacity to embrace a multitude of possible meanings, and their normative resonance" (Cornwall, 2007, p. 472). These types of buzzwords and vehicular concepts alike are politically powerful when it comes to advancing controversial and unpopular reforms, such as those involving education privatization (Srivastava, 2014). In fact, conceptual ambiguity partially explains the abovementioned left-right convergence around education privatization ideas in the context of the Third Way (cf. McLennan, 2004), as well as how, in countries like the United States, strange bedfellows, with apparently divergent interests, can work together in pro–school choice advocacy coalitions (cf. Apple & Pedroni, 2005; Bulkley, 2005).

Finally, although this book has focused on how the adoption of a range of educational policies can promote the privatization of education, it cannot be assumed that education privatization is always the consequence of deliberate policy decisions and educational reforms. Education privatization also stems from more general socioeconomic and cultural transformations and contingencies that go beyond the scope of educational policy. For instance, the economic expansion or recovery of the middle class or the emergence of an aspirational working class can result in an increase in the demand for private schooling (Narodowski & Moschetti, 2013). In different contexts, many families opt for private schools as a matter of social distinction, but also as a way to escape from what they consider as an overly standardized public education option (Belfield & Levin, 2002). Furthermore, as was evident in the case of *de facto* privatization, an increase in private education delivery can also be the result of inadequate educational planning, insufficient public school offerings, or both.

FINAL REMARKS: POLITICAL IMPLICATIONS, FUTURE DIRECTIONS

Education privatization is often presented as a change in policy instruments of a technical nature (for instance, vouchers as a financing tool, charter schools as a new modality of public education delivery, and so on), or as the increasing participation of private actors in education activities. However, it is much more than that. Education privatization, in its many facets, represents a drastic change in the main goals of education policy. Education privatization and the introduction of market mechanisms in education systems contribute to the individual and positional goals of education overshadowing the social and collective goals (such as the acquisition of a common culture and the promotion of social cohesion and equity) (Bellei & Orellana, 2015). Privatization also challenges the traditional ethos of key educational actors, with families becoming more demanding consumers, and schools and teachers becoming more entrepreneurial subjects. These changes in the goals and ethos of education institutions have important implications in the governance of education and, more broadly speaking, in the politics and economics of education.

From all this it follows that education privatization is a process that is contributing to a paradigmatic change in education policy. However, this is a change that needs to be seen as part of broader transformations in the field of public sector administration (*à la* new public management) and in the governance of public services (with current governance approaches increasingly conducive to public-private interactions and to private sector participation in both services delivery and policy-making spaces).

Despite the prevailing global pressures and conditions for privatizing education, this book has systematized a broad range of local contingencies that explain why these education privatization reform pressures do not translate into a linear and univocal process. Especially in those countries where education privatization initiatives are more debated and contested, pro-private sector reforms undergo an uneven trajectory, and are the object of back-and-forth dynamics. Even a country like Chile, which has gone so far in education market reforms, is currently introducing reforms to decommodify education (Falabella, 2015). These reforms, not with little difficulty, aim to disassemble some of the structural privatization features introduced to the educational system during the 1980s and 1990s. There is no doubt that future political economy research should not only focus on emerging education privatization processes, but also on the scope and challenges of educational deprivatization.

The gaps in education privatization literature identified in this book (see Box 11.1 earlier in this chapter) also indicate future research directions and themes that could be developed further. These include processes and dynamics of resistance to privatization, as well as the political economy of education privatization in Southern countries, emerging economies, and Eastern European countries, to name the most significant areas. Focusing on unexplored (or insufficiently explored) territories would probably allow a broadening of the categorization of pathways toward education privatization systematized to date.

Overall, more sophisticated explanations of how and why education privatization happens—such as those this book aims to formulate—are a necessary step to articulate informed policy and political responses to this increasingly complex phenomenon. In the context of the education privatization debate, TUs seem to play an important role—usually reactive more than proactive—in many places. Moreover, it is a role that is confined to the national or local scale of governance. In contrast, privatization advocates seem to be better articulated internationally, in part because they have the resources and the infrastructure to do so, but also because some of these advocates are international organizations themselves. The capacity to transit different political scales easily gives privatization advocates more opportunities to set global agendas and promote global discourses and norms. As argued by Herod (2001), within an increasingly globalized political economy, trade unions' strategies should be rooted in an analysis of the particular geographies of a struggle and their capacity to utilize their own power resources at particular scales, at particular moments, and for particular effects. The fact that the education privatization agenda has become increasingly globalized should make TUs and other civil society organizations more aware of the importance of organizing at least part of their strategies on a supranational scale.[8]

Finally, the cases analyzed in this book show that, independent of the different paths toward education privatization that have been identified here, some level of international convergence seems to prevail toward the adoption of endoprivatization measures in education systems. As outlined, endoprivatization policies such as school-based management, results-based accountability, and merit-based pay for teachers have penetrated in places as diverse as Nordic countries with strong welfare states, countries with a long tradition of PPPs in education, and countries that have restructured their educational systems according to drastic promarket principles. Future research should inquire into the nature of the relationship between endogenous and exogenous forms of privatization, as well as analyzing the multiple recontextualizations, enactments, and effects of this emerging policy trend in different educational settings.

Methodology
Key Components

This appendix develops some of the key components of the review methodology applied in the book—namely, the search terms used in the electronic search, the number of research products identified per source, the quality criteria used to discard some of the search products identified (Figure A.1), and the items included in the form that has been used to collect and organize the data.

SEARCH TERMS

The electronic search resulted from a combination of the following lists:

- **List A ("political economy terms"):** "Political economy" OR "government" OR "governance" OR "state" OR "ministry" OR "minister" OR "bureau" OR "department" OR "cabinet" OR "administration" OR "institution" OR "policy-mak*" OR "practitioner" OR "management" OR "steering" or "supervision" OR "control" OR "regulation" OR "planning" OR "politics of education" OR "education polic*" OR "economics of education" OR "policy implementation" OR "dissemination" OR "diffusion" OR "policy borrowing" OR "policy lending" OR "agenda setting" OR "advocacy" OR "lobbying" OR "globali*ation" OR "westernization" OR "Europeanization" OR "world society" OR "global arena" OR "multi-level govern*" OR "education system" OR "reform" OR "reshap*" OR "adapt*" OR "moderniz*" OR "enact*" OR "resource allocate*" OR "evaluat*" OR "decision mak*" OR "policy-practise" OR "institutionalism" OR "critical theory" OR "neoclassic economy*" OR "neoliberalism" OR "neo-liberalism" OR "human capital" OR "knowledge economy"
- **List B ("privatization reforms and policies"):** "Educational reform" OR "privati*ation" OR "endogenous privati*ation" OR "exogenous privati*ation" OR "school improvement" OR "quasi-market" OR "free market approach" OR "per-capita funding" OR "devolution" OR "performance management" OR "accountability" OR "performance monitor*" OR "education management" OR "benchmark" OR "new public management" OR "NPM" OR "public service paradigm"

OR "decentralization" OR "municipali*ation" OR "regulation" OR "deregulation" OR "liberalization" OR "flexibili*ation" OR "controlled decontrol! OR "school choice" OR "parent-chooser" OR "competition" OR "performance-oriented" OR "enrolment regulation" OR "public private partnership" OR "public-private partnership" OR "PPP" OR "partnership" OR "school voucher" OR "school-based management" OR "school autonomy" OR "curriculum reform" OR "private sector participation" OR "private-sector supply" OR "private sector supply" OR "for-profit basis" OR "private profit" OR "performance-related pay" OR "non-qualified teacher" OR "education service" OR "cola-i*ation" OR "commerciali*ation"

- **List C ("actors"):** "International organi*ation" OR "IO" OR "NGOs" OR "unions" OR "European Union" OR"EU" OR "OECD" OR "UNESCO" OR "World Bank" OR "WB" OR "International Monetary Fund" OR "IMF" OR "World Trade Organization" OR "WTO" OR "Education International" OR "IE" OR "Global Partnership for Education" OR "GPE" "aid agenc*" OR "nation-state" or "nation" or "international community" OR "civil society" OR "corporation" OR "foundation" OR "philantrop*" or "commercial company" OR "policy actor" OR "non-state actor" OR "global actor" OR "national government" OR "international agenc*" OR "multi-lateral agenc*"

- **List D ("education terms"):** "School" OR "schooling" OR "early children education" OR "early schooling" OR "elementary education" OR "basic education" OR "compulsory education" OR "primary education" OR "secondary education" OR "professional education" OR "vocational education" OR "vocational training" OR "professional training" OR "inclusive education" OR "special education needs" OR "comprehensive system" OR "learning" OR "academic achievement" OR "education achievement" OR "student achievement" OR "class size" OR "curriculum" OR "teachers training" OR "school organi*ation" OR "school management" OR "teaching" OR "tuition" OR "tutoring" OR "literacy" OR "numeracy" or "early school leaving" OR "teacher" OR "educator" OR "principal" OR "headmaster" OR "headmistress" OR "public education" OR "private education" OR "education funding" OR "education provision" OR "delivery of education" OR "students assessment" OR "students performance" OR "student test*"

NUMBER OF PRODUCTS IDENTIFIED/SELECTED PER SOURCE

Electronic Databases

Name	Results
Scopus	867
ASSIA	130
IBSS	260
ERIC	560
Total	1,817

Name	Results
Duplicate studies	469
Studies excluded during the title/abstract review	1,215
Studies excluded upon full-text review	42
Final selection	**91**

Gray Literature

Total	20
Studies excluded upon full-text review	9
Final selection	**11**

Hand Searching

Specialized journals	25
Information gaps (Unions/LFP/PPP/ actors–inter alia)	44
2015/2016	22
Total	**91**
Studies excluded during the title/abstract review	36
Final selection	**55**

Key Informants

Region/Topic	Results
Australia and New Zealand	13
United States	7
United Kingdom	9
Latin America	3
Teachers/unions	9
LFP	4
Belgium	5
Unions	3
Scandinavian countries	7
Latin America	3
The Netherlands/Belgium	7
Final selection	**70**

Primary studies included in the review	**227**

Figure A.1. Quality Criteria

	LEVEL	
Low	**Medium**	**High**
Quality: Validity		
• The document does not mention relevant literature to support its statements, or there are not references to earlier work in or significant contributions to the field. • The document does not clearly define the concepts. • The document draws conclusions without providing relevant evidence; inferences are unsupported.	• The document refers to relevant literature and reduces the ideological bias by referring to different approaches. • The document has a solid conceptual framework (central concepts are defined or their original sources are conveniently referred), but it oversimplifies some of the concepts or makes inaccurate inferences from primary or secondary data. • The methodology used in the research is made explicit.	• The document is based on relevant literature and a rigorous conceptual framework. • It reaches logical and reasoned conclusions, providing broad evidence. • The theoretical framework and the final conclusions are clearly and properly linked. • The methodology used is made explicit and adequately employed.
Quality: Relevance		
• The focus of the research does not match the topic of the review. • The review questions are addressed only in a very indirect way: Privatization is not the main subject, or the document deals with "privatization" but uses an approach distinct from political economy—e.g., impact evaluation, implementation, etc.)	• The topic of the review is addressed, but the document is related only partially to some of the review questions. • The objectives, research questions, or hypotheses of the paper correspond only partially to some of the review questions.	• The paper answers clearly one or more of the review inquiries. • The objectives, research questions, or hypotheses of the paper address one or more of the review questions.

ITEMS INCLUDED IN THE DATA COLLECTION FORM

General Data:

Title:

Authors:

Source type (*book/book chapter/journal article/report/working paper*):

Journal name (if applicable):

Reviewer:

Aim of the study/main questions:

Methods and methodology:

Addressed policies:

Geographical area:

Quality/validity (*low/medium/high*):

Quality/relevance (*low/medium/high*):

A. Theoretical Frame

B. Context

C. Actors Involved in the Policy Adoption Process

D. Mechanisms of Diffusion/Explaining the Adoption

E. Outputs/Reinterpretation

F. Comments on the Article (Validity/Relevance/etc.)

Notes

Chapter 1

1. Here, the category *private schools* refers to all educational institutions that are not operated by a public authority, regardless of whether they receive financial support from public authorities.

2. No data are available for less-developed countries in relation to this indicator.

3. Free trade agreements, such as the General Agreement on Trade in Services negotiated in the context of the World Trade Organization, constitute an important mechanism to open education markets to private providers internationally, although they are not necessarily the main driver of basic education privatization at the country level. These agreements/negotiations tend to focus on higher education, an education level in which commercial flows are more intense and lucrative. Higher education, however, is not covered directly in this book.

4. Nonetheless, the review incorporated some primary studies published after the search and screening stage to integrate the latest developments in the field.

Chapter 2

1. Definition adapted from Novelli, Higgins, Ugur, and Valiente (2014).

2. This chapter uses the external-global and internal-local concepts in a reciprocal way, while being aware that *external* and *internal* are more ambiguous categories; they could refer to variables that are external (or internal) to the government, to the education system, or to the country in question. The global-local categories are considered to be more appropriate for the type of debate raised here because of its clearer connotation of political and geographic scales.

3. Paraphrasing Bennett, policy convergence can be defined as "the tendency of [policy systems] to grow more alike, to develop similarities in structures, processes and performance" (Bennett, 1991, p. 215).

4. Nevertheless, the idea of a tax rate convergence has been questioned by several studies (see Hay, 2002; Holzinger & Knill, 2005).

5. The *cultural turn* refers to how culture and its multiple manifestations, including discourse and semiosis, are seen more and more in social sciences as universally constitutive of social relations and changes.

6. Institutions actually are an assemblage of ideational factors (such as social norms), regulations, and material resources (Campbell, 2004).

7. The iron triangle is an analytical concept mainly used in the U.S. context, which refers to the political interaction between interest groups, executive agencies, and Congress.

8. Nadler and Tushman (1995) also contribute to unpacking the concept of policy change by distinguishing between continuous improvement (incremental and anticipatory

change), reorientation (discontinuous and anticipatory change), simple adaptation (reactive and incremental change), and crisis re-creation (discontinuous and reactive change). http://www.theguardian.com/education/2016/mar/15/every-english-school-to-become-an-academy-ministers-to-announce

Chapter 3

1. Although this chapter uses the denomination *United Kingdom*, the literature analyzed mainly focuses on the cases of England and Wales.

2. Although Milton Friedman was an economist by training and did not have a background as an educationist or as an educational researcher, he was particularly interested in education affairs. In his book *Capitalism and Freedom*, published in 1962, he dedicated a specific chapter to the education sector entitled "The Role of Government in Education," arguing for school vouchers and choice.

3. Some authors use the terms *monetarism* or *liberal conservatism* instead of *neoliberalism*, but the latter is more common in political economy literature today.

4. *Thatcherism* is a term used to distinguish Thatcher's policy agenda from other forms of conservatism. Dale (1989) characterises it by its ideological foundations based on the neoliberal principles enounced by Milton Friedman and Friedrich Hayek. Thatcherism also qualified as *authoritarian populism* in the sense that it "recombines existing strands of conservatism (particularly those which appeal to the grass roots rather than the hierarchy of the Conservative Party); and it loosely knits these together with opportunistic reactions to contemporary problems" (Dale, 1989, p. 77).

5. *Monetarism* is a school of economic thinking that says that the government (through the central bank) should maintain a stable monetary policy, controlling the amount of money in circulation. In the context of the economic crisis of the 1970s, this economic theory was applied as a response to Keynesian fiscal policy, which was mainly demand-driven.

6. According to Hirschmann (1970), there are two possible responses of consumers in the face of quality issues with the services provided by the state: voice and exit. *Voice* consists of users addressing their quality concerns to the service provider directly, with the ultimate intention that the latter reacts and introduces improvements. *Exit* means that users end their relationship with the service provider and look for an alternative elsewhere.

7. Corporations are a very exceptional type of vocational education schools run by private companies that receive state funding, but not through the voucher system.

8. LOCE stands for the legislation's Spanish name, *Ley Orgánica Constitucional de Enseñanza*.

9. The 900 Schools Program, launched in 1990, was funded by the Swedish government with the objectives of facilitating Chile's transition to democracy and providing education opportunities to the poor.

10. In Spanish, MECE stands for *Mejoramiento de la Calidad y Equidad de la Educación*.

11. In fact, the possibility of cost-sharing for private subsidized schools was approved during the 1980s, but the legal changes introduced in 1993 allowed their effective implementation.

12. In Spanish, SIMCE stands for *Sistema de Medición de la Calidad de la Educación*.

13. The possibility of publishing the results of the national assessment was introduced in the last educational reform of the military dictatorship (1990), although it was not implemented until 1995.

14. *Sistema Nacional de Evaluación del Desempeño* (SNED).

15. Michael Barber was the government's chief adviser on school standards and director of the Standards and Effectiveness Unit during Tony Blair's first term as British prime minister (1997–2001).

16. Specialist Schools and city Academies were two new types of educational institutions funded by the central government and independent from the LEAs' control. The Specialist Schools program encouraged schools to specialize in a specific area (such as arts or science). In the case of city Academies, their main characteristic is that the government allows them to be sponsored by a private organization.

17. See https://www.jacobinmag.com/2015/08/chile-student-education-strikes-camila-vallejo-bachelet/.

18. See http://www.theguardian.com/education/2016/mar/15/every-english-school-to-become-an-academy-ministers-to-announce.

Chapter 4

1. Iceland, as well as the autonomous regions of Greenland and Faroes, are not discussed in this chapter because sufficient sources that focus on education privatization processes in these other Nordic territories were not identified.

2. Swedish social democrats have promoted both exogenous and endogenous forms of education privatization, whereas Norwegian social democrats have mainly focused on promoting so-called endogenous privatization.

3. See *Free schools: Lessons in store*, in goo.gl/008GsL (last retrieved February 2, 2016) and *The Swedish Model*, in www.economist.com/node/11535645?story_id=11535645 (last retrieved February 2, 2016).

4. This refers to a "voucher-type" system that has operated since 1849 through which the state covers 75–85% of the average costs per pupil in the public sector.

5. See www.theguardian.com/education/2013/may/31/free-schools-education.

Chapter 5

1. For an overview of privatization trends in Canada and Colombia, see Davidson-Harden and Majhanovich (2004) and Miñana (2010), respectively.

2. The impact of federalism (as a barrier to the spread of market reforms) applies to education, but not to other sectors, such as commerce, that are highly centralized in the United States. Nonetheless, federalism does play a dual role in the spread of vouchers at the state level (Klitgaard, 2008), since the absence of federal regulation on the matter enables some states to adopt voucher programs.

3. Osborne and Gaebler are two of the most important theorizers of the new public management doctrine. They became well known through their book, *Reinventing Government,* published in 1992, which became a *New York Times* best seller.

4. See *Black's Law Dictionary* (8th ed.). (2004). Saint Paul, MN: Thomson West.

5. One recent example of this occurred in Washington State, where the state Supreme Court ruled charters unconstitutional (*League of Women Voters, et al. v. State of Washington*, 2015).

6. However, and as discussed later in this chapter, kindred programs (broadly comparable to voucher schemes) are gaining momentum. Local or targeted voucher initiatives are also increasingly common, which suggests that, while the charter movement could have reached a plateau, voucher schemes are currently in an expansionary stage, especially in the form of targeted programs.

7. Magnet schools are public schools that offer a specialized or distinctive curriculum, intended to attract students from a variety of backgrounds (and sometimes from outside the attendance zone), and with the explicit purpose of ensuring cultural and socioeconomic diversity and avoiding segregation (Steel & Levine, 1994; U.S. Department of Education–Office of Innovation and Improvement, 2008).

8. In some states, in fact, the leaders of advocacy coalitions are openly high-profile politicians. Notable examples are California State Senator Gary Hart, who was the leader of

the charter schools' coalition, and governors in Massachusetts and Michigan, who have led statewide charter programs (Kirst, 2007).

9. At the same time, this state variation reflects the "lack of unity among charter advocates at the national level" (Bulkley, 2004, p. 17).

10. The idea seems to be consistent with Bulkley's considerations, when she notes that the most common source of data was the actual legislation adopted by other states (Bulkley, 2004, p. 17).

11. That is to say, the adoption or mere copying of a given program because it appears to work in another setting.

12. Elazar (1984) was one of the first authors to apply this concept. He identified three different state political cultures (traditionalistic, individualistic, and moralistic), which influence state political behavior independent of party affiliation.

13. According to the criteria established by the Center for Education Reform (2015), the strength of charter school law relies on market openness/market-oriented criteria, including schools' legal and fiscal autonomy and the diversity of chartering authorities.

14. Nonetheless, we have observed that, especially at the state level, specific charter modalities generate more controversy and political tension between Republicans and Democrats than others.

15. In the 2014–2015 academic year, there were up to 18 tax-credit scholarship programs, 8 individual tax-credit or deduction programs, and 2 education saving accounts, most of them having passed during the last 5 years (Alliance for School Choice, 2015; Friedman Foundation for Educational Choice, 2015).

Chapter 6

1. Indeed, in the literature on the topic, the term *low-fee* has progressively replaced that of *low-cost* because the latter is even more subjective than the former. According to Srivastava (2007, p. 4), if a school is to be considered low-fee, it should not charge a monthly tuition fee "exceeding about 1 day's earnings of a daily wage laborer at the primary and junior (elementary) levels, and about 2 days' earnings at the high school and intermediate (secondary) levels."

2. However, again, it is difficult to establish a clear barrier between for-profit and not-for-profit school operators. In many countries, despite schools not being legally allowed to operate on a for-profit basis, there are schools that are de facto for profit, in the sense that they have benefits and find alternative ways to channel them.

3. www.omega-schools.com/overview.php.

4. www.affordable-learning.com/what-is-affordable-learning/brief-history-of-affordable-learning.html#sthash.nnEBFoKZ.dpbs.

5. Unusually, even wide circulation media like *The Guardian* echoed this debate. See www.theguardian.com/sustainable-business/2015/mar/16/private-education-development-public-research-profit.

6. See www.ifc.org/wps/wcm/connect/industry_ext_content/ifc_external_corporate_site/industries/health+and+education/news/bridgeschools_feature.

7. See www.ifc.org/wps/wcm/connect/industry_ext_content/ifc_external_corporate_site/industries/health+and+education/news/events_presentations/education+conference+2014.

8. See www.theguardian.com/global-development/poverty-matters/2013/oct/04/uk-aid-private-schools-developing-world.

9. Source: www.affordable-learning.com/the-fund.html#sthash.vCIYqCs0.dpbs.

10. See www.idpfoundation.org/about/.

11. See *Global Education and Skills Conference (GESF) to Be Held Annually in the UAE Following the Inaugural Event and Will Become "The Davos of Education"* in

www.prnewswire.com/news-releases/global-education-and-skills-conference-gesf-to-be-held-annually-in-the-uae-following-the-inaugural-event-and-will-become-the-davos-of-education-198728571.html, and *Wise, le "Davos" de l'Education débute à Doha* in www.lexpress.fr/education/wise-le-davos-de-l-education-debute-a-doha1294982.html#6EX8ul6U.K.uKxv5Ks.99.

   12. www.bridgeinternationalacademies.com/company/about/.

Chapter 7

   1. Chile is another OECD country with very high levels of private enrollment in primary and secondary education. The case of Chile is analyzed in Chapter 3 in this volume.

   2. OECD uses the term *government-dependent private institution* and defines it as an institution controlled and managed by a nongovernment organization, or one whose governing board consists mostly of members not selected by a public agency and more than 50% of its core funding comes from government agencies (OECD, 2014).

   3. In the Dutch education context, private education is viewed as "state education," although it is managed by private institutions (Karsten, 1999). This is the reason why, in some statistical sources, private education in the Netherlands is assigned to the public education category.

   4. *Pillarization* (*vezuiling* in Dutch) is the term used to define the way in which Dutch society was organized. Wintle (2000, p. 141) defines it as "the way in which different social groups manage to co-exist in a stable political system."

   5. In the last few decades, Dutch society has experienced a marked process of secularization. According to the data provided by Dijkstra et al. (2004), in 1947, 17% of the population did not belong to any faith. In contrast, this percentage was 40% in 1995.

   6. Many authors (e.g., Dijkstra & Jungbluth, 1997; Karsten, 1994) have shown how the high level of segregation of the Dutch education system, particularly ethnic segregation, can be explained by the policies of freedom of school choice and the important presence of private providers in the education system.

   7. Belgian political governance is organized in two parallel structures. On the one hand, it is organized according to the different communities (namely, the Flemish, the French-speaking, and the German-speaking). The resulting governance bodies are responsible for culture, education, media, and social services. On the other hand, it is organized by region: Flemish, Brussels, and Walloon. The governments of these three regions have jurisdiction over economic development, housing, environment, and transport (De Rynck, 2005).

   8. In Belgium, private subsidized schools are operated by nonprofit organizations (NCEE, 2006).

   9. See the 1978 Spanish Constitution, p. 14, in https://www.boe.es/legislacion/documentos/ConstitucionINGLES.pdf.

   10. Although private subsidized schools are not allowed to charge fees to families for their education activities, on average around 30% of their funding come from families' voluntary contributions or other concepts such as materials or extracurricular activities (Villaroya, 2000).

   11. Olmedo (2013) identifies the following think tanks and organizations as advocates of market mechanisms in the Spanish education context: Fundación para el Análisis y Estudios Sociales (FAES), Institución Futuro, Fundación Burke, Fundación Europea Educación y Libertad (FUNDEL), and Asociación Española de Centros Privados de Enseñanza (ACADE).

   12. Currently, the Spanish state is organized into 17 regions or autonomous communities and two autonomous cities.

   13. *Ley Orgánica para la Mejora de la Calidad Educativa.*

Chapter 8

1. Interestingly, something similar happens with test-scores' crises such as the ones generated by the No Child Left Behind (NCLB) act, but also by the Program for International Assessment (PISA) in some places. These "crises" or "shocks" have often a manufactured nature and are associated with demands for continual school reform, including the possibility of subjecting schools to punitive action and privatization (Saltman, 2007).

2. Located in Baton Rouge, the capital of Louisiana, the BESE is the administrative policymaking body for elementary and secondary schools in the state.

3. According to this new definition, any school operated by a local school district and with a School Performance Score (SPS) below the state average was considered in "academic crisis" (in contrast with the prior threshold, located at an SPS of 60.0), and consequently susceptible to be taken over by the state (Adamson et al. 2015; Levin et al., 2010).

4. Data from Levin et al. (2010) for the 2009–2010 academic year.

5. Unlike RSD-run schools, OPSB-operated schools mainly comprised a few selective schools.

6. In fact, a national civil rights lawsuit was filed in 2010, representing special education students who had been denied access to public schools in New Orleans—charter schools, in most cases—apparently due to the financial cost of tailored programs (Buras, 2015).

7. Including the Eli and Edythe Broad Foundation, the Bill and Melinda Gates Foundation, and NewSchools Venture Fund.

8. DeBray et al. (2014) note that a recent class-action lawsuit ruled that teachers would have been wrongly dismissed. This large-scale termination was in fact declared illegal by the local appellate courts in 2012. However, the decision was reversed in 2012 by the Louisiana Supreme Court, and the U.S. Supreme Court refused to review the case (Adamson et al., 2015; see also nopsejustice.com/current_status.htm).

9. This index rank-averages the five most common segregation indexes.

10. *Programa de Educación con Participación de la Comunidad.*

11. *Fundación Salvadoreña para el Desarrollo Económico y Social.*

12. *Fundación Empresarial para el Desarrollo Educativo.*

13. However, the limited evidence on this case does not allow for generalizations, and makes it difficult to obtain consistent data on the scope of the privatization reforms.

14. This would be the case for prior contracts and projects, such as those directed at the integration of the *contras* into Nicaraguan civil society (Saltman, 2006).

Chapter 9

1. *Red Latinoamericana de Organizaciones de la Sociedad Civil por la Educación.*

2. However, this is not a totally new development. The conservative Lynde and Harry Bradley Foundation (established in 1942) is well known for having supported a number of influential promarket researchers, such as John E. Chubb and Terry M. Moe in the 1980s, as well as the emblematic school voucher program adopted in Milwaukee in 1990.

3. Bloomberg.net, edition of December 13, 2006.

4. It has been documented that conservative foundations are more eager to fund the operative costs of think tanks than are left-leaning foundations, which seem to be more inclined to commission and fund specific studies. Moreover, conservative foundations seem to be less concerned with the "rigour" or "neutrality" of the think tanks they support, and are more comfortable with "blurring boundaries between research and advocacy" (Rich, as cited in DeBray-Pelot et al., 2007, p. 214).

5. See nepc.colorado.edu/think-tank-review-project.

Chapter 10

1. For instance, in Spain, the Pedagogic Renovation Movements Federation, which comprises teachers advocating progressive pedagogies, was constituted in the early 1970s to resist the official education approach of General Francisco Franco's dictatorship. With the rise of democracy in the country, the movement focused on the defense of public education and on supporting school initiatives aimed at enhancing the quality of public education (Bonal, 2000).

2. By 2010, the partnership was meeting on a weekly basis, and phone calls and discussions were frequent between union and government officials.

Chapter 11

1. See Figures 1.1–1.3 in Chapter 1 in this volume.

2. Although the implications of privatization in terms of school segregation and inequalities are rather well-known. See Waslander et al. (2010).

3. Nonetheless, despite universal vouchers facing more opposition, nonuniversal voucher schemes (i.e., means-tested or special needs programs) and similar initiatives (including scholarship tax credits and education savings account programs) have advanced much further.

4. An ideal type, in a Weberian sense, is "a conception or a standard of something in its highest perfection." An ideal type "is formulated on the basis of facts collected carefully and analytically for empirical research. In this sense, ideal types are constructs or concepts that are used as methodological devices or tools in our understanding and analysis of any social problem" (Priyadarshini, n.d.).

5. To illustrate this idea, Merrill Lynch-Bank of America calculated in 2014 that the value of the education sector, globally speaking, is $4.3 trillion (see Robertson & Komljenovic, 2016).

6. See, for instance, a list of recent educational loans by the World Bank with PPP components in Mundy and Menashy (2014).

7. For instance, see www.edchoice.org/school-choice/programs/north-carolina-opportunity-scholarships/.

8. Recent international campaigns against education privatization organized by Education International and the Global Campaign for Education have adopted this approach. See, for instance, www.ei-ie.org/congress7/en/publications/resolutions/475-privatization-and-commercialization-in-and-of-education.

References

Adamson, F., Astrand, B., & Darling-Hammond, L. (2016). *Global educational reform: Privatization vs. public investments in national education systems.* New York, NY: Routledge.

Adamson, F., Cook-Harvey, C., & Darling-Hammond, L. (2015). *Whose choice? Student experiences and outcomes in the New Orleans school marketplace.* Stanford, CA: Stanford Center for Opportunity Policy in Education. Retrieved from edpolicy.stanford.edu/sites/default/files/publications/scope-report-student-experiences-new-orleans.pdf

Ahmed, H., & Sheikh, S. A. (2014). Determinants of school choice: Evidence from rural Punjab, Pakistan. *Lahore Journal of Economics, 19*(1), 1–30. Retrieved from 121.52.153.179/JOURNAL/LJE%20VOL%2019-1/Ahmed%20and%20Sheikh.pdf

Akers, J. M. (2012). Separate and unequal: The consumption of public education in post-Katrina New Orleans. *International Journal of Urban and Regional Research, 36*(1), 29–48. doi:10.1111/j.1468-2427.2011.01062.x

Akyeampong, K., & Rolleston, C. (2013). Low-fee private schooling in Ghana: Is growing demand improving equitable and affordable access for the poor? In P. Srivastava (Ed.), *Low-fee private schooling: Aggravating equity or mitigating disadvantage?* (pp. 37–64). Oxford, UK: Symposium Books.

Anderson-Levitt, K. M. (2003). *Local meanings, global schooling: Anthropology and world culture theory.* Basingstoke, UK/New York, NY: Palgrave Macmillan.

Andrabi, T., Das, J., & Khwaja, A. I. (2008). *A dime a day: The possibilities and limits of private schooling in Pakistan* (World Bank Policy Research Working Paper Number 4066). Washington, DC: World Bank. Retrieved from openknowledge.worldbank.org/bitstream/handle/10986/8871/wps4066.pdf?sequence=1&isAllowed=y

Apple, M. W., & Pedroni, T. C. (2005). Conservative alliance building and African American support of vouchers: The end of *Brown's* promise or a new beginning? *Teachers College Record, 107*(9), 2068–2105. doi:10.1111/j.1467-9620.2005.00585.x

Ashley, L. D., Mcloughlin, C., Aslam, M., Engel, J., Wales, J., Rawal, S., . . . Rose, P. (2014). *The role and impact of private schools in developing countries: A rigorous review of the evidence. Final report* (EPPI-Centre Education Rigorous Literature Review Reference Number 2206). London, UK: DfID. Retrieved from www.gov.uk/government/uploads/system/uploads/attachment_data/file/439702/private-schools-full-report.pdf

Aslam, M., & Kingdon, G. (2011). What can teachers do to raise pupil achievement? *Economics of Education Review, 30*(3), 559–574. doi:10.1016/j.econedurev.2011.01.001

Atasay, E., & Delavan, G. (2012). Monumentalizing disaster and wreak-construction: A case study of Haiti to rethink the privatization of public education. *Journal of Education Policy, 27*(4), 529–553. doi:10.1080/02680939.2012.662284

Au, W., & Ferrare, J. J. (2015). Other people's policy: Wealthy elites and charter school reform in Washington State. In W. Au & J. J. Ferrare (Eds.), *Mapping corporate education: Power and policy networks in the neoliberal state* (pp. 147–164). New York, NY: Routledge.

Au, W., & Lubienski, C. (2016). The role of the Gates Foundation and the philanthropic sector in shaping the emerging education market: Lessons from the U.S. on privatization of schools and education governance. In A. Verger, C. Lubienski, & G. Steiner-Khamsi (Eds.), *World yearbook of education 2016: The global education industry* (pp. 27–43). New York, NY: Routledge.

Avalos, B., & Assael, J. (2006). Moving from resistance to agreement: The case of the Chilean teacher performance evaluation. *International Journal of Educational Research, 45*(4/5), 254–266. doi:10.1016/j.ijer.2007.02.004

Balarin, M. (2015). The default privatization of Peruvian education and the rise of low-fee private schools: Better or worse opportunities for the poor? (Open Society Foundations/Privatisation in Education Research Initiative—Education Support Program Working Paper Number 56). London, UK: OSF. Retrieved from www.periglobal.org/sites/periglobal.org/files/WP65%20Peru.pdf

Ball, S. J. (1990). *Politics and policy-making in education: Explorations in policy sociology.* London, UK: Routledge.

Ball, S. J. (1998). Big policies/small world: An introduction to international perspectives in education policy. *Comparative Education, 34*(2), 119–130. doi:10.1080/03050069828225

Ball, S. J. (2008a). New philanthropy, new networks and new governance in education. *Political Studies, 56*(4), 747–765. doi:10.1111/j.1467-9248.2008.00722.x

Ball, S. J. (2008b). The legacy of ERA: Privatization and the policy ratchet. *Educational Management Administration Leadership, 36*(2), 185–199. doi:10.1177/1741143207087772

Ball, S.J. (2009). Privatising education, privatising education policy, privatising educational research: network governance and the "competition state", *Journal of Education Policy, 24*(1), 83–99. doi:10.1080/02680930802419474

Ball, S. J. (2012). *Global Education Inc.: New policy networks and the neoliberal imaginary.* New York, NY: Routledge.

Ball, S. J., & Exley, S. (2010). Making policy with "good ideas": Policy networks and the "intellectuals" of New Labour. *Journal of Education Policy, 25*(2). doi:10.1080/026809 30903486125

Ball, S. J., & Youdell, D. (2008). *Hidden privatisation in public education.* Brussels, Belgium: Education International. Retrieved from download.ei-ie.org/docs/IRISDocuments/Research%20Website%20Documents/2009-00034-01-E.pdf

Barber, M. (2013). The good news from Pakistan: How a revolutionary new approach to education reform in Punjab shows the way forward for Pakistan and development aid everywhere. London, UK: Reform. Retrieved from www.reform.uk/wp-content/uploads/2014/10/The_good_news_from_Pakistan_final.pdf

Bardach, E. (2006). Policy dynamics. In M. Moran, M. Rein, & R. E. Goodin (Eds.), *Oxford handbook of public policy* (pp. 336–366). Oxford, UK: Oxford University Press.

Barnett, M., & Finnemore, M. (2004). *Rules for the world: International organizations in global politics.* Ithaca, NY: Cornell University Press.

Bascia, N. (2014, March). *Privatisation and teacher union-governmental relations.* Paper presented at the annual conference of the Comparative & International Education Society (CIES), Toronto, Ontario, Canada.

Bascia, N., & Osmond, P. (2013). Teacher union governmental relations in the context of educational reform. Brussels, Belgium: Education International. Retrieved from download.ei-ie.org/Docs/WebDepot/Teacher_Union_Study.pdf

Baum, D. R. (2012). Education service contracting in the Philippines: Human rights as trumps, goals, or policy talk? *Educational Research for Policy and Practice, 11*(3), 189–206. doi:10.1007/s10671-011-9118-5

Baumgartner, F. R., & Jones, B. D. (1993). *Agendas and instability in American politics.* Chicago, IL: University of Chicago Press.

Béland, D. (2005). Ideas and social policy: An institutionalist perspective. *Social Policy & Administration, 39*(1), 1–18. doi:10.1111/j.1467-9515.2005.00421.x

Béland, D. (2010). The idea of power and the role of ideas. *Political Studies Review, 8*(2), 145–154. doi:10.1111/j.1478-9302.2009.00199.x

Belfield, C., & Levin, H. M. (2005). Vouchers and public policy: When ideology trumps evidence. *American Journal of Education, 111*(4), 548–567. doi:10.1086/431183

Bellei, C. (2007). The private-public school controversy: The case of Chile. In R. Chakrabarti & P. Peterson (Eds.), *School choice international: Exploring public-private partnerships* (pp. 165–192). Cambridge, MA: MIT Press.

Bellei, C., & Cabalin, C. (2013). Chilean student movements: Sustained struggle to transform a market-oriented educational system. *Current Issues in Comparative Education, 15*(2), 108–123. Retrieved from files.eric.ed.gov/fulltext/EJ1016193.pdf

Bellei, C., & Orellana, V. (2015). What does "education privatisation" mean? Conceptual discussion and empirical review of Latin American cases. *Education Support Program Working Paper 62*. London, UK: OSF.

Bellei, C., & Vanni, X. (2015). The evolution of educational policy, 1980–2014. In S. Schwartzman (Ed.), *Education in South America* (pp. 179–200). London, UK: Bloomsbury Academic.

Bennett, C. J. (1991). What is policy convergence and what causes it? *British Journal of Political Science, 21*(2), 215–233. doi:10.1017/S0007123400006116

Bhanji, Z. (2008). Transnational corporations in education: Filling the governance gap through new social norms and market multilateralism? *Globalisation, Societies and Education, 6*(1), 55–73. doi:10.1080/14767720701855618

Bhanji, Z. (2016). The business case for philanthropy, profits, and policy making in education. In K. Mundy, A. Green, R. Lingard, & A. Verger (Eds.), *Handbook of global policy and policy-making in education* (pp. 419–432). West Sussex, UK: Wiley-Blackwell.

Bishop, M., & Green, M. (2008). *Philanthrocapitalism: How the rich can save the world.* New York, NY: Bloomsbury Press.

Blomqvist, P. (2004). The choice revolution: Privatization of Swedish welfare services in the 1990s. *Social Policy & Administration, 38*(2), 139–155. doi:10.1111/j.1467-9515.2004.00382.x

Blossing, U., Imsen, G., & Moos, L. (2014). Schools for all: A Nordic model. In U. Blossing, G. Imsen, & L. Moos (Eds.), *The Nordic education model: "A school for all" encounters neo-liberal policy* (pp. 231–239). Dordrecht, the Netherlands: Springer.

Blyth, M. (2004). Structures do not come with an instruction sheet: Interests, ideas, and progress in political science. *Perspectives on Politics, 1*(4), 695–706. doi:10.1017/S1537592703000471

Böhlmark, A., & Lindahl, M. (2012). Independent schools and long-run educational outcomes: Evidence from Sweden's large scale voucher reform (IZA Discussion Paper Number 6683). Bonn, Sweden: Institute for the Study of Labor (IZA). Retrieved from ftp.iza.org/dp6683.pdf

Bold, T., Kimenyi, M., Mwabu, G., & Sandefur, J. (2010). Does abolishing fees reduce school quality? Evidence from Kenya (CSAE Working Paper WPS/2011-04). Oxford, UK: Centre for the Study of African Economies—University of Oxford. Retrieved from www.csae.ox.ac.uk/workingpapers/pdfs/csae-wps-2011-04.pdf

Bonal, X. (1995). Curriculum change as a form of educational policy legitimation: The case of Spain. *International Studies in Sociology of Education, 5*(2), 203–220. doi:10.1080/0962021950050205

Bonal, X. (1998). La política educativa: Dimensiones de un proceso de transformación (1976–1996). In J. Subirats & R. Gomà (Eds.), *Políticas públicas en España: Contenidos, redes de actores y niveles de gobierno* (pp. 153–175). Barcelona, Spain: Ariel.

Bonal, X. (2000). Interest groups and the state in contemporary Spanish education policy. *Journal of Education Policy, 15*(2), 201–216. doi:10.1080/026809300285908

Bonal, X. (2012). Education policy and school segregation of migrant students in Catalonia: The politics of non-decision-making. *Journal of Education Policy, 27*(3), 401–421. doi: 10.1080/02680939.2011.645168

Bonal, X., & Verger, A. (forthcoming). Education policy in times of austerity: The management of the global financial crisis within a Southern European education setting. In S. Robertson, R. Dale, & J. Komljenovic (Eds.), *Cultural political economy of education.* Cheltenham, UK: Edward Elgar.

Bourdieu, P. (1999). Rethinking the state: Genesis and structure of the bureaucratic field. In G. Steinmetz (Ed.), *State/culture: State-formation after the cultural turn* (pp. 53–75). Ithaca, NY: Cornell University Press.

Boyd, W. L. (2007). The politics of privatization in American education. *Educational Policy, 21*(1), 7–14. doi:10.1177/0895904806297728

Brans, B. J. (2013). Public private partnerships in Uganda: More perils than promises for universal secondary education. In A. Verger, H. K. Altinyelken, & M. de Koning (Eds.), *Global managerial education reforms and teachers: Emerging policies, controversies, and issues in developing countries* (pp. 74–90). Brussels, Belgium: Education International.

Bray, M. (2002). *The costs and financing of education: Trends and policy implications* (Education in Developing Asia, Volume 3). Manila/Hong Kong: Asian Development Bank/Comparative Education Research Centre—The University of Hong Kong. Retrieved from cerc.edu.hku.hk/wp-content/uploads/2013/11/costs_financing.pdf

Brogan, P. (2013). Education in global Chicago and the remaking of contemporary capitalism. *Canadian Geographer/Le Géographe Canadien, 57*(3), 303–310. doi:10.1111/cag.12024

Bulkley, K. (2005). Understanding the charter school concept in legislation: The cases of Arizona, Michigan, and Georgia. *International Journal of Qualitative Studies in Education, 18*(4), 527–554. doi:10.1080/09518390500137683

Bulkley, K. E. (2004). Reinventing an idea: The political construction of charter schools. *Educational Foundations, 18*(1), 5–31. Retrieved from files.eric.ed.gov/fulltext/EJ739888.pdf

Bulkley, K. E. (2007). Bringing the private into the public: Changing the rules of the game and new regime politics in Philadelphia public education. *Educational Policy, 21*(1), 155–184. doi:10.1177/0895904806297192

Bulkley, K. E., & Burch, P. (2011). The changing nature of private engagement in public education: For-profit and nonprofit organizations and educational reform. *Peabody Journal of Education, 86*(3), 236–251. doi:10.1080/0161956X.2011.578963

Buras, K. L. (2013). "We're not going nowhere": Race, urban space, and the struggle for King Elementary School in New Orleans. *Critical Studies in Education, 54*(1), 19–32. doi:10.1080/17508487.2013.741072

Buras, K. L. (2015). Gangsta raps, power gaps, and network maps: How the charter school market came to New Orleans. In W. Au & J. J. Ferrare (Eds.), *Mapping corporate education: Power and policy networks in the neoliberal state* (pp. 165–189). New York, NY: Routledge.

Burch, P. (2010). After the fall: Educational contracting in the USA and the global financial crisis. *Journal of Education Policy, 25*(6), 757–766. doi:10.1080/02680939.2010.508182

Cabalin, C. (2012). Neoliberal education and student movements in Chile: Inequalities and malaise. *Policy Futures in Education, 10*(2), 219–228. doi:10.2304/pfie.2012.10.2.219

Caddell, M. (2006). Private schools as battlefields: Contested visions of learning and livelihood in Nepal. *Compare, 36*(4), 463–479. doi:10.1080/03057920601024909

Calero, J., & Bonal, X. (1999). *Política educativa y gasto público en educación: Aspectos teóricos y una aplicación al caso español.* Barcelona, Spain: Pomares-Corredor.

Campbell, J. L. (1998). Institutional analysis and the role of ideas in political economy. *Theory and Society, 27*(3), 377–409. doi:10.1023/A:1006871114987

Campbell, J. L. (2004). *Institutional change and globalisation.* Princeton, NJ: Princeton University Press.

Carney, S. (2009). Negotiating policy in an age of globalization: Exploring educational "policyscapes" in Denmark, Nepal, and China. *Comparative Education Review, 53*(1), 63–88. doi:10.1086/593152

Carnoy, M. (2000). School choice? Or is it privatization? *Educational Researcher, 29*(7), 15–20. doi:10.3102/0013189X029007015

Carnoy, M. (2003). Las políticas educacionales de Chile desde una perspectiva internacional. In C. Cox (Ed.), *Políticas educacionales en el cambio de siglo: La reforma del sistema escolar de Chile* (pp. 115–124). Santiago de Chile: Editorial Universitaria.

Carroll, W. K., & Carson, C. (2003). The network of global corporations and elite policy groups: a structure for transnational capitalist class formation?.*Global Networks, 3*(1), 29–57. doi:10.1111/1471-0374.00049

Carter, B., Stevenson, H., & Passy, R. (2010). *Industrial relations in education.* New York, NY: Routledge.

Cave, T., & Rowell, A. (2014). *A quiet word: Lobbying, crony capitalism, and broken politics in Britain.* London, UK: The Bodley Head-Vintage.

Center for Education Reform. (2015). Charter School Laws Across the States: 2015 Rankings and Scorecard. Washington, DC: Center for Education Reform. Retrieved from www.edreform.com/wp-content/uploads/2015/04/CharterLaws2015.pdf

Cerny, P. G. (2010) The competition state today: from raison d'État to raison du Monde, *Policy Studies,* 31:1, 5–21, doi:10.1080/01442870903052801

CfBT. (2011). Preliminary study into low-fee private schools and education—Final report. Reading, PA: CfBT/DfID. Retrieved from r4d.dfid.gov.uk/pdf/outputs/mis_spc/60912-GyanShalaFinalReport.pdf

Chubb, J. E., & Moe, T. T. (1990). *Politics, markets, and America's schools.* Washington, DC: Brookings Institution.

Cierniak, K., Stewart, M., & Ruddy, A. (2015). *Mapping the growth of statewide voucher programs in the United States.* Bloomington, IN: Center for Evaluation and Education Policy—Indiana University, School of Education. Retrieved from ceep.indiana.edu/projects/PDF/Statewide_Vouchers_CEEP_EPB.pdf

Clarke, J., Gewirtz, S., & McLaughlin, E. (Eds.). (2000). *New managerialism, new welfare?* London, UK: Sage.

Codd, J. (2005). Teachers as "managed professionals" in the global education industry: The New Zealand experience. *Educational Review, 57*(2), 193–206. doi:10.1080/0013191042000308369

Colyvas, J. A., & Jonsson, S. (2011). Ubiquity and legitimacy: Disentangling diffusion and institutionalization. *Sociological Theory, 19*(1), 27–53. doi:10.1111/j.1467-9558.2010.01386.x

Connell, R. (2013). The neoliberal cascade and education: An essay on the market agenda and its consequences. *Critical Studies in Education, 54*(2), 99–112. doi:10.1080/17508487.2013.776990.

Corbalán Pössel, F., & Corbalán Carrera, P. (2012). El rol del think-tank Libertad y Desarrollo en la consolidación de la educación neoliberal en Chile. *Profesorado, 16*(3), 191–212. Retrieved from www.redalyc.org/articulo.oa?id=56725002010.

Cornwall, A. (2007). Buzzwords and fuzzwords: Deconstructing development discourse. *Development in Practice, 17*(4–5), 471–484. doi:10.1080/09614520701469302

Cowen Institute for Public Education Initiatives. (2012). *Private schools and choice: The Student Scholarships for Education Excellence pilot program in Orleans Parish*. New Orleans, LA: Cowen Institute for Public Education Initiatives—Tulane University. Retrieved from www.coweninstitute.com/wp-content/uploads/2012/04/Private-Schools-and-Choice-April-20121.pdf

Cox, C. (2003). Las políticas educacionales de Chile en las últimas dos décadas del siglo XX. In C. Cox (Ed.), *Políticas educacionales en el cambio de siglo: La reforma del sistema escolar de Chile* (pp. 73–146). Santiago de Chile: Editorial Universitaria.

Cox, C., & Avalos, B. (1999). Educational change programmes and international co-operation: The case of Chile. In K. King, & L. Buchert (Eds.), *Changing international aid to education: Global patterns and national contexts* (pp. 280–297). Paris, France: UNESCO Publishing/Norrag.

Crouch, C. (2003). *Commercialisation or citizenship: Education policy and the future of public services* (Fabian Ideas Number 606). London: Fabian Society. Retrieved from www.fabians.org.uk/wp-content/uploads/2012/04/CommercialisationOrCitizenship.pdf

Cuéllar-Marchelli, H. (2003). Decentralization and privatization of education in El Salvador: Assessing the experience. *International Journal of Educational Development, 23*(2), 145–166. doi:10.1016/S0738-0593(02)00011-1

Dahal, M., & Nguyen, Q. (2014). Private non-state sector engagement in the provision of educational services at the primary and secondary levels in South Asia: An analytical review of its role in school enrollment and student achievement (World Bank Policy Research Working Paper Number 6899). Washington, DC: World Bank—South Asia Region, Education Unit. doi:10.1596/1813-9450-5185. Retrieved from openknowledge.worldbank.org/bitstream/handle/10986/18786/WPS6899.pdf?sequence=1&isAllowed=y

Dale, R. (1989). *The state and education policy*. Philadelphia, PA: Open University Press.

Dale, R. (1999). Specifying globalisation effects on national policy: A focus on the mechanisms. *Journal of Education Policy, 14*(1), 1–17. doi:10.1080/026809399286468

Dale, R. (2000). Globalisation and education: Demonstrating a "common world educational culture" or locating a "globally structured educational agenda"? *Educational Theory, 50*(4), 427–448. doi:10.1111/j.1741-5446.2000.00427.x

Dale, R. (2001). Constructing a long spoon for comparative education: Charting the career of the "New Zealand model." *Comparative Education, 37*(4), 493–500. doi:10.1080/03050060120091274

Dale, R. (2005). Globalisation, knowledge economy, and comparative education. *Comparative Education, 41*(2), 117–149. doi:0.1080/03050060500150906

Dale, R. (2012). Global education policy: Creating different constituencies of interest and different modes of valorisation. In A. Verger, M. Novelli, & H. K. Altinyelken (Eds.), *Global education policy and international development: New agendas, issues, and policies* (pp. 287–300). London, UK/New York, NY: Bloomsbury Academic.

Davidson-Harden, A., & Majhanovich, S. (2004). Privatisation of education in Canada: A survey of trends. *International Review of Education/Internationale Zeitschrift für Erziehungswissenschaft/Revue Internationale de l'Education, 50*(3/4), 263–287. Retrieved from www.jstor.org/stable/4151599

De Rynck, S. (2005). Regional autonomy and education policy in Belgium. *Regional & Federal Studies, 15*(4), 485–500. doi:10.1080/13597560500230664

De Rynck, S., & Dezeure, K. (2006). Policy convergence and divergence in Belgium: Education and health care. *West European Politics, 29*(5), 1018–1033. doi:10.1080/01402380600968927

DeBray, E., Scott, J., Lubienski, C., & Jabbar, H. (2014). Intermediary organizations in charter school policy coalitions: Evidence from New Orleans. *Educational Policy, 28*(2), 175–206. doi:10.1177/0895904813514132

DeBray-Pelot, E. H., Lubienski, C. A., & Scott, J. T. (2007). The institutional landscape of interest group politics and school choice. *Peabody Journal of Education, 82*(2/3), 204–230. doi:10.1080/01619560701312947

Delannoy, F. (2000). *Education reforms in Chile, 1980–1998: A lesson in pragmatism* (Country Studies—Education Reform and Management Publication Series, Volume 1, Number 1). Washington, DC: World Bank. Retrieved from www-wds.worldbank.org/external/default/WDSContentServer/WDSP/IB/2000/09/01/000094946_00081805551098/Rendered/PDF/multi_page.pdf

Department for International Development (DfID). (2013). *Education position paper: Improving learning, expanding opportunities.* London, UK: Department for International Development. Retrieved from www.gov.uk/government/uploads/system/uploads/attachment_data/file/225715/Education_Position_Paper_July_2013.pdf

Dijkstra, A. B., & Jungbluth, P. (1997, July). *The Institutionalization of Social Segmentation? Segregation of Schooling in the Netherlands.* Paper presented at the World Congress of the International Institute of Sociology (IIS), Cologne.

Dijkstra, A. B., Dronkers, J., & Karsten, S. (2004). Private schools as public provision for education: School choice and market forces in the Netherlands. In P. J. Wolf & S. Macedo (Eds.), *Educating citizens: International perspectives on civic values and school choice* (pp. 67–90). Washington, DC: Brookings Institution Press.

Dixon, P., Tooley, J., & Schagen, I. (2013). The relative quality of private and public schools for low-income families living in slums of Nairobi, Kenya. In P. Srivastava (Ed.), *Low-fee private schooling: Aggravating equity or mitigating disadvantage?* (pp. 83–104). Oxford, UK: Symposium Books.

Dobbin, F., Simmons, B., & Garrett, G. (2007). The global diffusion of public policies: Social construction, coercion, competition, or learning? *Annual Review of Sociology, 33,* 449–472. doi:10.1146/annurev.soc.33.090106.142507

Dobbins, M. (2011). Explaining different pathways in higher education policy in Romania and the Czech Republic. *Comparative Education, 47*(2), 223–245. doi:10.1080/03050068.2011.555116

Drezner, D. W. (2001). Globalisation and policy convergence. *International Studies Review, 3*(1), 53–78. doi:10.1111/1521-9488.00225

Dupriez, V., & Maroy, C. (2003). Regulation in school systems: A theoretical analysis of the structural framework of the school system in French-speaking Belgium. *Journal of Education Policy, 18*(4), 375–392. doi:10.1080/0268093032000106839

Education International. (2009). *Public private partnerships in education.* Brussels, Belgium: Education International. Retrieved from download.ei-ie.org/Docs/WebDepot/PUBLIC%20PRIVATE%20PARTNERSHIP.Pdf

Edwards, Jr., D. B. (2013). The development of global education policy: A case study of the origins and evolution of El Salvador's EDUCO program (Doctoral dissertation). Available from ProQuest Dissertations & Theses Global. (Accession Order No 3590614).

Edwards, Jr., D. B. (2015). Rising from the ashes: How the global education policy of community-based management was born from El Salvador's civil war. *Globalisation, Societies and Education, 13*(3), 411–432. doi:10.1080/14767724.2014.980225

Edwards, Jr., D. B. (2016). A perfect storm: The political economy of community-based management, teacher accountability, and impact evaluations in El Salvador and the global reform agenda. In W. C. Smith (Ed.), *The global testing culture: Shaping education policy, perceptions, and practice* (pp. 25–42). Oxford, UK: Symposium Books.

Edwards, Jr., D. B., & Klees, S. J. (2012). Participation in international development and education governance. In A. Verger, M. Novelli, & H. K. Altinyelken (Eds.), *Global education policy and international development: New agendas, issues and policies* (pp. 55–76). London, UK/New York, NY: Bloomsbury Academic.

Elazar, D. J. (1984). *American federalism: A view from the states* (3rd ed.). New York, NY: Harper Row.

Elinder, M., & Jordahl, J. (2013). Political preferences and public-sector outsourcing. *European Journal of Political Economy, 30*(2013), 43–57. doi:10.1016/j.ejpoleco.2013.01.003

EPPI-Centre. (2010). *EPPI-Centre methods for conducting systematic reviews.* London, UK: Evidence for Policy and Practice Information and Co-ordinating Centre. Retrieved from eppi.ioe.ac.uk/cms/LinkClick.aspx?fileticket=hQBu8y4uVwI%3D.

Esping-Andersen, G. (1985). *Politics against markets: The social democratic road to power* (pp. 145ff). Princeton, NJ: Princeton University Press.

Esping-Andersen, G. (1990). *The three worlds of welfare capitalism.* Cambridge/Oxford, UK: Cambridge Polity Press/Blackwell Publishing.

Espínola, V., & de Moura, C. (1999). *Economía política de la reforma educacional en Chile: La reforma vista por sus protagonistas.* Washington, DC: Banco Iberoamericano de Desarrollo. Retrieved from publications.iadb.org/bitstream/handle/11319/282/Econ om%c3%ada%20pol%c3%adtica%20de%20la%20reforma%20educacional%20en %20Chile.pdf?sequence=1

Exley, S. (2012). The politics of educational policy making under New Labour: An illustration of shifts in public service governance. *Policy & Politics, 40*(2), 227–244. doi:10.1332/030557312X640031

Fairbrother, P. (1996). Workplace trade unionism in the state sector. In P. Ackers, C. Smith, & P. Smith (Eds.), *The new workplace trade unionism* (pp. 110–148). London, UK: Routledge.

Falabella, A. (2015). School markets in Chile and the emergence of the new public management: The fabric of policies between a neoliberal dictatorship regime and center-left democratic governments (1979–2009). *Educaçao & Sociedade, 36*(132), 699–722.

Farah, I., & Rizvi, S. (2007). Public–private partnerships: Implications for primary schooling in Pakistan. *Social Policy & Administration, 41*(4), 339–354. doi:10.1111/j.1467-9515.2007.00557.x

Fennell, S. (2013). Low-fee private schools in Pakistan: A blessing or a bane? In P. Srivastava (Ed.), *Low-fee private schooling: Aggravating equity or mitigating disadvantage?* (pp. 65–82). Oxford, UK: Symposium Books.

Fennell, S., & Malik, R. (2012). Between a rock and a hard place: The emerging educational market for the poor in Pakistan. *Comparative Education, 48*(2), 249–261. doi:10.1080 /03050068.2011.608900.

Fitz, J., & Beers, B. (2002). Education management organisations and the privatisation of public education: A cross-national comparison of the USA and Britain. *Comparative Education, 38*(2), 137–154. doi:10.1080/03050060220140j18

Fitz, J., & Hafid, T. (2007). Perspectives on the privatization of public schooling in England and Wales. *Educational Policy, 21*(1), 273–296. doi:10.1177/0895904806297193

Fourcade-Gourinchas, M., & Babb, S. L. (2002). The rebirth of the liberal creed: Paths to neoliberalism in four countries. *American Journal of Sociology, 108*(3), 533–579. doi:10.1086/367922

Friedman, M. (1955). The role of government in education. In R. A. Solo (Ed.), *Economics and the public interest* (pp. 123–144). New Brunswick, NJ: Rutgers University Press.

Friedman, M. (1962). *Capitalism and freedom.* Chicago, IL: Chicago University Press.

Friedman, M. (2005, December 5). The promise of vouchers. *Wall Street Journal*, p. A20.

Fulge, T., Bieber, T., & Martens, K. (2016). Rational intentions and unintended consequences: On the interplay between international and national actors in education policy. In K. Mundy, A. Green, R. Lingard, & A. Verger (Eds.), *Handbook of global policy and policy-making in education* (pp. 553–469). West Sussex, UK: Wiley-Blackwell.

Fusarelli, L. D., & Johnson, B. (2004). Educational governance and the new public management. *Public Administration and Management, 9*(2), 118–127. Retrieved from www .spaef.com/file.php?id=192

Gauri, V. (1998). *School choice in Chile: Two decades of educational reform.* Pittsburgh, PA: University of Pittsburgh Press.

Giddens, A. (1998). *The third way: The renewal of social democracy.* Cambridge, MA: Polity Press.

Giles, C. (2006). Sustaining secondary school visions over time: Resistance, resilience, and educational reform. *Journal of Educational Change, 7*(3), 179–208. doi:10.1007/s10833-005-5727-1

Gillard, D. (2011). *Education in England: A brief history.* Retrieved from www.education england.org.uk/history

Gillies, J., Crouch, L., & Flórez, A. (2010). *Strategic review of the EDUCO Program.* El Salvador: USAID-EQUIP2. Retrieved from www.equip123.net/docs/e2-EDUCO_Strategic_Review.pdf

Gindin, J., & Finger, L. (2013). *Promoting education quality: The role of teachers' unions in Latin America.* Paper commissioned for the EFA Global Monitoring Report 2013/2014, Teaching and learning: Achieving quality for all. Retrieved from scholar.harvard.edu/files/lesliefinger/files/unesco_paper.pdf

Goldie, D., Linick, M., Jabbar, H., & Lubienski, C. (2014). Using bibliometric and social media analyses to explore the "echo chamber" hypothesis. *Educational Policy, 28*(2), 281–305. doi:10.1177/0895904813515330.

Gough, D., Oliver, S., & Thomas, J. (2013). Learning from research: Systematic reviews for informing policy decisions—A quick guide. A paper for the Alliance for Useful Evidence. London, UK: Nesta. Retrieved from www.alliance4usefulevidence.org/assets/Alliance-FUE-reviews-booklet-3.pdf

Gough, D., Thomas, J., & Oliver, S. (2012). Clarifying differences between review designs and methods. *Systematic Reviews, 1*(28). Retrieved from link.springer.com/content/pdf/10.1186%2F2046-4053-1-28.pdf

Govinda R., & Bandyopadhyay, M. (2008). *Access to elementary education in India: Analytical overview* (CREATE Working Paper). Brighton, UK: University of Sussex—Centre for International Education. Retrieved from sro.sussex.ac.uk/2145/1/India_CAR.pdf .

Grek, S. (2010). Governing by numbers: The Pisa "effect" in Europe. *Journal of Education Policy, 24*(1), 23–37. doi:10.1080/02680930802412669 .

Grek, S., Lawn, M., Lingard, B., Ozga, J., Rinne, R., Segerholm, C., & Simola, H. (2009). National policy brokering and the construction of the European education space in England, Sweden, Finland, and Scotland. *Comparative Education, 45*(1), 5–21. doi:10.1080/03050060802661378

Griera, M. (2007). The education battle: The role of the Catholic Church in the Spanish education system. In G. Grace & J. O'Keefe (Eds.), *International handbook of Catholic education: Challenges for school systems in the 21st century* (pp. 291–310). Dordrecht, the Netherlands: Springer Netherlands.

Gunter, H. M. (Ed.). (2010). *The state and education policy: The academies programme.* London, UK: Bloomsbury Publishing.

Gunter, H. M., & Forrester, G. (2009). School leadership and education policy-making in England. *Policy Studies, 30*(5), 495–511. doi:10.1080/01442870902899947

Gunter, H., & Mills, C. (2016). Knowledge production and the rise of consultocracy in education policymaking in England. In A. Verger, C. Lubienski, & G. Steiner-Khamsi (Eds.), *World yearbook of education 2016: The global education industry* (pp. 125–141). New York, NY: Routledge.

Haas, P. (2004). When does power listen to truth? A constructivist approach to the policy process. *Journal of European Public Policy, 11*(4), 569–592. doi:10.1080/1350176042000248034

Hall, P. A. (1993). Policy paradigms, social learning, and the state: The case of economic policymaking in Britain. *Comparative Politics, 25*(3), 275–296. doi:10.2307/422246

Hall, P. A., & Taylor, R. C. R. (1996). Political science and the three new institutionalisms. *Political Studies, 44*(5), 936–957. doi:10.1111/j.1467-9248.1996.tb00343.x

Härmä, J. (2010). *School choice for the poor? The limits of marketisation of primary education in rural India* (CREATE–Pathways to Access Research Monograph Number 23). Brighton, UK: University of Sussex–Centre for International Education; Consortium for Educational Access, Transitions, and Equity. Retrieved from www.create-rpc.org/pdf_documents/PTA23.pdf

Härmä, J. (2011). Low-cost private schooling in India: Is it pro poor and equitable? *International Journal of Educational Development, 31*(4), 350–356. doi:10.1016/j.ijedudev.2011.01.003

Härmä, J. (2013). *Private responses to state failure: The growth in private education (and why) in Lagos, Nigeria* (NCSPE Occasional Paper Number 215). New York, NY: National Center for the Study of Privatization in Education, Teachers College, Columbia University. Retrieved from www.ncspe.org/publications_files/OP215.pdf

Härmä, J., & Adefisayo, F. (2013). Scaling up: Challenges facing low-fee private schools in the slums of Lagos, Nigeria. In P. Srivastava (Ed.), *Low-fee private schooling: Aggravating equity or mitigating disadvantage?* (pp. 129–152). Oxford, UK: Symposium Books.

Härmä, J., & Rose, P. (2012). Is low-fee private primary schooling affordable for the poor? Evidence from rural India. In S. L. Robertson, K. Mundy, A. Verger, & F. Menashy (Eds.), *Public-private partnerships in education: New actors and modes of governance in a globalizing world* (pp. 243–258). Cheltenham/Northampton, UK: Edward Elgar.

Harris, D. N., Herrington, C. D., & Albee, A. (2007). The future of vouchers: Lessons from the adoption, design, and court challenges of Florida's three voucher programs. *Educational Policy, 21*(1), 215–244. doi:10.1177/0895904806297209

Hartney, M., & Flavin, P. (2011). From the schoolhouse to the statehouse: Teacher union political activism and U.S. state education reform policy. *State Politics & Policy Quarterly, 11*(3), 251–268. doi:10.1177/1532440011413079

Harvey, D. (2003). *The new imperialism.* Oxford, UK: Oxford University Press.

Harvey, D. (2005). *A brief history of neoliberalism.* New York, NY: Oxford University Press.

Hatcher, R. (2001). Getting down to business: Schooling in the globalised economy. *Education and Social Justice, 3*(2), 45–59.

Hatcher, R. (2006). Privatization and sponsorship: The re-agenting of the school system in England. *Journal of Education Policy, 21*(5), 599–619. doi:10.1080/02680930600866199

Hatcher, R., & Jones, K. (2006). Researching resistance: Campaigns against academies in England. *British Journal of Educational Studies, 54*(3), 329–351. doi:10.1111/j.1467-8527.2006.00350.x

Hay, C. (1999). Crisis and the structural transformation of the state: Interrogating the process of change. *British Journal of Politics & International Relations, 1*(3), 317–344

Hay, C. (2001). The "crisis" of Keynesianism and the rise of neoliberalism in Britain: An ideational institutionalist approach by Colin Hay. In J. L. Campbell & O. K. Pedersen (Eds.), *The rise of neoliberalism and institutional analysis* (pp. 193–218). Princeton, NJ: Princeton University Press.

Hay, C. (2002). *Political analysis: A critical introduction.* Basingstoke, UK: Palgrave.

Heise, M. (2012). Law and policy entrepreneurs: Empirical evidence on the expansion of school choice policy. *Notre Dame Law Review, 87*(5), 1917–1940. Retrieved from works.bepress.com/michael_heise/31

Held, D., & Leftwich, A. (1984). A discipline of politics? In A. Leftwich (Ed.), *What is politics?* (pp. 139–159). Oxford, UK: Basil Blackwell.

Held, D., McGrew, A., Goldblatt, D., & Perraton, J. (1999). *Global transformations: Politics, economics and culture.* Stanford, CA: Stanford University Press.

Henig, J. R. (2008). *Spin cycle: How research gets used in policy debates: The case of charter schools.* New York, NY: Russell Sage Foundation.

Herod, A. (2001). *Labor geographies: Workers and the landscapes of capitalism*. New York, NY: Guilford Press.

Heyneman, S. P., & Stern, J. M. B. (2014). Low-cost private schools for the poor: What public policy is appropriate? *International Journal of Educational Development, 35*, 3–15. doi:10.1016/j.ijedudev.2013.01.002

Hirschmann, A. O. (1970). *Exit, voice and loyalty*. Cambridge, MA: Harvard University Press.

Hodge, G. A., Greve, C., & Boardman, A. E. (Eds.). (2010). *International handbook on public-private partnerships*. Cheltenham/Northampton, UK: Edward Elgar.

Hogan, A., Sellar, S., & Lingard, B. (2015). Network restructuring of global edu-business: The case of Pearson's efficacy framework. In W. Au & J. J. Ferrare (Eds.), *Mapping corporate education: Power and policy networks in the neoliberal state* (pp. 43–64). New York, NY: Routledge.

Hojman, D. E. (1993). *Chile: The political economy of development and democracy in the 1990s*. London, UK: Palgrave Macmillan.

Holyoke, T. T., Henig, J. R., Brown, H., & Lacireno-Paquet, N. (2009). Policy dynamics and the evolution of state charter school laws. *Policy Sciences, 42*(1), 33–55. doi:10.1007/s11077-009-9077-3

Holzinger, K., & Knill, C. (2005). Causes and conditions of cross-national policy convergence. *Journal of European Public Policy, 12*(5), 775–796. doi:10.1080/13501760500161357

Immergut, E. M. (2006). Historical-institutionalism in political science and the problem of change. In A. Wimmer & R. Kössler (Eds.), *Understanding change: Models, methodologies, and metaphors* (pp. 237–259). Basingstoke, UK/New York, NY: Palgrave Macmillan.

Imsen, G., & Volckmar, N. (2014). The Norwegian school for all: Historical emergence and neoliberal confrontation. In U. Blossing, G. Imsen, & L. Moos (Eds.), *The Nordic education model: "A school for all" encounters neo-liberal policy* (pp. 35–55). Dordrecht, the Netherlands: Springer.

International Finance Corporation. (2001). *Handbook on public private partnerships in education*. Washington, DC: IFC/EdInvest. Retrieved from www.ifc.org/wps/wcm/connect/Topics_Ext_Content/IFC_External_Corporate_Site/EdInvest_Home/PublicPrivatePartnerships/

James, E. (1984). Benefits and costs of privatized public services: Lessons from the Dutch educational system. *Comparative Education Review, 28*(4), 605–624. doi:10.1086/446470.

Jessop, B. (1993). Towards a Schumpeterian workfare state? Preliminary remarks on post-Fordist political economy. *Studies in Political Economy, 40*, 7–39

Jessop, B. (1998). The rise of governance and the risks of failure: The case of economic development. *International Social Science Journal, 50*(155), 29–45. doi:10.1111/1468-2451.00107

Jessop, B. (2010). Cultural political economy and critical policy studies. *Critical Policy Studies, 3*(3/4), 336–356. doi:0.1080/19460171003619741

Jessop, B. (2015). A cultural political economy approach to the governance of global social policy. In A. Kaasch & K. Martens (Eds.), *Actors and agency in global social governance* (pp. 18–42). Oxford, UK: Oxford University Press.

Jimenez, E., & Sawada, Y. (2003). *Does community management help keep kids in schools? Evidence using panel data from El Salvador's EDUCO program* (CIRJE Discussion Paper CF-236). Tokyo, Japan: Center for International Research on the Japanese Economy–University of Tokyo. Retrieved from www1.worldbank.org/prem/poverty/ie/dime_papers/541.pdf

Johnston, J. B. (2014). Resisting charters: A comparative policy development analysis of Washington and Kentucky, 2002–2012. *Sociology of Education, 87*(4), 223–240. doi:10.1177/0038040714546756

Junemann, C., Ball, S., & Santori, D. (2016). Joined-up policy: Network connectivity and global education governance. In K. Mundy, A. Green, R. Lingard, & A. Verger (Eds.), *Handbook of global policy and policy-making in education* (pp. 535–553). West Sussex, UK: Wiley-Blackwell.

Kalimullah, N. A., Ashraf, K. M., & Ashaduzzaman, M. M. (2012). New public management: Emergence and principles. *Bangladesh University of Professionals Journal, 1*(1), 1–22. Retrieved from www.bup.edu.bd/journal/1-22.pdf

Karsten, S. (1994). Policy on ethnic segregation in a system of choice: The case of the Netherlands. *Journal of Education Policy, 9*(3), 211–225. doi:10.1080/0268093940090302

Karsten, S. (1999). Neoliberal education reform in the Netherlands. *Comparative Education, 35*(3), 303–317. Retrieved from www.jstor.org/stable/3099481

Keck, M. E., & Sikkink, K. (1998). *Activists beyond borders: Advocacy networks in international politics.* Ithaca, NY: Cornell University Press.

Kenny, L. W. (2005). *The public choice of educational choice* (NCSPE Occasional Paper Number 108). New York, NY: National Center for the Study of Privatization in Education, Teachers College, Columbia University. Retrieved from www.ncspe.org/publications_files/OP108.pdf

Kingdon, J. W. (1995). *Agendas, alternatives, and public policies* (2nd ed.). New York, NY: HarperCollins College.

Kirst, M. C. (2007). Politics of charter schools: Competing national advocacy coalitions meet local politics. *Peabody Journal of Education, 83*(2/3), 184–203. doi:10.1080/016 19560701312939

Kitaev, I. (2007). Education for all and private education in the developing and transitional countries. In P. Srivastava & G. Walford (Eds.), *Private schooling in less economically developed countries: Asian and African perspectives* (pp. 89–110). Oxford, UK: Symposium Books.

Kjaer, P., & Pedersen, O. K. (2001). Translating liberalization: Neoliberalism in the Danish negotiated economy. In J. L. Campbell & O. K. Pedersen (Eds.), *The rise of neoliberalism and institutional analysis* (pp. 219–248). Princeton, NJ: Princeton University Press.

Klees, S. J. (2008). A quarter century of neoliberal thinking in education: Misleading analyses and failed policies. *Globalisation, Societies, and Education, 6*(4), 311–348. doi:10.1080/14767720802506672

Klein, N. (2007). *The shock doctrine: The rise of disaster capitalism.* New York, NY: Metropolitan Books/Henry Holt.

Klitgaard, M. B. (2007). Do welfare state regimes determine public sector reforms? Choice reforms in American, Swedish, and German schools. *Scandinavian Political Studies, 30*(4), 444–468. doi:10.1111/j.1467-9477.2007.00188.x

Klitgaard, M. B. (2008). School vouchers and the new politics of the welfare state. *Governance, 21*(4), 479–498. doi:10.1111/j.1468-0491.2008.00410.x

Knill, C. (2005). Introduction: Cross-national policy convergence: Concepts, approaches, and explanatory factors. *Journal of European Public Policy, 12*(5), 764–774. doi:10.1080/13501760500161332

Korten, D. C. (1995). *When corporations rule the world.* London, UK: Earthscan.

Kvist, J., & Greve, B. (2011). Has the Nordic welfare model been transformed? *Social Policy & Administration, 45*(2), 146–160. doi:10.1111/j.1467-9515.2010.00761.x .

Labaree, D. F. (2007). *Education, markets, and the public good: The selected works of David F. Labaree.* New York, NY: Routledge.

Larsson, B., Letell, M., & Thörn, H. (2012). Transformations of the Swedish welfare state: From social engineering to governance? Basingstoke, UK: Palgrave Macmillan.

League of Women Voters, et al. v. State of Washington. No. 89714-0 (Wash. 2015).

Lejano, R. P., & Shankar, S. (2013). The contextualist turn and schematics of institutional fit: Theory and a case study from southern India. *Policy Sciences, 46*(1), 83–102. doi:10.1007/s11077-012-9163-9

Lenschow, A., Liefferink, D., & Veenman, S. (2005). When the birds sing: A framework for analysing domestic factors behind policy convergence. *Journal of European Public Policy, 12*(5), 797–816. doi:10.1080/13501760500161373

Levin, H. M., Daschbach, J., & Perry, A. (2010). A diverse education provider: New Orleans. In B. Bulkley, J. Henig, & H. M. Levin (Eds.), *Between public and private: Politics, governance, and the new portfolio models for urban school reform* (pp. 165–191). Cambridge, MA: Harvard Education Press.

Lewin, K. M. (2007). *The limits to growth of non-government private schooling in sub-Saharan Africa* (CREATE–Pathways to Access Research Monograph Number 5). Brighton, UK: University of Sussex–Centre for International Education. Retrieved from sro.sussex. ac.uk/1833/1/PTA5.pdf

Lingard, B., Rawolle, S., & Taylor, S. (2005). Globalizing policy sociology in education: Working with Bourdieu. *Journal of Education Policy, 20*(6), 759–777. doi:10.1080/026 80930500238945 10.1086/231174

Lubienski, C. (2003). Instrumentalist perspectives on the "public" in public education: Incentives and purposes. *Educational Policy, 17*(4), 478–502. doi: 10.1177/08959048 03254964

Lubienski, C., Scott, J., & DeBray, E. (2014). The politics of research production, promotion, and utilization in educational policy. *Educational Policy, 28*(2), 131–144. doi:10. 1177/0895904813515329

Lubienski, C., Weitzel, P., & Lubienski, S. T. (2009). Is there a "consensus" on school choice and achievement? Advocacy research and the emerging political economy of knowledge production. *Educational Policy, 23*(1),161–193. doi:10.1177/0895904808328532

Luengo, J. J., & Saura, G. (2012). Mecanismos endógenos de privatización encubierta en la escuela pública: Políticas educativas de gestión de resultados y rendición de cuentas en Andalucía. *Profesorado,16*(3), 133–148. Retrieved from www.redalyc.org/articulo. oa?id=56725002007

Lundahl, L. (2002). Sweden: Decentralization, deregulation, quasi-markets—and then what? *Journal of Education Policy, 17*(6), 687–697. doi:10.1080/0268093022000032328

Lundahl, L., Erixson-Arreman, I. E., Holm, A. S., & Lundström, U. (2013). Educational marketization the Swedish way. *Education Inquiry, 4*(3), 497–517. doi:10.3402/edui. v4i3.22620.

Lupton, R. (2011). "No change there then!": The onward march of school markets and competition. *Journal of Educational Administration and History, 43*(4), 309–323. doi:10.10 80/00220620.2011.606894

Maranto, R. (2005). A tale of two cities: School privatization in Philadelphia and Chester. *American Journal of Education, 111*(2), 151–190. doi:10.1086/426836

Marginson, S. (1993). *Education and public policy in Australia.* Cambridge, UK: Cambridge University Press.

Maroy, C. (2009). Convergences and hybridization of educational policies around "postbureaucratic" models of regulation. *Compare, 39*(1), 71–84. doi:10.1080/030579208019 03472

Maroy, C., & Vaillancourt, S. (2013). Le discours syndical face à la nouvelle gestion publique dans le système éducatif Québécois. *Education et Sociétés, 2*(32), 93–108. doi:10.3917/ es.032.0093

Marshall, C., Mitchell, D. E., & Wirt, F. (1985). Assumptive worlds of education policy makers. *Peabody Journal of Education, 62*(4), 90–115. doi:10.1080/01619568509538493

Martens, K., Rusconi, A., & Leuze, K. (Eds.). (2007). *New arenas of education governance: The impact of international organizations and markets on educational policy making.* Basingstoke, UK/New York, NY: Palgrave Macmillan.

Martins, E. M. (2013). *Movimento todos pela educação: Um projeto de nação para a educação brasileira* (Master dissertation). Retrieved from Biblioteca Digital da UNICAMP (Accession Order No 000915751).

Martins, E. M., & Krawczyk, N. R. (2016) Entrepreneurial influence in Brazilian education policies: The case of todos pela educação. In A. Verger, C. Lubienski, & G. Steiner-Khamsi (Eds.), *World yearbook of education 2016: The global education industry* (pp. 78–89). New York, NY: Routledge.

Martinsson, J. (2011). *Global norms: Creation, diffusion, and limits* (CommGAP Discussion Paper). Washington, DC: The International Bank for Reconstruction and Development/ The World Bank–Communication for Governance and Accountability Program. Retrieved from www-wds.worldbank.org/external/default/WDSContentServer/WDSP/IB/2011/10/18/000333037_20111018024736/Rendered/PDF/649860WP00PUBLIC0 0Box361550B0GlobalNorms.pdf

Maurer, M. (2012). Structural elaboration of technical and vocational education and training systems in developing countries: The cases of Sri Lanka and Bangladesh. *Comparative Education, 48*(4), 487–503. doi:10.1080/03050068.2012.702011

McLennan, G. (2004). Travelling with vehicular ideas: The case of the third Way, Economy and Society, 33(4), 484–499. doi:10.1080/0308514042000285251

McNulty, B. (2011). The education of poverty: Rebuilding Haiti's school system after its "total collapse." *Fletcher Forum of World Affairs, 35*(1), 109–126. Retrieved from fletcher.tufts.edu/Fletcher-Forum/Archives/~/media/Fletcher/Microsites/Fletcher %20Forum/PDFs/2011winter/McNulty.pdf

Mehrotra, S., & Panchamukhi, P. R. (2007). Universalizing elementary education in India: Is the private sector the answer? In P. Srivastava & G. Walford (Eds.), *Private schooling in less economically developed countries: Asian and African perspectives* (pp. 129–153). Oxford, UK: Symposium Books.

Menashy, F. (2014). Theorizing privatization in education: Comparing conceptual frameworks and the value of the capability approach. *Current Issues in Comparative Education, 16*(1), 13–25. Retrieved from www.tc.columbia.edu/i/a/document/30408_16_1_ Francine_Menashy.pdf

Meyer, H. D., & Benavot, A. (2013). Introduction: PISA and the globalization of education governance: Some puzzles and problems. In H. D. Meyer & A. Benavot (Eds.), *PISA: Power and policy: The emergence of global educational governance* (pp. 9–26). Oxford, UK: Symposium Books.

Meyer, J. W., Boli, J., Thomas, G. M., & Ramirez, F. O. (1997). World society and the nation-state. *American Journal of Sociology, 103*(1), 144–181. doi:10.1086/231174

Miller, P., Craven, B., & Tooley, J. (2014). Setting up a free school: Successful proposers' experiences. *Research Papers in Education, 29*(3), 351–371. doi:10.1080/02671522.2014.885734

Miñana, C. (2010). Políticas neoliberales y neoinstitucionales en un marco constitucional adverso: Reformas educativas en Colombia 1991–2010. *FLACSO Argentina–Propuesta Educativa, 34.* Retrieved from www.propuestaeducativa.flacso.org.ar/archivos/ dossier_articulos/44.pdf

Mintrom, M. (2000). *Policy entrepreneurs and school choice.* Washington, DC: Georgetown University Press.

Mintrom, M., & Vergari. S. (1996). Advocacy coalitions, policy entrepreneurs, and policy change. *Policy Studies Journal, 24*(3), 420–434. doi:10.1111/j.1541-0072.1996.tb01638.x

Mizala, A. (2007). *La economía política de la reforma educacional en Chile* (Serie Estudios Socio/Económicos Number 36). Santiago de Chile: Corporación de Estudios para Latinoamérica (CIEPLAN). Retrieved from cieplan.cl/media/publicaciones/ archivos/153/Capitulo_1.pdf

Mizala, A., & Schneider, B. R. (2014). Negotiating education reform: Teacher evaluations and incentives in Chile (1990–2010). *Governance, 27*(1), 87–109. doi:10.1111/gove.1 2020.

Moe, T. M. (2001). *Schools, vouchers, and the American public.* Washington, DC: Brookings Institution.

Møller, J., & Skedsmo, G. (2013). Modernising education: New public management reform in the Norwegian education system. *Journal of Educational Administration and History, 45*(4), 336–353. doi:10.1080/00220620.2013.822353

Mundy, K., & Menashy, F. (2012). The role of the International Finance Corporation in the promotion of public-private partnerships for educational development. In S. L. Robertson, K. Mundy, A. Verger, & F. Menashy (Eds.), *Public-private partnerships in education: New actors and modes of governance in a globalizing world* (pp. 81–103). Cheltenham/Northampton, UK: Edward Elgar.

Mundy, K., & Menashy, F. (2014). The World Bank and private provision of schooling: A look through the lens of sociological theories of organizational hypocrisy. *Comparative Education Review, 58*(3), 401–427. doi:10.1086/676329

Nadler, D. A., & Tushman, M. (1995). Types of organizational change: From incremental improvement to discontinuous transformation. In D. A. Nadler, R. B. Shaw, & A. E. Walton (Eds.), *Discontinuous change: Leading organizational transformation* (pp. 15–34). San Francisco, CA: Jossey-Bass.

Nambissan, G. B., & Ball, S. (2010). Advocacy networks, choice, and private schooling of the poor in India. *Global Networks, 10*(3), 324–343. doi:10.1111/j.1471-0374.2010.00291.x

Narodowski, M., & Moschetti, M. (2013). The growth of private education in Argentina: Evidence and explanations. *Compare: A Journal of Comparative and International Education, 45*(1), 47–69. doi:10.1080/03057925.2013.829348

Narodowski, M., Moschetti, M., & Alegre, S. (2013). Radiografía de las huelgas docentes en la Argentina: Conflicto laboral y privatización de la educación. Retrieved from www .clarin.com/educacion/Radiografia-Argentina-Conflicto-Narodowski-Moschetti_ CLAFIL20130710_0005.pdf

National Center on Education and the Economy (NCEE). (2006). An Overview of Education on Flemish Belgium. Retrieved from http://www.ncee.org/wp-content/ uploads/2013/10/Belgium-Education-Report3.pdf

National Conference of State Legislatures. (2015). School voucher laws: State-by-state comparison. Retrieved from www.ncsl.org/documents/educ/StateByStateVoucher Comparison.pdf

Niemerg, M. (2013). *International support to low-cost private schools.* Chicago, IL: INP Foundation Inc. Retrieved from www.idpfoundation.org/wp-content/uploads/2013/ 07/Funding-Paper-FINAL.pdf

Novelli, M., Higgins, S., Ugur, M., & Valiente, O. (2014). *The political economy of education systems in conflict-affected contexts: A rigorous literature review* (EPPI-Centre Education Rigorous Literature Review Reference Number 2209). London, UK: DfID. Retrieved from r4d.dfid.gov.uk/pdf/outputs/HumanDev_Evidence/Political_Economy_ Education_2014_Novelli_report.pdf

Nusche, D., Braun, H., Haláz, G. & Santiago. P. (2014). *OECD reviews of evaluation and assessment in education: Netherlands 2014.* Paris, France: OECD Publishing.

O'Keefe, J. E. (2013). The role of an epistemic community in Haitian education reform post-earthquake 2010 (Master dissertation). Retrieved from ecommons.luc.edu/ luc_theses/index.4.html

Offe, C. (1987). Democracy against the welfare state? Structural foundations of neo-conservative political opportunities. *Political Theory, 15*(4), 501–537. doi:0.1177/ 0090591787015004002

Olmedo, A. (2008). De la participación democrática a la elección de centro: Las bases del cuasimercado en la legislación educativa Española. *Education Policy Analysis Archives/Archivos Analíticos de Políticas Educativas, 16*(21), 1–35. Retrieved from www.redalyc.org/articulo.oa?id=275020545020.

Olmedo, A. (2013). Policy-makers, market advocates, and edu-businesses: New and renewed players in the Spanish education policy arena. *Journal of Education Policy, 28*(1), 55–76. doi:10.1080/02680939.2012.689011

Olmedo, A. (2014). From England with love … ARK, heterarchies, and global "philanthropic governance." *Journal of Education Policy, 29*(5), 575–597. doi:10.1080/02680 939.2013.859302

Olmedo, A., & Santa Cruz, E. (2013). Neoliberalism, policy advocacy networks, and think tanks in the Spanish educational arena: The case of FAES. *Education Inquiry, 4*(3), 473–496. doi:10.3402/edui.v4i3.22618

Oppenheimer, A. (2010). *Basta de histórias! A obsessão Latino-Americana com o passado e as 12 chaves do futuro.* Rio de Janeiro, Brazil: Objetiva.

Organisation for Economic Co-operation and Development (OECD). (2006). Education at a Glance 2006: OECD Indicators. Paris, France: OECD Publishing. Retrieved from https://www.oecd.org/education/skills-beyond-school/37376068.pdf

Organisation for Economic Co-operation and Development (OECD). (2012). Education at a Glance 2012: OECD Indicators. Paris, France: OECD Publishing. Retrieved from www.oecd.org/edu/EAG%202012_e-book_EN_200912.pdf

Organisation for Economic Co-operation and Development (OECD). (2014). Education at a Glance 2014: OECD Indicators. Paris, France: OECD Publishing. Retrieved from www.oecd.org/edu/Education-at-a-Glance-2014.pdf

Osborne, D., & Gaebler, T. (1992). *Reinventing government: How the entrepreneurial spirit is transforming the public sector.* Reading, PA: Addison-Wesley

Paredes, R., & Ugarte, G. (2009). Should students be allowed to miss? (MPRA Paper Number 15583.) Munich, Germany: Munich Personal RePEc Archive. Retrieved from mpra. ub.uni-muenchen.de/15583/1/MPRA_

Patrinos, H. A. (2010). Private education provision and public finance: The Netherlands (World Bank Policy Research Working Paper Number 5185). Washington, DC: World Bank–Human Development Network, Education Team. doi:10.1596/1813-9450-5185. Retrieved from elibrary.worldbank.org/doi/abs/10.1596/1813-9450-5185.

Patrinos, H. A. (2013). Private education provision and public finance: The Netherlands. *Education Economics, 21*(4), 392–414. doi:10.1080/09645292.2011.568696

Patrinos, H. A., Barrera-Osorio, F., & Guáqueta, J. (2009). The role and impact of public-private partnerships in education. Washington, DC: World Bank. Retrieved from siteresources.worldbank.org/EDUCATION/Resources/278200-1099079877269/ 547664-1099079934475/547667-1135281523948/2065243-1239111225278/Role_ Impact_PPP_Education.pdf

Pearson PLC. (2015). Where are the low-cost schools? Retrieved from www.affordable-learning.com/resources/where-are-the-low-cost-schools.html

Peck, J., & Theodore, N. (2010). Mobilizing policy: Models, methods, and mutations. *Geoforum, 41*(2), 169–174. doi:0.1016/j.geoforum.2010.01.002

Petticrew, M., & Roberts, H. (2006). *Systematic reviews in the social sciences: A practical guide.* Oxford, UK: Blackwell Publishing.

Phillips, K. D., & Stambach, A. (2008). Cultivating choice: The invisible hands of educational opportunity in Tanzania. In M. Forsey, S. Davis, & G. Walford (Eds.), *The globalisation of school choice?* (pp. 145–164). Oxford, UK: Symposium Books.

Phillipson, B. (2008). *Low-cost private education: Impacts on achieving universal primary education.* London, UK: Commonwealth Secretariat.

Pinto, L. E. (2012). Hidden privatization in education policy as "quick fixes" by "hired guns": Contracting curriculum policy in Ontario. *Critical Policy Studies, 6*(3), 261–281. doi:1 0.1080/19460171.2012.717782

Pollitt, C., & Bouckaert, G. (2004). *Public management reform: A comparative analysis.* Oxford, UK: Oxford University Press.

Pollock, A. M. (2005). *NHS plc: The privatisation of our health care.* London, UK: Verso.

Poole, L., & Mooney, G. (2006). Privatizing education in Scotland? New Labour, modernization, and "public" services. *Critical Social Policy, 26*(3), 562–586. doi:10.1177/0261018306065609

Poole, W. (2007). Neo-liberalism in British Columbia education and teachers' union resistance. *International Electronic Journal for Leadership in Learning, 11*(24). Retrieved from iejll.journalhosting.ucalgary.ca/index.php/ijll/article/view/679

Poole, W. L. (2001). The teacher unions' role in 1990s educational reform: An organizational evolution perspective. *Educational Administration Quarterly, 37*(2), 173–196. doi:10.1177/00131610121969280.

Poppema, M. (2012). School-based management in post-conflict Central America: Undermining civil society and making the poorest parents pay. In A. Verger, M. Novelli, & H. K. Altinyelken (Eds.), *Global education policy and international development: New agendas, issues, and policies* (pp. 161–180). London, UK/New York, NY: Bloomsbury Academic.

Prieto, M., & Villamor, P. (2012). Libertad de elección, competencia y calidad: Las políticas educativas de la Comunidad de Madrid. *Profesorado, 16*(3), 149–166. Retrieved from www.redalyc.org/articulo.oa?id=56725002008

Priyadarshini, S. (n.d.). *Weber's "ideal types": Definition, meaning, purpose, and use.* Retrieved from www.yourarticlelibrary.com/sociology/webers-ideal-types-definition-meaning-purpose-and-use/43758/

Quiggin, J. (2006). Economic constraints on public policy. In M. Moran, M. Rein, & R. E. Goodin (Eds.), *The Oxford handbook of public policy* (pp. 529–542). Oxford, UK: Oxford University Press.

Rangvid, B. S. (2008). Private school diversity in Denmark's national voucher system. *Scandinavian Journal of Educational Research, 52*(4), 331–354. doi:10.1080/00313830802184491

Ravitch, D. (2006, July 30). Bill Gates, the nation's superintendent of schools. *Los Angeles Times*, p. M3

Reid, A. (2013). Renewing the public and the role of research in education. *The Australian Educational Researcher, 40*(3), 281–297. doi:10.1007/s13384-013-0116-x

Renzulli, L. A., & Roscigno, V. J. (2005). Charter school policy, implementation, and diffusion across the United States. *Sociology of Education, 78*(4), 344–365. doi:10.1177/003804070507800404

Rich, A. (2004). *Think tanks, public policy, and the politics of expertise.* Cambridge, UK: Cambridge University Press.

Riep, C. B. (2014). Omega schools franchise in Ghana: "Affordable" private education for the poor or for-profiteering? In I. Macpherson, S. Robertson, & G. Walford (Eds.), *Education, privatisation, and social justice: Case studies from Africa, South Asia, and South East Asia* (pp. 259–278). Oxford, UK: Symposium Books.

Rinne, R. (2000). The globalisation of education: Finnish education on the doorstep of the new EU millennium. *Educational Review, 52*(2), 131–142. doi:10.1080/713664043

Rinne, R., Kivirauma, J., & Simola, H. (2002). Shoots of revisionist education policy or just slow readjustment? The Finnish case of educational reconstruction. *Journal of Education Policy, 17*(6), 643–658. doi:10.1080/0268093022000032292

Risse, T. (2000). "Let's argue!" Communicative action in world politics. *International Organization, 54*(1), 1–39. doi:10.1162/002081800551109

Rizvi, F., & Lingard, B. (2009). *Globalizing education policy.* London, UK: Routledge.

Robertson, S. L. (2005). Re-imagining and rescripting the future of education: Global knowledge economy discourses and the challenge to education systems. *Comparative Education, 41*(2), 151–170. Retrieved from www.jstor.org/stable/30044529

Robertson, S. L. (2012). The Strange Non-Death of Neoliberal Privatization in the World Bank's Education Strategy 2020. In S. Klees, N. Stromquist, & J. Samoff (Eds.), *A Critical Review of The World Banks Education Strategy 2020* (pp. 189–206). Rotterdam: Sense Publishers.

Robertson, S. L., Bonal, X., & Dale, R. (2002). GATS and the education service industry: The politics of scale and global reterritorialization. *Comparative Education Review, 46*(4), 472–495. Retrieved from www.jstor.org/stable/10.1086/343122

Robertson, S. L., & Dale, R. (2015). Toward a "critical cultural political economy" account of the globalising of education. *Globalisation, Societies, and Education, 13*(1), 149–170. doi:10.1080/14767724.2014.967502

Robertson, S. L., & Komljenovic, J. (2016). Unbundling the university and making higher education markets. In A. Verger, C. Lubienski, & G. Steiner-Khamsi (Eds.), *World yearbook of education 2016: The global education industry* (pp. 211–227). New York, NY: Routledge.

Robertson, S. L., & Verger, A. (2012). Governing education through public private partnerships. In S. L. Robertson, K. Mundy, A. Verger, & F. Menashy (Eds.), *Public-private partnerships in education: New actors and modes of governance in a globalizing world* (pp. 21–42). Cheltenham/Northampton, UK: Edward Elgar.

Rose, P., & Adelabu, M. (2007). Private sector contributions to education for all in Nigeria. In P. Srivastava & G. Walford (Eds.), *Private schooling in less economically developed countries: Asian and African perspectives* (pp. 67–88). Oxford, UK: Symposium Books.

Ryan, J. E., & Heise, M. (2002). The political economy of school choice. *Yale Law Journal, 111*(8), 2043–2136. doi:10.2307/797643

Sabatier, P., & Jenkins-Smith, H. (Eds.). (1993). *Policy change and learning: An advocacy coalition approach*. Boulder, CO: Westview Press.

Sabatier, P. A. (Ed.). (1999). *Theories of the policy process*. Boulder, CO: Westview Press.

Salinas, D., & Fraser, P. (2012). Educational opportunity and contentious politics: The 2011 Chilean student movement. *Berkeley Review of Education, 3*(1). Retrieved from escholarship.org/uc/item/60g9j416

Saltman, K. J. (2006). Creative Associates International: Corporate education and "democracy promotion" in Iraq. *Review of Education, Pedagogy, and Cultural Studies, 28*(1), 25–65. doi:10.1080/10714410600552795

Saltman, K. J. (2007). Schooling in disaster capitalism: How the political right is using disaster to privatize public schooling. *Teacher Education Quarterly, 34*(2), 131–156. Retrieved from www.jstor.org/stable/20866825

Santa Cruz, E., & Olmedo, A. (2012). Neoliberalismo y creación de "sentido común": Crisis educativa y medios de comunicación en Chile. *Profesorado, 16*(3), 145–168. Retrieved from www.redalyc.org/articulo.oa?id=56725002009

Santori, D., Ball, S. J., & Junemann, C. (2015). Education as a site of network governance. In W. Au & J. J. Ferrare (Eds.), *Mapping corporate education: Power and policy networks in the neoliberal state* (pp. 23–42). New York, NY: Routledge.

Sarangapani, P. M., & Winch, C. (2010). Tooley, Dixon, and Gomathi on private education in Hyderabad: A reply. *Oxford Review of Education, 36*(4), 499–515. doi:10.1080/030 54985.2010.495465

Saura, G. (2015). Think tanks y educación. Neoliberalismo de FAES en la LOMCE. *Archivos Analíticos de Políticas Educativas, 23*(107). Retrieved from http://dx.doi.org/10.14507/ epaa.v23.2106

Sawada, Y. (2000). Community participation, teacher effort, and educational outcome: The case of El Salvador's EDUCO program (William Davidson Institute Working Paper Number 307). Ann Arbor, MI: William Davidson Institute at the University of

Michigan. Retrieved from deepblue.lib.umich.edu/bitstream/handle/2027.42/39691/
wp307.pdf?sequence=3&isAllowed=y

Sayer, A. (2001). For a critical cultural political economy. *Antipode, 33*(4), 687–708. doi:10.
1111/1467-8330.00206

Schmidt, V. A., & Radaelli, C. M. (2004). Policy change and discourse in Europe: Conceptual and methodological issues. *West European Politics, 27*(2), 183–210. doi:10.10
80/0140238042000214874

Schriewer, J. (2004). Multiple internationalities: The emergence of a world-level ideology and
the persistence of idiosyncratic world-views. In J. Schriewer, C. Charle, & P. Wagner
(Eds.), *Transnational intellectual networks: Forms of academic knowledge and the search
for cultural identities* (pp. 473–533). Frankfurt, Germany/New York, NY: Campus Verlag.

Scott, J. (2009). The politics of venture philanthropy in charter school policy and advocacy.
Educational Policy, 23(1), 106–136. doi:10.1177/0895904808328531

Scott, J., & Jabbar, H. (2014). The hub and the spokes: Foundations, intermediary organizations, incentivist reforms, and the politics of research evidence. *Educational Policy,
28*(2), 233–257. doi:10.1177/0895904813515327

Sergiovanni, T. J. (1992). *Moral leadership: Getting to the heart of school improvement*. New
York, NY: Maxwell Macmillan.

Solhaug, T. (2011). New public management in educational reform in Norway. *Policy
Futures in Education, 9*(2), 267–279. doi:10.2304/pfie.2011.9.2.267

Srivastava, P. (2007). Neither voice nor loyalty: School choice and the low-fee private
sector in India (NCSPE Research Publications Series, Occasional Paper 134). New
York, NY: National Center for the Study of Privatization in Education–Teachers
College, Columbia University. Retrieved from www.ncspe.org/publications_files/
OP134_2.pdf

Srivastava, P. (2008). The shadow institutional framework: Towards a new institutional understanding of an emerging private school sector in India. *Research Papers in Education, 23*(4), 451–475. doi:10.1080/02671520701809783

Srivastava, P. (2010). Privatization and education for all: Unravelling the mobilizing frames.
Development, 53(4), 522–528. doi:10.1057/dev.2010.88

Srivastava, P. (2014, March). Contradictions and the persistence of the mobilizing frames
of privatization: Interrogating the global evidence on low-fee private schooling. Paper
presented at the annual conference of the Comparative & International Education
Society (CIES), Toronto, Ontario, Canada.

Srivastava, P. (2016). Questioning the global scaling up of low-fee private schooling:
The nexus between business, philanthropy, and PPPs. In A. Verger, C. Lubienski, &
G. Steiner-Khamsi (Eds.), *World yearbook of education 2016: The global education in-
dustry* (pp. 248–263). New York, NY: Routledge.

Srivastava, P., & Baur, L. (2016). New global philanthropy and philanthropic governance in
education in a post-2015 world. In K. Mundy, A. Green, R. Lingard, & A. Verger (Eds.),
Handbook of global policy and policy-making in education (pp. 433–448). West Sussex,
UK: Wiley-Blackwell.

Steel, L., & Levine, R. (1994). *Educational innovations in multiracial contexts: The growth
of magnet schools in American education*. Palo Alto, CA/Washington, DC: American
Institutes for Research in the Behavioral Sciences/Department of Education, Office of
the Under Secretary. Retrieved from files.eric.ed.gov/fulltext/ED370232.pdf

Steiner-Khamsi, G. (2010). The politics and economics of comparison. *Comparative Education Review, 54*(3), 323–342. doi:10.1086/653047

Steiner-Khamsi, G. (2012a). For all by all? The World Bank's global framework for education. In S. J. Klees, J. Samoff, & N. P. Stromquist (Eds.), *The World Bank and
education: Critiques and alternatives* (pp. 3–20). Rotterdam, the Netherlands: Sense
Publishers.

Steiner-Khamsi, G. (2012b). Understanding policy borrowing and lending: Building comparative policy studies. In G. Steiner-Khamsi & F. Waldow (Eds.), *World yearbook of education 2012: Policy borrowing and lending in education* (pp. 3–17). New York, NY: Routledge.

Stevenson, H. (2007). Restructuring teachers' work and trade union responses in England: Bargaining for change? *American Educational Research Journal, 44*(2), 224–251. doi:10.3102/0002831207302194

Stevenson, H., & Carter, B. (2009). Teachers and the state: Forming and reforming "partnership." *Journal of Educational Administration and History, 41*(4), 311–326. doi:10.1080/00220620903211547

Stoddard, C., & Corcoran, S. P. (2007). The political economy of school choice: Support for charter schools across states and school districts. *Journal of Urban Economics, 62*(1), 27–54. doi:10.1016/j.jue.2006.08.006

Stone, D. (2004). Transfer agents and global networks in the "transnationalization" of policy. *Journal of European Public Policy, 11*(3), 545–566. doi:10.1080/1350176041000016 94291

Suleiman, E. N., & Waterbury, J. (Eds.). (1990). *The political economy of public sector reform and privatization.* Boulder, CO: Westview Press.

Takayama, K. (2012). Exploring the interweaving of contrary currents: Transnational policy enactment and path-dependent policy implementation in Australia and Japan. *Comparative Education, 48*(4), 505–523. doi:10.1080/03050068.2012.721631

Telhaug, A. O., Mediås, O. A., & Aasen, P. (2006). The Nordic model in education: Education as part of the political system in the last 50 years. *Scandinavian Journal of Educational Research, 50*(3), 245–283. doi:10.1080/00313830600743274

Termes, A., Bonal, X., Verger, A., & Zancajo, A. (2015). Public-private partnerships in Colombian education: The equity and quality implications of "Colegios en concesión." *Education Support Program Working Paper* 66. London, UK: OSF. Retrieved from www.periglobal.org/sites/periglobal.org/files/WorkingPaper66%20PPPs.pdf

Terzian, S. G., & Boyd, D. C. (2004). Federal precedents and the origins of the charter school movement in Florida, USA, 1981–1996. *Journal of Educational Administration and History, 36*(2), 135–144. doi:10.1080/0022062042000255900.

Tooley, J. (2007). Educating Amaretch: Private schools for the poor and the new frontier for investors. *Economic Affairs, 27*(2), 37–43. doi:10.1111/j.1468-0270.2007.00728.x

Tooley, J. (2013). Challenging educational injustice: "Grassroots" privatisation in South Asia and sub-Saharan Africa. *Oxford Review of Education, 39*(4), 446–463. doi:10.108 0/03054985.2013.820466

Tooley, J. (2016). Pring on privatisation. In M. Hand & R. Davies (Eds.), *Education, ethics, and experience: Essays in honour of Richard Pring* (pp. 62–74). New York, NY: Routledge.

Tooley, J., & Longfield, D. (2015). The role and impact of private schools in developing countries: A response to the DFID-commissioned "rigorous literature review." London, UK: Pearson. Retrieved from research.pearson.com/content/plc/prkc/uk/open-ideas/en/articles/role-and-impact-of-private-schools/_jcr_content/par/article-downloadcompo/file.res/150330_Tooley_Longfield.pdf

UNESCO. (2009). *Overcoming inequality: Why governance matters* (EFA Global Monitoring Report 2009). Paris, France: UNESCO. Retrieved from www.unesco.org/education/gmr2009/press/EFA_GMR_complet.pdf

UNESCO Institute of Statistics. (2015). Distribution of enrolment by type of institution: Percentage of enrollment in primary education in private institutions, 1990 to 2015. Retrieved from data.uis.unesco.org/Index.aspx?queryid=136#

U.S. Census Bureau. (2002). *Racial and ethnic residential segregation in the United States: 1980–2000.* Washington, DC: U.S. Government Printing Office. Retrieved from www.census.gov/hhes/www/housing/housing_patterns/pdf/censr-3.pdf

U.S. Census Bureau. (2015). *Poverty rates by county, 1960 to 2010.* Retrieved from www .census.gov/hhes/www/poverty

U.S. Department of Education, National Center for Education Statistics. (2015). *Public elementary and secondary charter schools and enrollment, by state: Selected years, 1999–2000 to 2011–2012.* Retrieved from nces.ed.gov/programs/digest/d13/tables/dt13_216.90.asp

U.S. Department of Education, Office and Innovation and Improvement. (2008). Creating and sustaining successful K–8 magnet schools. Washington, DC: U.S. Department of Education. Retrieved from www2.ed.gov/admins/comm/choice/magnet-k8/magnetk-8.pdf

Vaillant, D. (2005). *Education reforms and teachers' unions: Avenues for action* (IIEP Fundamentals of educational planning 82). Paris, France: UNESCO–International Institute for Educational Planning. Retrieved from unesdoc.unesco.org/images/ 0014/001410/141028e.pdf

van der Tuin, M., & Verger, A. (2013). Evaluating teachers in Peru: Policy shortfalls and policy implications. In A. Verger, H. K. Altinyelken, & M. de Koning (Eds.), *Global managerial education reforms and teachers: Emerging policies, controversies, and issues in developing countries* (pp. 127–140). Brussels, Belgium: Education International.

van Fleet, J. (2012). A disconnect between motivations and education needs: Why American corporate philanthropy alone will not educate the most marginalized. In S. L. Robertson, K. Mundy, A. Verger, & F. Menashy (Eds.), *Public-private partnerships in education: New actors and modes of governance in a globalizing world* (pp. 158–181). Cheltenham/Northampton, UK: Edward Elgar.

Vandenberghe, V. (1999). Combining market and bureaucratic control in education: An answer to market and bureaucratic failure? *Comparative Education, 35*(3), 271–282. doi:10.1080/03050069927829

Vavrus, F. (2004). The referential web: Externalisation beyond education in Tanzania. In G. Steiner-Khamsi (Ed.), *The global politics of educational borrowing and lending* (pp. 141–153). New York, NY: Teachers College Press.

Vergari, S. (2007). The politics of charter schools. *Educational Policy, 21*(1), 15–29. doi:10. 1177/0895904806296508

Verger, A. (2012). Framing and selling global education policy: The promotion of public-private partnerships for education in low-income contexts. *Journal of Education Policy, 27*(1), 109–130. doi:10.1080/02680939.2011.623242

Verger, A., & Bonal, X. (2012). "All things being equal?" Policy options, shortfalls, and absences in the World Bank education strategy 2020. In S. J. Klees, J. Samoff, & N. P. Stromquist (Eds.), *The World Bank and education: Critiques and alternatives* (pp. 125–142). Rotterdam, the Netherlands: Sense Publishers.

Verger, A., & Curran, M. (2014). New public management as a global education policy: Its adoption and re-contextualization in a Southern European setting. *Critical Studies in Education, 55*(3), 253–271. doi:10.1080/17508487.2014.913531

Verger, A., & VanderKaaij, S. (2012). The national politics of global policies: Public-private partnerships in Indian Education. In A. Verger, M. Novelli, & H. K. Altinyelken (Eds.), *Global education policy and international development: New agendas, issues, and policies* (pp. 245–266). London, UK/New York, NY: Bloomsbury Academic.

Verger, A., Lubienski, C., & Steiner-Khamsi, G. (2016). The emergence and structuring of the global education industry: Towards an analytical framework. In A. Verger, C. Lubienski, & G. Steiner-Khamsi (Eds.), *World yearbook of education 2016: The global education industry* (pp. 3–24). New York, NY: Routledge.

West, A. & Currie, P. (2008). The role of the private sector in publicly-funded schooling in England: finance, delivery and decision making. *Policy and Politics, 36* (2), 191–207

Villarroya, A. (2000). La financiación de los centros concertados (C.I.D.E.–Investigación Number 147). Madrid, Spain: Ministerio de Educación, Cultura y Deporte; Centro de Investigación y Documentación Educativa. Retrieved from redined.mecd.gob.es/xmlui/bitstream/handle/11162/61450/00820072000029.pdf?sequence=1

Viteritti, J. P. (2005). School choice: How an abstract idea became a political reality. *Brookings Papers on Education Policy, 8*, 137–173. Retrieved from www.jstor.org/stable/20062557

Volckmar, N., & Wiborg, S. (2014). A social democratic response to market-led education policies: Concession or rejection? In U. Blossing, G. Imsen, & L. Moos (Eds.), *The Nordic education model: "A school for all" encounters neo-liberal policy* (pp. 117–131). Dordrecht, the Netherlands: Springer.

Walford, G. (2013). Low-fee private schools: A methodological and political debate. In P. Srivastava (Ed.), *Low-fee private schooling: Aggravating equity or mitigating disadvantage?* (pp. 199–213). Oxford, UK: Symposium Books.

Walford, G. (2015). The globalisation of low-fee private schools. In J. Zajda (Ed.), *Second international handbook on globalisation, education and policy research* (pp. 309–320). Dordrecht, the Netherlands: Springer Netherlands.

Waslander, S., Pater, C., & van der Weide, M. (2010). Markets in education: An analytical review of empirical research on market mechanisms in education (OECD Education Working Paper Number 52). Paris, France: OECD Publishing. doi:10.1787/5km4pskmkr27-en

West, A., & Bailey, E. (2013). The development of the academies programme: "Privatising" school-based education in England, 1986–2013. *British Journal of Educational Studies, 61*(2), 137–159. doi:10.1080/00071005.2013.789480.

Weyland, K. (2005). Theories of policy diffusion lessons from Latin American pension reform. *World Politics, 57*(2), 262–295. doi:0.1353/wp.2005.0019

Whitty, G., & Power, S. (2000). Marketization and privatization in mass education systems. *International Journal of Educational Development, 20*(2), 93–107

Wiborg, S. (2013). Neo-liberalism and universal state education: The cases of Denmark, Norway, and Sweden, 1980–2011. *Comparative Education, 49*(4), 407–423. doi:10.1080/03050068.2012.700436

Wiborg, S. (2015). Privatizing education: Free school policy in Sweden and England. *Comparative Education Review, 59*(3), 473–497. Retrieved from www.jstor.org/stable/10.1086/681928

Windle, J. (2014). The rise of school choice in education funding reform: An analysis of two policy moments. *Educational Policy, 28*(2), 306–324. doi:10.1177/0895904813513151

Wintle, M. (2000). Pillarisation, consociation and vertical pluralism in the Netherlands revisited: A European view. *West European Politics, 23*(3), 139–152. doi:10.1080/0140238 0008425387

Wong, K. K., & Shen, F. X. (2002). Politics of State-Led Reform in Education: Market Competition and Electoral Dynamics. *Educational Policy, 16*(1), 161–192. doi:10.1177/0895904802016001009

World Bank (2011). *Learning for all: Investing in people's knowledge and skills to promote development: World Bank Group education strategy, 2020.* Washington, DC: World Bank. Retrieved from siteresources.worldbank.org/EDUCATION/Resources/ESSU/Education_Strategy_4_12_2011.pdf

Young, T. V. (2011). Teachers unions in turbulent times: Maintaining their niche. *Peabody Journal of Education, 86*(3), 338–351. doi:10.1080/0161956X.2011.579019

Zilbersheid, U. (2008). The Dovrat report: Transforming Israel's education system into a combination of public social assistance and privatization. *Israel Affairs, 14*(1), 118–134. doi:10.1080/13537120701706021.

Index

References followed by the letter *f* refer to figures. Notes are designated by the page number and note number.

Aasen, P., 55
Academies, 48, 51, 51n16, 52, 54n18, 139, 163, 172
Academization, 163
Access to education, 91, 95, 97, 102, 191
Accommodationist effect, 82
Accountability, 8, 43, 51, 63, 81, 124, 129, 130, 147, 192, 195
Accumulation by dispossession, 119–120
Act 9 (Louisiana State), 121
Act 35 (Louisiana State), 122
Act on Private Schools (Norway), 66
Actors; domestic, 16, 20, 133, 150; international, 30, 95, 96, 129, 133; nongovernmental actors, 83, 129, 137; nonstate actors, 24, 78, 100, 137–157, 166, 177, 190
Adam Smith Institute, 46, 139
Adamson, F., 64, 121, 122, 122n3, 123, 124, 125, 126, 126n8
Adefisayo, F., 89, 93, 95
Adelabu, M., 94
Administrative viability, 21, 28, 30
Advocacy, corporate, 144–146
Advocacy coalitions, 16, 20, 24, 77–78, 80, 80n8, 83, 183, 190, 193
Affordability, 30, 91, 93–94
African-American parents/families/middle-class, 78, 79, 126
Agenda-setting, 18, 31, 76, 138, 156, 175,
Ahmed, H., 90
Aid: bilateral aid agency, 96; conditionality, 30, 44; international aid community, 44, 95
Akers, J. M., 119, 121, 123, 126
Akyeampong, K., 93, 94
Albee, A., 71
Allende, Salvador, 39
Ambiguity; conceptual ambiguity, 87, 183, 193; legal ambiguity, 75–76, 117, 180, 184

American Federation of Teachers (AFT), 81
American Recovery and Reinvestment Act (2009), 74
Amplification, 120, 121, 133
A Nation at Risk, 71, 86
Andalusia, Spain, 115, 116
Anderson-Levitt, K. M., 18
Andrabi, T., 93
Apple, M. W., 3, 70, 79, 80, 149, 193
Argentina, 162, 171, 195
Arizona, 79, 142
Ashaduzzaman, M. M., 8
Ashley, L. D., 5, 92, 93, 94
Ashraf, K. M., 8
Asian Development Bank (ADB), 144
Aslam, M., 93
Asociación Española de Centros Privados de Enseñanza (ACADE), 114n11
Assael, J., 161
Assisted Places Scheme (APS), 46, 48
Astrand, B., 64
Atasay, E., 119, 120, 121, 123, 127
Au, W., 147, 149
Austerity, 21, 57, 66, 111
Australia; low-fee private schools, 96; the media, 140; selection of policy changes, 190; teachers' unions, 162; think tanks, 139
Authoritarian populism, 36n3
Avalos, B., 44, 161
Azim Premji Foundation (APF), 149

Babb, S. L., 37, 39, 46, 53, 139
Back door privatization, 120, 121
Bailey, E., 51, 139
Balarin, M., 92, 94
Ball, S. J., 8, 9f, 19, 20, 21, 24, 25, 35, 45, 47, 49, 91, 97, 98, 137, 139, 140, 142, 145, 150, 151, 152, 156, 178, 190

Bandhyopadhyay, M., 93
Bangladesh, 96
Barber, M., 50, 50n15, 97–98, 100, 101, 151, 152, 156
Bardach, E., 27, 29
Barnett, M., 17
Barrera-Osorio, F., 9, 99
Bascia, N., 159, 160, 162, 163, 167, 171, 174
Baum, D. R., 95
Baumgartner, F. R., 16, 27
Baur, L., 149
Beers, B., 7, 46, 71, 76, 145, 166
Béland, D., 24, 25, 190
Belfield, C., 75, 76, 82, 85, 145, 153, 154, 172
Belgium; communautarization of education,
    111–112; historical origins of PPPs, 110–111;
    nonprofit schools, 112n8; percentages of
    enrollment by type of institution, 111f;
    political governance, 112n7; public-private
    partnerships, 104–105, 109–112, 116–118, 180,
    184; School Pact, 110–112; selection of policy
    changes, 189; teachers' unions, 160
Bellei, C., 8, 40, 43, 169, 170, 193
Bellirive, Jean-Max, 128
Benavot, A., 17
Bennett, C. J., 16n3
Bennett, David, 156
Berlin Wall, 56
Berman, 23
Bhanji, Z., 146, 149, 150
Bharti Foundation, 150
Bicameralism, 72
Bieber, T., 20
Bilateral aid agency, 96
Bill and Melinda Gates Foundation, 125n7,
    147–148, 149
Bishop, M., 102
Black Alliance for Educational Options (BAEO),
    79, 147–148
Blaine amendments, 76
Blair, Tony, 49, 50, 50n15, 51, 139, 152, 156
Blomqvist, P., 60
Bloomberg, Michael, 127, 148, 152
Blossing, U., 55
Blyth, M., 31
Boardman, A. E., 9
Board of Elementary and Secondary Education
    (BESE), 121, 121n2, 122, 123, 127, 143
Böhlmark, A., 59
Bold, T., 94
Boli, J., 18
Bolick, Clint, 73
Boltanski, 173
Bonal, X., 22, 96, 103, 104n1, 113, 114, 115, 165,
    173, 188, 191

Bouckaert, G., 22
Bourdieu, P., 20
Boyd, D. C., 71, 73, 74
Boyd, W. L., 25, 71, 73, 74, 75, 76, 85, 138, 140, 141,
    142, 154, 190
Brans, B. J., 100
Braun, H., 107
Bray, M., 96
Brazil, 145–146
Bridge International Academies (BIA), 97, 99
British Columbia, 160, 164
Broad Foundation, 125n7, 127, 147–148
Brogan, P., 173
Brown, Gordon, 50
Brown, H., 82–83, 145, 168
Brown v. Board of Education, 80
Budde, R., 81
Budgetary restrictions, 117
Buffett, Warren, 147
Bulkley, K. E., 74, 80, 81, 82n10, 83, 84, 138, 142,
    143, 145, 149, 184, 193
Buras, K. L., 119, 122, 124, 125, 125n6, 126, 127
Burch, P., 74, 145, 149
Bureaucracy, 22, 70, 78, 109
Bureaucratization, 64
Bush, George H. W., 71
Bush, George W., 74, 155
Business community/sector, 24, 37, 48, 138, 145, 150
Business Foundation for Educational Development
    (FEPADE), 129

Cabalin, C., 169, 170
Caddell, M., 95
Calero, J., 113, 114
Calvinists, 106–107, 117
Campbell, J. L., 23n6, 25, 31
Canada; consultancy, 151; irregular process of
    privatization, 69, 69n1, 183; low-fee private
    schools, 96; selection of policy changes, 190;
    teachers' unions, 159–160
Capitalism, 43, 50, 132
Carney, S., 25
Carnoy, M., 43, 45, 53, 71, 118
Carroll, W. K., 22
Carson, C., 22
Carter, B., 159, 162, 163, 166, 173, 185
Catalonia, Spain, 115–116, 165
Catastrophe, privatization by way of, 119–133;
    constant features, 119–121; El Salvador,
    postconflict, 128–131; Haiti after the
    earthquake, 127–128; Iraq, postwar, 131–132;
    natural disasters, 121–128; overview, 181;
    postconflict reform, 128–132; post-Hurricane
    Katrina, 121–128

Catastrophism, 188
Catchment areas, 107, 115, 118
Catholics, 106–107
Cave, T., 140, 141, 144–145, 147, 148, 152
Center for British Teachers (CfBT), 144
Center for Education Reform, 148
Center for Independent Studies, 139
Center for Policy Studies (CPS), 46, 139, 155–156
Cerny, P. G., 186
Chandler Corporation, 98
Charter Management Organizations (CMOs), 78, 124, 125, 147, 149
Charter schools; Colombia, 191; promotion in the U.S., 65–74, 179–180; enrollment in the U.S., 77f; legislation, 76f; malleability of a policy idea, 80–82; New Orleans, 121–126, 184; vouchers vs., 72–74, 83–86, 183, 191
Charter Schools Initiative (I-1240), 149
Cherry-picking, 139, 153, 154
Chicago Boys, 38, 40
Chicago School of Economics, 37
Chile; consultants, 151; education privatization, 37–45, 178, 181, 182; enrollment by school typology, 42f, 104n1; incentive pay, 161; media and privatization, 140, 171; neoliberal influence, 36–37; Pinochet dictatorship, 38–42; privatization expansion in the nineties, 42–45; students' movement, 169–170; retention, of policy changes, 191; selection of policy changes, 189; teachers' unions, 159-161, 171, 174; think tanks, 139
Choice in the United States; advocacy coalitions and new alliances, 77–78; background of reforms, 69; charter schools, 72–74, 80–82; charter schools vs. vouchers, 76–86; debate origins, 70–72; disadvantaged students, 79–80; legal ambiguity, 75–76; new civil rights groups, 79; scaling up privatization, 69–88, 179–180, 183; spatial diffusion, 82–83
Christian Democratic party; Belgium, 110, 111, 112; Chile, 43; Denmark, 63; The Netherlands, 109;
Chubb, John E., 71, 147n2
Church-run schools, 90
Cierniak, K., 85, 86, 127
City Technology College (CTC), 51, 139
Civil disobedience, 164
Civil rights; frame, 80; groups, 3, 16, 20, 79–80, 84, 115, 139, 145, 158, 171, 172–173; movement, 79–80, 148
Civil servants, 29, 41, 145, 151
Civil society organization (CSO), 6, 78, 92, 165, 170, 194
Clarke, J., 8
Clemet, Kristin, 63

Cleveland, Ohio, 74, 85
Clinton, Bill, 72, 73, 74, 128, 155
Codd, J., 171
Coercion, 26, 39
Colegio de Profesores, 44, 161, 171, 174
Colombia; uneven process of privatization, 69, 69n1, 183; retention of policy changes, 191
Colyvas, J. A., 28
Communautarization of Belgium education, 111–112
Compartmentalization. See Pillarization
Competition, 18, 28, 35–41, 46, 47, 48, 50, 51, 53, 60, 63, 65, 67, 71, 72, 73, 81, 86, 115, 116, 123, 140, 147, 151, 152, 177, 178, 181, 182, 189, 190
Compulsive Competitive Tendering (CCT), 47, 48
Confederación de Estudiantes de Chile (CONFECH), 170
Conflict; armed/violent, 128–132; political, 95
Confrontational model, 160
Connecticut, 143, 165, 166
Connell, R., 140, 162
Conservative Party, conservatives;; Denmark, 62, 168; Finland, 55; The Netherlands, 109; Nordic countries: 57, 58, 182; Norway; 63; Spain, 115; Sweden, 59, 62, 65; UK, 46–49, 155–156, 178
Constituency, 19, 20, 27, 29, 84, 87, 161, 174, 180
Consultants/consultancy/consultocracy, 96, 98, 128, 141, 142, 144, 150–151, 183, 190
Consumerism, 140, 191
Contracting out, 7, 9
Cook-Harvey, C., 121
Cooptation, 29, 30, 166
Corbalan Carrera, P., 139
Corbalan Pössel, F., 139
Corcoran, S. P., 79, 83
Cornwall, A., 193
Corporations; advocacy, 144–146; consultancy, 150–151; corporate social responsibility, 149–150; philanthropy, 146–150
Cost-sharing policy, 44, 44n10, 45, 54
Court cases; Brown v. Board of Education, 80; League of Women Voters, et al. v. State of Washington, 75n5; Pierce v. Society of Sisters, 75; Zelman v. Simmons-Harris, 75, 84
Cowen Institute for Public Education Initiatives, 127
Cox, C., 39, 40, 41, 44
Creative Associates International (CAI), 131
Crisis; financial, 21, 30, 57, 188; economic, 21, 37, 38, 40, 57, 111, 117, 187, 188; educational, 27, 46, 53, 71, 86; legitimacy, 57, 64, 67, 179, 182
Cristiani, Alfredo, 129
Crouch, C., 49
Crouch, L., 130
Cuéllar-Marchélli, H., 130
Cultural diversity. See Diversity

Cultural Political Economy (CPE), 177–195; approach, 26, 31, 187; *de facto* privatization, 180; different paths toward education privatization, 182*f*–184*f*; retention of policy changes, 190–193; selection of policy solutions, 188–190; trajectories of education privatization, 177–185; variation, policy moment, 75, 187–188
Cultural turn, 23, 23n5
Culture and low-fee private schools, 94–95
Curran, M., 115, 116, 165
Currie, 52

Dahal, M., 100
Dale, R., 18, 19, 20, 22, 26, 29, 36n3, 156
Darling-Hammond, L., 64, 121
Daschbach, J., 121, 143
Data collection form, 200, 201
Davidson-Harden, A., 69n1
DeBray-Pelot, E. H., 73, 74, 75, 78, 79, 80, 84, 85, 124, 125, 126, 126n8, 127, 138, 139, 140, 148n4, 149, 153, 155, 190
Decentralization; Belgium, 110; Chile, 40, 41, 42, 140, 151; El Salvador, 130; Finland, 64; Iraq, 131; The Netherlands, 107; New Orleans, 122; Norway, 63; Spain, 115, 173; Sweden, 59, 191; US, 70, 76, 180
Decision-makers, 16, 29, 31, 137, 139, 141, 156, 187
Decision-making chain, 61, 72
Delannoy, F., 39
Delavan, G., 119, 120, 121, 123, 127
Demand for education, 7, 97, 183
Democracy promotion, 131, 132
Democratic exceptionality, 181, 192
Democratic Party, Democrats (US): 72-74, 81, 82, 84, 179
Democrats for Education Reform, 127
Demonstrations, 115, 164–165, 169
de Moura, C., 38
Denmark; education privatization, 55, 62–63, 182; global neoliberal ideas, 56–57; new social democracy and welfare state modernization, 64, 65; party politics, 58; retention of new policies, 29; teachers' unions, 168
Department for International Development (DFID), 92, 93, 96–97, 101, 180
Department of Education (US), 74
De Rynck, S., 110–112, 111*f*, 112n7
Desegregation policies, 80
Deutsche Bank Foundation, 99
Development goals, 17, 20, 95, 97, 180, 192
Dezuere, K., 112
Dictatorship, 36, 37–45, 45n12, 53, 112-113, 117, 139, 158n1, 165, 169, 171, 191

Dijkstra, A. B., 107, 108, 108nn6
Disadvantaged families, 50, 71, 79–80, 102
Distinction. *See* Social distinction
Diversification, 56, 59, 60, 67, 109, 177, 179, 182, 189
Dixon, P., 92
Dobbin, F., 21, 23, 26
Dobbins, M., 19
Documentaries, 140
Domestic, local or internal drivers of change, 16, 16n2, 19, 30, 87, 187
Domestic forces, 6
Donor, 90, 100–102, 144, 146, 147, 149, 177
Drezner, D. W., 16
Drivers; external or global drivers, 15, 16, 17, 18, 19, 20, 30; ideational (soft) drivers, 15, 20–26, 30, 186; local or internal drivers, 16, 16n2, 19, 30, 87, 187; material (hard) drivers, 15, 20–26, 30
Dronkers, J., 107
Dual education system, 113–114
Duncan, Arne, 127
Dupriez, V., 110
Dutch. *See* Netherlands, the
Dutch Reformed (Church), 106, 117

Echo-chamber effect, 154–155, 190
Economy; CPE. *See* Cultural Political Economy (CPE); economic factors as driver of change, 21, 186
Ecuador, 159, 162
Edison Schools Inc., 81
Education Act (The Netherlands), 106–107
Educational crisis, 27, 46, 53, 71, 86
Education for All (EFA), 89, 90, 92, 95, 97, 98, 101, 102, 183, 188
Education-for-development field, 90, 92, 142, 149
Education ideology, 25
Education Industry Association, 145
Education-industry links, 9
Education International, 52
Education materials, 9
Education privatization; de facto privatization, 89–103, 180, 183; defined, 7–10; endogenous privatization, 8, 9*f*; exogenous privatization, 8, 9*f*; historical PPPs, 104–118, 180–181, 184; in Nordic social democratic welfare states, 55–68, 179, 182; new public management, 8; policies, 7–10; public-private partnerships, 8–9; scaling-up privatization, 69–88, 179–180, 183; as a state reform, 35–54, 178, 182; via disaster/catastrophe, 119–133, 181, 184
Education provision, 4, 55, 130, 144, 180
Education Reform Act (ERA), 46–48, 51, 155–156

Education saving accounts, 86n15, 180n3
Education Sector Reform Plan of Action
     (Pakistan), 101
Edupreneurs, 95, 98, 102, 180, 183
Edwards, Jr., D. B., 128, 129, 130, 131
Efficiency, 3, 36, 38, 40, 47, 50, 51, 53, 71, 73, 95,
     100, 177, 189

Egalitarianism, 66
Elazar, D. J., 83n12
Elinder, M., 28, 188
Elites, 22, 80, 115, 139, 189
El Salvador, 119, 120, 128–131, 181, 184, 188
Empathy Schools, 92
Endogenous privatization, 8, 9f, 115, 116, 195
England. See United Kingdom
EPPI-Centre, 10f
Erixson-Arreman, I. E., 59
Esping-Andersen, G., 22, 55
Espínola, V., 38
European Union (EU), 17, 57, 182
Evaluation of the education system, 41
Evidence; evidence-based policy/advocacy, 172,
     175, 192; selective use, 102, 154, 155, 189, 190
Exit (consumer response), 40n5, 94
Exley, S., 139, 151, 152, 155, 156, 160, 171
Exogenous privatization, 8, 9f, 63, 115, 195
Expansion of education, 100, 111, 113, 117, 169,
     170, 180, 184
Expenditure on education, 11, 4, 5f, 173
Expert knowledge, 30, 175
External or global drivers of change, 15, 16, 17, 18,
     19, 20, 30

Fairbrother, P., 163
Faith-based institutions, 104–109, 117, 118, 180,
     184, 189
Falabella, A., 43, 45, 194
Families; African-American, 126; disadvantaged,
     50, 71, 79–80, 102; family associations, 3; low-
     income, 90, 92–96, 100, 180; middle-class, 71,
     96, 108; minority, 71, 79
Farah, I., 101
Federalism, 72, 72n2
Feldt, Kjell-Olof, 65
Fennell, S., 92, 93, 190
Ferrare, J. J., 147, 149
Financial crisis, 21, 30, 188
Finger, L., 159, 162, 171, 172
Finland; global neoliberal ideas, 56–57; new social
     democracy and welfare state modernization,
     66; path toward privatization, 55, 64, 66, 179,
     182; teachers' unions, 160
Finnemore, M., 17

First Amendment (US), 75–76
Fitz, J., 7, 36, 46, 47, 48, 49, 50, 51, 52, 71, 76, 145,
     152, 166
Flavin, P., 165, 172
Flórez, A., 130
For profit providers/operators, 56, 59, 61, 81, 90n2,
     107, 143, 169
Forrester, G., 8
Foundations, 3, 24, 80, 124, 127, 139, 146, 150,
     153, 155, 184, 190; Azim Premji Foundation,
     149; Bharti Foundation, 150; Bill and Melinda
     Gates Foundation, 125n7, 147–148, 149;
     Broad Foundation, 125n7, 127, 148; Business
     Foundation for Educational Development,
     129; Deutsche Bank Foundation, 99; Friedman
     Foundation for Educational Choice, 86n15;
     Heritage Foundation, 123, 138, 148, 155;
     Innovation Development Progress Foundation,
     98; Lynde and Harry Bradley Foundation,
     147n2; Orient Global Foundation, 98; Qatar
     Foundation, 98; Salvadoran Foundation for
     Economic and Social Development, 129; W. K.
     Kellogg Foundation, 99
Fourcade-Gourinchas, M., 36, 37, 39, 46, 53, 139
Fragmented centralization, 47, 48
Framing, 25, 30, 77, 138, 156, 165, 168
Franco, Francisco, 104, 113, 158n1, 165
Fraser, P., 170
Freedom of instruction/teaching, 109–110, 113, 184
Freedom of school choice, 70, 71, 72, 86, 107, 108,
     109, 123, 182, 183, 184. See also Choice in the
     United States
Free market, 35, 38, 56, 61, 75, 80, 91, 131
Free Schools, 48, 59, 66, 68
Free Schools Act (Norway), 63
Frente Farabundo Martí para la Liberación Nacional
     (FMLN), 129
Friedman, Milton; Capitalism and Freedom, 36n1;
     influence in privatization in Chile and the
     United Kingdom, 35; privatization by way of
     catastrophe, 123; scaling up privatization, 70,
     71, 82, 86
Friedman Foundation for Educational Choice, 86n15
Fulge, T., 20
Fundación Burke, 114n11
Fundación Empresarial para el Desarrollo Educativo,
     129n12
Fundación Europea Educación y Libertad
     (FUNDEL), 114n11
Fundación para el Análisis y Estudios Sociales
     (FAES), 114n11
Fundación Salvadoreña para el Dessarrollo
     Económico y Social, 129n11
Fusarelli, L. D., 145

Gaebler, T., 73, 73n3
Garrett, G., 21
Gates, Bill, 147–148
Gauri, V., 39, 42, 43
General Agreement on Trade in Services
        (GATS), 9n3
Georgia, 142
Gewirtz, S., 8
Ghana, 89, 90, 92, 98, 183
Giddens, A., 50, 189
Giles, C., 158
Gillard, D., 52
Gillies, J., 130
Gindin, J., 159, 162, 171, 172
Global Business Coalition for Education (GBCE), 146
Global Campaign of Education (GCE), 194n8
Global or external drivers of change, 15, 16, 17, 18,
        19, 20, 30
Global education agenda, 6, 178
Global Education and Skills Conference, 98, 98n11
Global Education Inc., 98
Global education policy field, 20
Global forces, 185
Global governance, 12
Global-local divide, 16–20
Globally Structured Education Agenda (GSEA), 18
Goldblatt, D., 19
Goldie, D., 153, 154
Gough, D., 10, 10*f*
Gove, Michael, 152
Governmental allies, 167–168
Government-dependent private institution, 104n2
Govinda, R., 93
Grant-maintained schools, 47, 48, 51
Grassroots privatization, 95
Gray Ghost Ventures, 99
Great Britain. *See* United Kingdom
Green, M., 102
Grek, S., 20, 25
Greve, B., 67
Greve, C., 9
Griera, M., 114
Guáqueta, J., 9, 99
Guatemala, 131
Gunter, H. M., 8, 25, 51, 151

Haas, P., 24
Hafid, T., 36, 46, 47, 48, 49, 50, 51, 52, 145, 152
Haiti; low-fee private schools, 96; privatization by
        way of earthquake, 119, 120, 127–128, 143,
        181, 184, 188
Haláz, G., 107
Hall, P. A., 22, 25, 26, 28
Hard drivers of change, 15, 20-26, 30

Härmä, J., 89, 93, 94, 95, 152
Harris, D. N., 71, 79, 80
Hart, Gary, 80n8
Hartney, M., 165, 172
Harvard University, 144
Harvey, D., 36, 40, 119, 186
Hatcher, R., 50, 51, 52, 152, 172
Hay, C., 21n4, 23, 25, 26, 27, 31, 188
Hayek, Friedrich, 36n3
Heise, M., 70, 71, 84, 85
Held, D., 6, 19
Henig, J. R., 82–83, 145, 153, 168
Heritage Foundation, 123, 138, 148, 155
Herod, A., 194
Herrington, C. D., 71
Heterarchies, 24
Heyneman, S. P., 94
Higgins, S., 15n1
Higher education, 10, 44, 170
High-income countries, 4
Hirschmann, A. O., 40, 40n5
Hispanic Council for Reform and Educational
        Options (HCREO), 79, 148
Historical institutionalist studies, 19
Hodge, G. A., 9, 150
Hogan, A., 152
Hojman, D. E., 38
Holm, A. S., 59
Holyoke, T. T., 82–83, 145, 168
Holzinger, K., 21n4
Honduras, 131
Hong-Kong and Shangai Banking Corporation
        (HSBC), 98
Horne, 24
Human right, education as, 3
Hurricane Katrina, 119, 120, 121–127, 143, 147, 188

Ideal types, 12, 181, 181n4
Ideas, the role of, 23-26
Ideational (soft) drivers of change, 15, 20–26, 30
Ideological road to neoliberalism, 37, 53
IFC Private Education Conference, 96, 96n6,
        96n7, 98
Immergut, E. M., 22
Imposition, 17, 26, 88
Improving the Quality and Equity of Education
        (MECE), 44, 44n9
Imsen, G., 55, 56, 57, 63, 66
Incentives; private providers, 41; schemes/pay for
        teachers, 8, 45, 159, 160, 161; school choice,
        78, 81
Incentives to private school consumption, 7, 9, 178
Income level (countries) and enrollment in private
        institutions, 4, 4*f*

Incremental change, 27n8
Independent schools, 65
India; advocacy for school choice and private
    education, 145, 149–150; low-fee private
    schools, 89, 90, 91, 92, 94, 98, 100, 140, 143;
    School Choice Campaign, 24
Individualization, 56, 68
Individual tax-credit programs, 86n15
Industrial action, 163, 164–165, 171, 192
Industrial Credit and Investment Corporation of
    India (ICICI) Bank, 149
Inequalities, 5-6, 41, 44, 45, 54, 65, 108, 113, 149,
    169, 170, 177n2
Inflation, 37
Innova Schools, 99
Innovation, 50, 81, 97, 109, 152

Innovation Development Progress (IDP)
    Foundation, 98
Inquiry into privatization processes, 3–7
Institución Futuro, 114n11
Institute of Economic Affairs (IEA), 46, 139
Institutional; architecture, 87; arrangements, 189;
    constraints, 18, 20–21; factors, 61, 70, 132, 187,
    191; frameworks, 101; structure, 22
Institutionalist theory, 19, 21, 72, 189
Institutionalization, 28–29, 104, 113
Inter-American Development Bank (IADB), 128,
    143, 146
Interest groups, 3, 20, 24n7, 83, 115, 117, 171,
    172–173, 175, 184, 190
Intermediary organization, 139–140
Internal or local drivers of change, 15, 16-20, 30
International aid community, 44, 95
International and Private Schools Education
    Forum, 98
International community, 18, 22, 90, 95, 102
International events, 91, 98
International Finance Corporation (IFC), 96, 96n6,
    96n7, 98, 99, 144, 180
International organization (IO), 3, 11, 16, 17, 20,
    26, 57, 95, 98, 102, 120, 128, 130, 133, 141, 142,
    144, 153, 156, 175, 177, 182, 194
Iraq, 120, 131–132, 184, 188
Ireland, 160
Iron triangle, 24, 24n7
Irreversibility, 118, 120, 121
Isomorphism, 83
Israel, 160

Jabbar, H., 125, 139, 146, 147, 148, 153, 155
James, E., 105, 106, 107, 108f
Jenkins-Smith, H., 77
Jessop, B., 24, 26, 27, 28, 29, 31, 186, 187

Jimenez, E., 131
Johnson, B., 145
Johnston, J. B., 168
Jones, B. D., 16, 27
Jones, K., 172
Jones, Kira Orange, 127
Jonsson, S., 28
Jordahl, J., 28, 188
Joseph, Keith, 155
Journalists, 24, 146
Judicial challenge, judicialization, 75, 164, 183
Junemann, C., 97, 98, 99, 150, 151, 190
Jungbluth, P., 108n6

Kalimullah, N. A., 8
Kalyvas, 110
Karsten, S., 104n3, 106, 107, 108n6, 109
Keck, M. E., 20, 24
Kenny, L. W., 85
Kenya, 89, 90, 97, 99, 183
Keynesianism, 40, 50, 65, 189
Kingdon, G., 93
Kingdon, J. W., 16, 141
Kirst, M. C., 76, 78, 81, 83, 84, 80n8, 138, 142, 154
Kitaev, I., 90
Kivirauma, J., 56
Kjaer, P., 23, 29, 31, 58
Klees, S. J., 36, 130
Klein, Joel, 148
Klein, N., 132, 181
Klitgaard, M. B., 22, 57, 58, 60, 61, 65, 67, 71, 72,
    72n2, 75, 78, 85, 163–164, 191, 192
Knill, C., 16, 21, 21n4
Knowledge economy, 18
Knowledge Is Power Program (KIPP),
    147–148, 149
Knowledge production, 138, 139, 148, 153, 175,
    176, 192
Kolderie, Ted, 81, 142
Komljenovic, J., 186n5
Korten, D. C., 21
Krawczyk, N. R., 146
Kvist, J., 67

Labaree, D. F., 186
Labour Party (UK): 49-52, 54. *See also* New Labour
Lacireno-Paquet, N., 82–83, 145, 168
Larsson, B., 56
Latin America, 38, 39; low-fee private schools, 89;
    teachers' unions, 171, 172
Latin American Network of Civil Society
    Organizations for Education (REDUCA), 146
Law on Education Quality Improvement
    (LOMCE), 116

League of Women Voters, et al. v. State of Washington, 75n5
LEAP Science and Maths Schools, 99
Learning outcomes, 93, 94, 95, 102, 147
Leftwich, A., 6
Legatum Global Development, 98
Legitimation, 18, 22, 54, 120, 133
Leigh, Gustavo, 39–40
Lejano, R. R., 189
Lenschow, A., 21
Letell, M., 56
Leuze, K., 17
Levin, H. M., 75, 76, 82, 85, 121, 122, 122nn4, 123*f*, 124, 125, 126, 143, 145, 153, 154, 172, 193
Levine, R., 79n7
Lewin, K. M., 89
Ley Orgánica Constitucional de Enseñanza (LOCE), 41, 42, 42n7
Ley Orgánica del Derecho a la Educación (LODE), 114
Ley Orgánica del Estatuto de Centros Escolares (LOECE), 113–114
Ley Orgánica para la Mejora de la Calidad Educativa (LOMCE), 116, 116n13
LFPS. *See* Low-fee private schools (LFPSs)
Liberal conservatism, 36n2. *See also* Neoliberalism
Liberal democracies, 16, 53, 131
Liberalization of the education sector, 7, 9*f*, 59, 60, 105, 182
Liberal Party; Denmark, 63; The Netherlands, 106
Libertad y Desarrollo (LyD), 139
Liefferink, D., 21
Lindahl, M., 59
Lindbom, 61
Lingard, B., 18, 19, 20, 152
Linguistic minorities. *See* Minority groups
Linick, M., 153
Lobby groups, 16, 20, 145
Lobbying (activity), 144, 145, 147, 167, 172
Local, domestic or internal drivers of change, 15, 16–20, 30
Local Education Authorities (LEAs), 47–48, 51
Lock-in effect, 29
Longfield, D., 92
Louisiana. *See* New Orleans, Louisiana
Low-fee private schools (LFPSs), 89–103; affordability, 93–94; chains, 99; criteria for choosing, 94–95; defined, 89; global promotion of, 95–101; growing demand for, 90–95; growth of, 89–90; media for promotion of, 140; overview, 180; public-private partnerships, 99–101
Low-income countries, 4, 89–103, 142, 154, 180, 183, 190

Lubienski, C., 7, 28, 71, 73, 86, 125, 138, 139, 140, 149, 153, 154, 186, 190
Lubienski, S. T., 71, 153
Luengo, J. J., 116
Lundahl, L., 57, 58, 59, 65, 67
Lundström, U., 59
Lupton, R., 45, 47, 50, 51
Lynde and Harry Bradley Foundation, 147n2

Madrid, Spain, 115
Magnet school, 79, 79n7
Majhanovich, S., 69n1
Malawi, 89
Malik, R., 93, 190
Managerialism, 8, 57, 66, 156, 165
Maranto, R., 143
Marginson, S., 8
Market maker, 190
Market oriented reforms/policies, 48, 53, 69, 137, 149, 152, 158, 160, 168, 181
Maroy, C., 8, 110, 159, 166, 172, 173, 174
Marshall, C., 16
Martens, K., 17, 20
Martins, E. M., 145, 146
Martinsson, J., 177
Material (hard) drivers of change, 15, 20–26, 30
Maurer, M., 19
McGrew, A., 19
McKinsey, 150, 152, 156
McLaughlin, E., 8
McLennan, G., 193
McNulty, B., 128, 143
Media, 29, 51, 79, 123, 139, 148, 154, 157; promoting educational privatization, 140–141; students' movement, 169-170; teachers' unions, 171, 173
Mediås, O. A., 55
Mehrotra, S., 93, 94
Mejoramiento de la Calidad y Equidad de la Educación (MECE), 44, 44n9
Menashy, F., 96, 101, 190n6
Merit-based pay. *See* Incentives
Merrill Lynch Bank of America, 186n5
Mexico, 159
Meyer, H. D., 17
Meyer, J. W., 18
Mezzacappa, 141
Michigan, 81, 80n8, 142
Microsoft, 146
Middle-class families, 71, 96, 108
Middle-income countries, 4
Millennium Development Goals (MDGs), 95, 101, 183
Miller, P., 95

Mills, C., 151
Milwaukee, 80, 85
Miñana, C., 69n1
Minnesota, 73, 76, 142
Minority; disadvantage groups, 79, 80; ethnic, 3;
    families, 71, 79
Mintrom, M., 24, 141, 142
Mitchell, D. E., 16
Mizala, A., 44, 45, 161, 170, 172, 174
Modernization of the public sector, 49
Modernization of the welfare state, 64–66
Moe, T. M., 71, 84, 85, 147n2, 172
Møller, J., 57, 63, 191
Monetarism, 36n2, 37n4
Mooney, G., 49, 50
Moos, L., 55
Moschetti, M., 193
Mugabe, Robert, 152
Multi-scalar, 6, 18–20, 87, 187
Mundy, K., 96, 190n6
Municipalization, 36, 41, 43–44, 59, 64, 66, 129.
    See also Decentralization

Nadler, D. A., 27n8
Nambissan, G. B., 24, 140, 142, 145, 150, 190
Narodowski, M., 171, 193
Nathan, Joe, 81, 142
National Alliance for Public Charter Schools, 147–148
National Center on Education and the Economy
    (NCEE), 112n8
National Conference of State Legislatures, 76f
National Education Association (NEA), 168
Natural disaster, 121–128, 188
Negotiation model, 160
Neoliberalism; doctrine, 36; history of, 36; influence
    in education (UK and Chile), 36–37, 53;
    material-ideational divide, 25; New Orleans,
    Louisiana, 126–127; Nordic countries, 56–57,
    68; public-private partnerships, 104, 109,
    114, 168, 180
Nepal, 131
Netherlands, the; education system features, 107;
    enrollment percentages by type of institution,
    108f; historical public-private partnerships,
    104–109, 104n3, 116–118, 180, 184; recent
    trends in privatization, 109
Networks, transnational advocacy networks
    (TANs), 24, 149–150
New Labour, 49–52, 54, 139, 151, 152, 160
New Leaders for New Schools, 147–148
New Orleans, Louisiana; privatization by way of
    natural disasters, 119, 120, 126–127, 181, 184;
    school management evolution, 123f; voucher
    schemes, 85

New public management (NPM), 8, 57, 63, 66, 81,
    115, 156, 159, 193
NewSchools Venture Fund, 125n7
New Teachers for New Schools, 124
New Zealand; private actors in promotion of
    privatization, 156; state reform, 178, 182;
    teachers' unions, 171
Nguyen, Q., 100
Niemerg, M., 96, 97
Nigeria, 89, 90, 91, 97, 99, 183
900 Schools Program, 44, 44n8
No Child Left Behind Act (NCLB); and post-
    Katrina New Orleans, 120n1, 126; and
    privatization advocates, 155; scaling-up
    privatization, 74, 76, 83
Nongovernment organization (NGO);
    accountability of private education, 177; low-
    fee private schools, 90; post-Katrina New
    Orleans, 124; schools for the poor, 150
Nordic countries, education privatization in,
    55–68, 179, 182; Denmark. See Denmark;
    Finland. See Finland; global neoliberal ideas,
    56–57; Norway. See Norway; party politics,
    58; political stability and policy continuity,
    57–58; social democracy and welfare state
    modernization, 64–66; social democratic
    model of the welfare state, 55–56; Sweden. See
    Sweden
Norway; education privatization, 55-56, 63, 66, 182;
    global neoliberal ideas, 56–57; Municipal Act,
    63; new social democracy and welfare state
    modernization, 66; party politics, 58; retention
    of policy changes, 191; teachers' unions, 160
Nova Scotia, 159–160, 165, 168
Novelli, M., 15n1
Nusche, D., 107

Obama, Barack, 74
Offe, C., 22
Office of Innovation and Improvement, 74
O'Keefe, J. E., 128, 143
Oliver, S., 10, 10f
Olmedo, A., 24, 25, 113, 114, 114n11, 115, 140,
    171, 190
Omega Schools, 92, 99, 103
Omidyar Network, 99
Oppenheimer, A., 145–146
Opportunity International, 98
Opportunity scholarships, 192
Opposition to privatization. See Resistance to
    privatization
Orellana, V., 8, 193
Organisation for Economic Co-operation and
    Development (OECD); Chile, 104n1;

global-local divide, 17; government-dependent private institution, defined, 104n2; historical PPPs, 104, 109; Nordic path toward privatization, 57, 64; paths toward education privatization, 182f–184f; private expenditure of education institutions, 4, 5f
Orient Global Education Fund, 98
Orient Global Foundation, 98
Orleans Parish School Board (OPSB), 122, 123, 125
Osborne, D., 73
Osmond, P., 159, 160, 162, 171, 174
Outcomes-based incentives, 8. *See also* Incentives

Pakistan, 89, 96, 97, 100, 101, 183
Panchamukhi, P. R., 93, 94
Parapolitical sphere, 24, 190
Paredes, R., 40
Parental associations, 59
Parent-teachers' associations. *See* Parental associations
Partnerships. *See* Public-private partnership (PPP)
Passy, R., 162, 185
Pastorek, Paul, 127, 143
Pater, C., 5
Path-dependence, 21, 164, 179
Paths toward privatization; different paths toward education privatization, 11, 12, 178, 181, 182f–184f; historical public-private partnerships, 104–118, 180–181; low-fee private schools, 89–103, 180; Nordic countries, 55–68, 179; scaling up privatization, 69–88, 179–180; state reform, 35–54, 178–179; by way of catastrophe, 119–133, 181
Patrinos, H. A., 9, 99, 100, 106, 107
Pavez, Jorge, 174
Pay-for-performance schemes, 9, 45, 146, 153, 167. *See also* incentives
Pearson, PLC, 89, 92, 97, 98, 99, 141, 146, 152, 180
Pearson Affordable Learning Fund (PALF), 92, 97
Peck, J., 19
Pedersen, O. K., 23, 29, 31, 58
Pedroni, T. C., 3, 70, 79, 80, 149, 193
Penguin Revolution, 169–170
Per capita funding, 35, 41, 48, 182
Performance-based incentives. *See* Incentives
Performance-related pay, 9f, 45, 146. *See also* incentives
Per pupil funding, 130. *See also* Per capita funding
Perraton, J., 19
Perry, A., 121, 143
Peru; low-fee private schools, 89, 183; teachers' unions, 159, 162
Petrilli, Michael, 155
Petticrew, M., 10f

Philanthropy, philanthropic organizations, 24 78, 102, 139, 177, 183; New Orleans, 124, 125, 127, 181, 184; promoting privatization, 144, 146-150
Phillips, K. D., 18
Phillipson, B., 89
Pierce v. Society of Sisters, 75
Pillarization, 106, 106n4, 109
Pinochet, Augusto; dictatorship of Chile, 37–42; neoliberalism, 36–37
Pinto, L. E., 150, 151
Policy; global policy, 18, 20, 23, 24, 192; networks, 17, 24, 138, 141, 155; paradigm, 25; policy scape, 25; sociology studies, 18–19; subsystem, 24
Policy change; endoprivatization, 178; exoprivatization, 178; external or global drivers. *See* external drivers; ideational (soft) drivers. *See* drivers; internal, domestic or local drivers. *See* drivers; material (hard) drivers. *See* drivers; structuring mechanisms, 27–29, 30; theories, 18–19
Policy convergence; causal drivers, 17; defined, 16n3
Policy entrepreneurs, 24, 28, 91, 95, 98, 101, 141–144, 148, 150, 152, 153, 155, 181, 183, 190
Policy Exchange, 139
Policy scape, 25
Policy mechanisms, 17, 27–29, 30, 31, 132, 187–193
Political economy, 15–32; advantages of use, 6; cultural political economy, 26, 30, 31–32, 177-195
Political imaginaries, 25, 30
Political/institutional/policy stability, 29, 57, 58, 78
Political parties; Christian Democratic party (The Netherlands, Belgium, Chile). *See* Christian Democratic party; Conservative party (UK, Sweden, Norway, Spain, Denmark). *See* Conservative Party, Conservatives; Democratic Party (U.S.). *See* Democratic Party, Democrats; Labour Party (U.K.). *See* Labour Party; Liberal Party (Denmark, The Netherlands). *See* Liberal Party; Republican Party (U.S.). *See* Republican Party, Republicans; right-wing parties, 45, 62, 67, 113; Social Democratic Party (Denmark, Finland, Norway, Spain, Sweden). *See* Social Democratic Party, Social Democrats
Political viability, 77, 83, 87
Politicization of research, 151–155
Politics; charter schools in the U.S., 72–74; charter schools vs. vouchers, 83–86; CPE. *See* Cultural Political Economy (CPE); as driver of policy change, 22–23; party politics in the Nordic region, 57–66
Pollitt, C., 22

Pollock, A. M., 50
Poole, W. L., 49, 50, 159–160, 164, 165, 166, 168, 173–174
Poor families, 90, 92–96, 100, 180. *See also* Families
Poppema, M., 130
Positional good, education as a, 186, 193
Poverty, 126
Power, S., 8
PPP. *See* Public-private partnership (PPP)
Pragmatic transition, 37
Pratham, 149
Presidentialism, 72
Prieto, M., 115
Private Finance Initiative (PFI), 51–52
Private foundations. *See* Foundations
Private institutions; enrollment according to countries level of income, 4, 4*f*; enrollment according to world regions, 4, 5*f*; private expenditure on education institutions, 4, 5*f*
Private schools, defined, 4n1
Private Sector Education Group (PSEG), 145
Priyadarshini, S., 181n4
Programa de Educación con Participación de la Comunidad (EDUCO), 128-131, 129n10
Program for International Student Assessment (PISA); global-local divide, 17; Nordic path toward privatization, 57, 64, 179, 182; test scores, 120n1; variation of policy changes, 188
Public good, education as a, 3, 115, 158, 191
Public opinion, 16, 30, 25, 57, 70, 132, 140, 147, 156, 190
Public-private partnership (PPP); Belgium, 104–105, 109–112, 116–118; contracts, 8–9; historical PPPs, 104–118, 180-181, 184; from low-fee private schools to, 99–101, 103, 180, 183; The Netherlands, 104–109, 116–118; Spain, 104–105, 112–118; Third Way, 50
Public relations campaigns, 147, 163, 165
Public sentiments, 25, 30
Public services, state's role in delivery of, 178–179
Public subsidies to private schools, 9*f*, 45, 63, 109
Punctuated equilibrium, 26, 59
Punjab, Pakistan, 97, 100, 101

Qatar Foundation, 98
Quality education, 70, 90–92, 102, 116, 146, 159
Quasi-market, 39, 107, 114, 117, 140, 154, 182, 187
Quebec, Canada, 159, 174
Quiggin, J., 21

Race to the bottom, 21, 30
Race to the Top, 74, 76, 125
Racial achievement gap, 148–149
Radaelli, C. M., 24

Ramirez, F. O., 18
Rangvid, B. S., 62
Rankings (school rankings), 9*f*, 45, 115
Ravitch, D., 148
Rawolle, S., 20
Reagan, Ronald, 58, 70, 71, 72
Reaganomics, 71
Reconstruction, 119–123, 128, 131, 132, 133, 181, 184
Recontextualization, 6, 19, 20, 66, 195
Recovery Schools District (RSD), 121–127, 143
Redefinition of the normalcy, 121, 127
Red Latinoamericana de Organizaciones de la Sociedad Civil por la Educación (REDUCA), 146, 146n1
Rees, Nina Shokraii, 155
Reform trajectories, 5, 14
Reframing. *See* Framing
Regulatory competition, 17
Reid, A., 153
Religion; Belgium, 109–111; historical public-private partnerships, 104, 105, 116 -118; low-fee private schools and, 94–95; minorities. *See* Minority groups; the Netherlands, 105–109; Spain, 112–114
Renzulli, L. A., 71, 79, 81, 82, 83, 84
Repression, 29, 39, 53, 181
Republican Party, Republicans (US): 72-74, 80, 82, 84, 87, 132, 183
Research, politicization of, 151–155
Research gaps, 185
Research production and management, 165–166, 175
Research products identified/selected per source, 197-199
Resistance to privatization, 158–176; conditions of influence for unions, 167–175; unions' models of engagement, 158–162; union strategies, 162–167, 192
Retention of policy changes, 27, 28–29, 187, 190–193
Revolving doors mechanism, 155–156
Rich, A., 138, 139, 148n4, 153
Riep, C. B., 93, 98, 99, 152
Right-wing parties, 45, 62, 67, 113
Rinne, R., 56, 57, 58, 64, 66
Risse, T., 24
Rizing Schools Program, 98
Rizvi, F., 18, 19
Rizvi, S., 101
Roberts, H., 10*f*
Robertson, S. L., 8, 18, 22, 25–26, 144, 147, 150, 154, 155, 186n5
Rolleston, C., 93, 94
Roscigno, V. J., 71, 79, 81, 82, 83, 84
Rose, P., 93, 94
Rotherham, Andy, 155

Rothstein, 65
Rowell, A., 140, 141, 144–145, 147, 148, 152
Ruddy, A., 85, 127
Rural areas, 94, 130
Rusconi, A., 17
Ryan, J. E., 71

Sabatier, P. A., 16, 24, 77
Salinas, D., 170
Saltman, K. J., 119, 120, 120n1, 121, 123, 126, 127, 131, 131n14, 132, 188
Salvadoran Foundation for Economic and Social Development (FUSADES), 129
Santa Cruz, E., 114, 140, 171, 190
Santiago, P., 107
Santori, D., 97, 98, 150, 151, 190
Sarangapani, P. M., 94
Saura, G., 115, 116
Sawada, Y., 131
Sayer, A., 15
Scaling up privatization, 69–88, 179–180, 183
Scandinavian. *See* Nordic countries
Schagen, I., 92
Schmidt, V. A., 24
Schneider, B. R., 161, 170, 172, 174
Scholastic Assessment Test, 83
School; autonomy, 47–48, 63–64, 66, 74, 107, 109, 116, 192; choice. *See* Choice in the United States; facilities, 9, 52; fees, 4, 44, 46, 66, 93, 94, 114, 130; leadership, 63, 66, 116; suburban, 84
School-based management, 8, 9f, 130, 165, 184, 195
School-in-a-box model, 99
School Pact (Belgium), 109–112
School Performance Score (SPS), 122n3
Schools' social composition, 93, 94, 186
School Standards and Frameworks Act (UK), 51
Schriewer, J., 25
Schumpeterian Workfare State, 186
Scott, J., 73, 125, 138, 139, 146, 147, 148, 149, 155, 190
Secularization, 108n5, 118
Segregation; racial, 80, 124, 126; religious, 105, in schools, 65–66, 103, 125
Selection of policy changes, 27, 28, 187, 188–190
Selective practices, 125
Self-referentiality, 154–155
Sellar, S., 152
Semiosis, 15, 21, 25–26, 27, 31, 133
Sergiovanni, T. J., 16
Shankar, S., 189
Shanker, A., 81
Sheikh, S. A., 90
Shen, F. X., 73
Sikkink, K., 20, 24
Simmons, B., 21

Simola, H., 56
Sinapi Aba Trust, 98
Sistema de Medición de la Calidad de la Educación (SIMCE), 45, 45n11
Sistema Nacional de Evaluación del Desempeño (SNED), 45n13
Skedsmo, G., 57, 63, 191
Slum areas, 94
Small-scale reform/policies, 86, 87, 183
Smash-and-grab privatization, 120, 131
Social democracy welfare states. *See* Nordic Countries
Social Democratic Party, Social Democrats; Denmark, 62–63; Finland, 66; Norway, 63; Spain, 117, 114, 165; Sweden, 58–62, 65; welfare state model, 55–68, 182
Social distinction, 95, 102, 193
Socialists, Denmark, 63
Social Liberal Party (Denmark), 63
Social movement, 78, 158, 165, 172
Social segmentation. *See* Pillarization
Soft drivers of change, 15, 20–26, 30
Solhaug, T., 57, 58, 65
South Asia, 89, 102
Southern countries, 3, 89, 103, 185, 194
Spain; Andalusia, 115, 116; Catalonia, 115, 165; historical origins of PPPs, 112–114; interest groups, 115; Madrid, 115; Pedagogic Renovation Movements Federation, 158n1; public-private partnerships, 104–105, 112–118, 180, 184; selection of policy changes, 189, 190; teachers' unions, 164–165; recent trends in privatization, 114–116, 173
Spatial diffusion, 82–83
Specialist Schools Program, 51, 171
Srivastava, P., 89, 89n1, 91, 92, 93, 98, 99, 100, 102, 103, 149, 152, 188, 193
Stambach, A., 18
Standardization, 45, 99, 103, 132, 147
Standardized assessments/evaluation/testing, 9, 20, 27, 63, 64, 74, 93, 116
State reform in education privatization, 35–54, 178–178, 182; background, 35–36; Chile, 35–45; neoliberal influence in education, 36–37; United Kingdom, 45–52
Steel, L., 79n7
Steiner-Khamsi, G., 20, 23, 25, 28, 150, 186
Stern, J. M. B., 94
Stevenson, H., 159, 162, 185
Stewart, M., 85, 127
Stoddard, C., 79, 83
Stone, D., 26
Strange bedfellows, 3, 80, 193
Strategic alliances, 165

Strike; framing strategies and, 168; industrial action, 164–165; negotiations, 162; public image and, 171; right to, 160, 164; teacher evaluations, 159
Strom, 150
Structural Adjustment Programs (SAPs), 144
Students' association/movements/organizations, 158, 169–170
Sub-Saharan Africa, 4, 89, 94, 96, 102, 144
Suburban schools, 84
Suleiman, E. N., 23
Sweden; education privatization, 55, 67, 179, 182; global neoliberal ideas, 56–57; new social democracy and welfare state modernization, 64, 65–66; party politics, 58–62, 58n2; retention of policy changes, 191; selection of policy changes, 189; teachers' unions, 160, 163–164; voucher scheme, 56
Systematic literature review (SLR), 6–7, 10–12, 10f, 178, 181, 185

Takayama, K., 19
Targeted vouchers, 46, 84, 85, 87
Tax-credit scholarship programs, 86n15
Taylor, R. C. R., 22
Taylor, S., 20
Teacher-pupil ratio, 93
Teachers; evaluation, 8, 159–161; labor conditions and rights, 3, 41, 92, 110, 160, 161, 163, 164, 165, 166, 167; labor deregulation, 41; organizations, 84, 158, 164, 171. See also Teachers' union; professional status, 163; recruitment, 126, 143; salaries, 45, 113, 158, 161; training, 92, 113, 131, 178
Teachers' unions (TUs); accountability of private education, 177; Chile, 40–41, 42, 44, 140, 161, 171, 174; conditions of influence, 167–175; industrial action. See Strike; legitimacy, 156, 167–171; membership, 126, 166, 167, 168; models of engagement with the government, 158–162; public relations campaigns, 165; research production, 165–166; resisting privatization, 158–176, 192; strategies and repertoires of action, 162–167
Teach for America (TFA), 99, 124, 126, 147–148
TeachNOLA, 124, 126
Telhaug, A. O., 55
Termes, A., 191
Terzian, S. G., 71, 73, 74
Thatcher, Margaret; Center for Policy Studies, 155; influence on Nordic conservatives, 58; state reform, 35, 45–49, 53; think tanks, 46, 139
Thatcherism, 36, 36n3, 45–52, 53
Theodore, N., 19

Think tanks; Chile, 139; conservative, 3, 123, 138–139; intermediary organization, 139–140; promoting privatization, 138-140, 138; Think Tank Review Project, 154; Third Way. See Third Way; United Kingdom, 46, 139, 151, 155–156; United States, 74, 78, 138–139
Third Way; bridging the ideological divide, 189; consultants, 151; Nordic path toward privatization, 62; retention of policy changes, 193; state reform, 49, 50; think tanks, 139
Thomas, G. M., 18
Thomas, J., 10, 10f
Thörn, H., 56
Todos Pela Educação (TPE), 145–146
Tooley, James, 89, 90, 93, 95, 99; low-fee private schools, 90–92, 97, 98; private actors in promotion of privatization, 140, 142, 150, 152
Trade agreements, 9, 17
Trade unions, accountability of private education, 177. See also Teachers' unions (TUs)
Transnational advocacy network (TAN), 24, 149–150
Transnational corporations, 95, 149, 183
Trends in International Mathematics and Science Study (TIMSS), 57
Tuin, 159
Tuition tax credits, 84
Tushman, M., 27n8
2020 Education Sector Strategy, 96

Uganda, 99, 100, 131
Ugarte, G., 40
Ugur, M., 15n1
Uncommon Schools, 149
UNESCO, 4f, 5f, 6, 129, 131
UNESCO Institute of Statistics, 4f, 5f
UNICEF, 129
United Kingdom; academization, 163; conservative reform, 46–48; consultants, 151; Department for International Development (DFID). See Department for International Development (DFID); education privatization as a state reform, 35–37, 45–52, 178; low-fee private schools, 96, 180; neoliberal influence in education, 36–37; New Labour, 49–52; politicization of research, 155; selection of policy changes, 189, 190; teachers' unions, 159, 160, 162, 171, 172; think tanks, 46, 139, 151, 155–156; Third Way. See Third Way
United Nations, 17, 84, 95, 131
United States; choice. See Choice in the United States; corporate advocacy, 145; low-fee

private schools, 96; philanthropy, 146–149; politicization of research, 153–154; retention of policy changes, 191; selection of policy changes, 189, 190; teachers' unions, 166; think tanks, 138–139
United States Agency for International Development (USAID), 129, 131, 132
Urban Institute, 123
U. S. Department of Education-National Center for Education Statistics, 77f

Vaillancourt, S., 159, 166, 172, 173, 174
Vaillant, D., 159, 161, 174
Valiente, O., 15n1
Vallas, Paul, 121, 128, 142–143
Vallas Group Inc., 128, 143
Vandenberghe, V., 106, 117
VanderKaaij, S., 100
van der Weide, M., 5
Van Fleet, J., 149
Vanni, X., 43
Variation of policy changes, 27–28, 187–188
Vavrus, F., 20
Veenman, S., 21
Venture philanthropy, 146–150
Vergari, S., 24, 78, 81, 141, 154
Verger, A., 8, 28, 96, 100, 115, 116, 141, 142, 144, 154, 155, 159, 165, 186, 188, 191, 192
Vernacularization, 19
Vested interest, 101, 141, 171, 172–173, 178
Veto; opportunity/point, 22, 29, 30, 72, 87, 132, 184; players, 29, 132, 179, 191
Villamor, P., 115
Villarroya, A., 114, 114n10
Viteritti, J. P., 71, 72
Voice (consumer response), 40, 40n5
Volckmar, N., 56, 57, 62, 63, 66
Voluntary sector, 49
Voucher programs. See Voucher schemes
Vouchers; charter schools vs., 83–86; First Amendment challenges to, 75–76; legislation, 76f; reforms in Sweden, 56, 60, 61, 163; targeted, 46, 84, 85, 87; universal, 37, 85, 87, 180

Waiting for Superman, 140, 166, 171
Walford, G., 95
Washington State, 149
Washington Coalition for Public Charter Schools, 149
Waslander, S., 5, 177n2
Waterbury, J., 23
Weitzel, P., 71, 153
Welfare regimes, 15, 22, 61, 66–67, 191
Welfare states; legitimacy crisis, 57, 64, 67, 179, 182; modernization, 64–66
West, A., 51, 52, 139
Weyland, K., 23, 24
White, John, 127
Whitty, G., 8
Wiborg, S., 57, 58, 59, 62, 63, 64, 65, 66, 168, 189
Winch, C., 94
Windle, J., 139, 190
Window of (political opportunity), 13, 28, 47, 88, 188
Wintle, M., 106n4
Wipro, 149
Wirt, F., 16
W. K. Kellogg Foundation, 99
Wong, K. K., 73
World Bank; global-local divide, 17; low-fee private schools, 96, 100, 101; private actors in promotion of privatization, 144, 155, 156; privatization by way of catastrophe, 128, 129, 130, 131; state reform, 44, 182
World Bank Group, 96. See also World Bank
World Culture Theory, 18, 25
World Innovation Summit for Education (WISE), 98
World regions and enrollment in private institutions, 4, 5f
World Society Theory, 18. See also World Culture Theory
World Trade Organization, 9n3

Youdell, D., 8, 9f, 137, 178
Young, T. V., 74, 164, 166, 167, 171, 175

Zancajo, A., 191
Zelman v. Simmons-Harris, 75, 84
Zilbersheid, U., 160

About the Authors

Antoni Verger is associate professor at the Department of Sociology of the Universitat Autònoma de Barcelona. A former postdoctoral fellow at the Amsterdam Institute for Social Science Research (University of Amsterdam), Dr. Verger's research has specialized in the study of the relationship between global governance institutions and education policy, with a focus on the dissemination, enactment, and effects of education privatization, public–private partnerships, and quasi-market policies in education. Currently, he is coordinating two European research projects related to these matters: "Public-Private Partnerships in Educational Governance" (Marie S. Curie Grant, 2013–2016) and "Reforming Schools Globally: A Multiscalar Analysis of Autonomy and Accountability Policies in the Education Sector" (ERC StG, 2016–2021).

Clara Fontdevila holds a degree in sociology from the Universitat Autònoma de Barcelona and a master's degree in discourse studies from the Universitat Pompeu Fabra. At the present time, she is a PhD candidate at the Department of Sociology of the Universitat Autònoma de Barcelona, with a thesis project on the post-2015 global education agenda. Previously, she has collaborated in different projects of the Globalisation, Education, and Social Policies (GEPS) research center, as well as with Education International. Her research focuses on private-sector engagement in education, education and development, and the global governance of education.

Adrián Zancajo is a graduate in economics from the Autonomous University of Barcelona (UAB) and has a master's degree in educational research from the same university. Currently, he is a PhD candidate in sociology at UAB, writing a thesis on the Chilean education market. In the context of the GEPS research center, Zancajo is participating in the competitive research projects "The New Quasi-market Reforms in Education in Latin America" (EDUMERCAL) and "Public-Private Partnerships in Educational Governance" (EDUPARTNER). He has also conducted research for Education International, the Open Society Foundations, and UNESCO. His main areas of interest are education privatization policies, educational inequalities, and the evaluation of educational policies.